THE INSIDE STORY OF THE END OF AN ERA

SOPHIE ALDRED & MIKE TUCKER

DOCTOR WHO BOOKS

First published in Great Britain in 1996 by
Doctor Who Books
an imprint of Virgin Publishing Ltd
332 Ladbroke Grove
London W10 5AH

ISBN: 1 85227 574 X

Cover photographs, and some internal photographs by Robin Prichard.

Layout and typesetting by Mark Stammers Design, London, SM5 4LY

Printed and bound by BPC Paulton Books Ltd, Aylesbury, Great Britain

ABOUT THE COVER

When we were commissioned to write this book the first thing that struck me was that it would be nice to try and do
something new for the cover. My initial idea was to set up a photograph of Sophie, dressed as Ace, sitting in front of a huge
explosion.

Having sold the idea to Peter and Rebecca, our cost conscious editors, I did some rough visuals and set about finding a
suitable location for the shoot. I eventually decided to go back to the quarry where we had shot *Delta and the Bannermen* but,
although the location was ideal, the amount of money that would be needed to set up the shot eventually proved prohibitive.

Undaunted, I came up with a cheaper solution – Ace standing alongside a burning Dalek, casually tossing a can of Nitro into
the air. We set up the shoot in the car park of the visual effects department at North Acton, the Dalek rigged with gas jets to
make the flames a little more controllable. Although the shoot went well, the casual tossing of a can of Nitro while smiling at the
camera proved far more difficult than initially expected and several baseball bat alternatives were done!

At the same session we shot some rather special stills of Sophie as the New Adventures version of Ace. It had been a project
that several people had mentioned over the years and the book seemed to be a good excuse to finally get it together. Armed
with a rubber suit, several large guns, some Daleks and a bottle of Perv-o-shine we did several variations on a theme, though as
Rebecca pointed out, we now have a really good set of reference photographs just as the character of Ace has been written out
of the book series!

Mike Tucker

Photographer: Robin Prichard. Make-up: Paige Bell. Costume: Ssh
Ace's belt: Robert Allsopp. Guns: Mike Tucker.
Baseball bat loaned by Andrew Beech.

CONTENTS

Acknowledgements

Sophie's:
Vince, for everything
All those family and friends
who've put up with off-screen Ace

Mike's:
Mum, Dad, Gran and Andy
Robert, who deserves this book more than me.
Helen, for encouragement
Roz

Thanks to:
Mary Del Castillo & Jill Shardlow
Peter Wragg & Tony Harding
Bobbie Mitchell
Everyone at the effects department, particularly the Boys from the Dwarf
Peter, Bex and Andy at Virgin
Gary Russell
Mark Stammers
JNT and Gary
Sylvester
All at Marvel, past and present, especially John and Gary
Andrew Beech and the Panopticon Posse
Marc, Ben, Andrew and Ian – splendid chaps, all of them!
Angela and Martin, for the best writing environment in the world.
Everyone who has contributed to this book in any way
The entire 'Dr Who Family'
The fans

Quotes from Sylvester McCoy, Andrew Carmel, Marc Platt and
Ben Aaronovitch were taken from interviews conducted at 'Doctor in the Dome' in Morecambe in 1994

**This book is dedicated to the memories of
RICHARD CROFT and TIP TIPPING**

Foreword

Without doubt, Ace is one of the most popular companions ever to appear in *Doctor Who*.

However, it's no good pretending that the role would have been as successful with just any old actress playing the part. Nor would she have been so successful without the contributions of many other TV professionals: Ian Briggs and Andrew Cartmel on much of the character's conception, director Chris Clough and myself on the casting, the late Richard Croft's original costume design, make-up ladies, guest artistes and all the other unsung heroes who contributed in large and small ways to the character that evolved from a single sheet of foolscap paper.

In particular, Sylvester McCoy encouraged the rapport between the Doctor and Ace, and indeed between Sylvester and Sophie Aldred.

Few would disagree that their TV relationship was fully rounded, yet never predictable; complex, then again simple; intense one minute, almost casual the next; as decoratively diverse as the badges on the character's jacket.

How so many people contributed to Ace is contained in this fascinating view of one part of the series that is loved by so many.

The multi-talented Sophie Aldred herself, and Mike Tucker, a respected member of the BBC Visual Effects Department, a regular on *Doctor Who* during my tenure, and whose nickname may not be published in a tome such as this, are bridge partners, as it were.

In their and others' pack of observations, memories and anecdotes, Sophie is Queen and Mickey is King. There are a few Knaves and one or two Jokers – but only one Ace!

John Nathan-Turner
Producer *Doctor Who* 1979-90

Introduction by Sophie Aldred

THE CALL FROM MY AGENT CAME. 'They're looking for someone for three episodes of *Doctor Who* who looks young for their age and can ride a motorbike.' My agent had written 'has own leathers' on the back of my publicity photo which intrigued Chris Clough, the director, so he'd asked me down to an audition from Manchester. I was appearing in the back row of the chorus in *Fiddler on the Roof* starring Topol at the Opera House, and now I was to audition along with many other hopefuls for the part of Ray in *Delta and the Bannermen* or Ace in *Dragonfire*.

As I was often asked my age in pubs when I was really twenty-five, I knew I fulfilled the baby-face factor and I was also good at sight reading in auditions after years of reading bedtime stories to my brother. So when I saw the page of script handed to me at Union House reception, I felt a buzz of excitement.

'Ray' it said in the top left-hand corner. And then followed a speech I now know as Ace's from *Dragonfire* with the line: 'Each night, I'd walk home, and I'd look up at the stars through the gaps in the clouds. And I'd try to imagine where I really came from.'

I sat in a corner, too excited to concentrate fully, my eyes straying to the walls adorned with photos of successful BBC series. I began a daydream in which I was the star of some well known programme and people were asking for my autograph at Tesco's.

'Sophie Aldred?' A voice shook my ego from its reverie. I jumped up and followed a woman to a large room on the second floor. Chris Clough welcomed me with a smile. We discussed the state of children's theatre in Britain – one of my hobby horses – and I was being very grown up until I remembered that I was meant to be portraying a sixteen-year-old. Chris asked me to read 'Ray's' speech, having told me a little of the character which I later found out was Ace. She sounded like just my cup of tea!

I got a recall. Two weeks later I was sitting on a London-bound train again, preparing to meet the producer, John Nathan-Turner. My first impression of John was of a powerful man who knew exactly what he wanted – I was quite scared of him, in fact. Chris Clough was there as well, selling me to JNT; I remember him mentioning that I had my own motorbike leathers and me laughing feebly. John asked me to read the 'Ray' piece for him a second time with a different expression and emphasis. I left Shepherd's Bush feeling that I hadn't made much of a mark.

Three weeks later I'd all but forgotten the audition, and when I remembered that my agent had asked me to ring her that day, we were halfway through the show. I rang her from the backstage payphone, interrupting her tea.

'You've got the job,' she said rather crossly, 'but it's a bit more complicated than that. Let me ring you back.' I put the phone down and caught my breath. Three episodes of *Doctor Who* – my first stab at television! Then she rang back, apologised for her annoyance and explained that she'd been trying to contact me urgently all day. 'There's a possibility they may want you to take over as the new *Doctor Who* girl, so congratulations!'

I replaced the receiver with trembling hand, and turned to John Scott Martin who was standing by the 'phone.

'I've got the job!' I told him.

'I thought you might,' he said. Smiling, he reached into the pocket of his costume and handed me a Dalek postcard. 'I've had this ready for a while,' he said 'I had a good feeling.' I turned the card over. 'Welcome to the family,' it said. 'You will not be exterminated.'

I grinned from ear to ear as my good news passed amongst the company, and on-stage backslapping and discreet congratulations ensued. Later, Topol congratulated me and told my mother, who had come to visit me, 'I knew she was going to be a star!'

Weeks later, back in London, I waited to sign my contract and for the scripts to arrive, just to make sure it was going to happen. Three episodes of *Dragonfire,* by Ian Briggs, arrived in the post, and I marked up my part with fluorescent pen, delighted with the characterisation and, let's face it, the size of the part. **S**

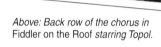

Above: Back row of the chorus in Fiddler on the Roof *starring Topol.*

Above: Congratulations postcard from a Dalek.

Sophie Aldred

Introduction by Mike Tucker

SINCE *DOCTOR WHO* BEGAN IN 1963 IT HAS CONSTANTLY put demands on all of the BBC design departments, but, as with any science fiction/fantasy programme, that demand has been particularly heavy on the visual effects department.

it was midway through the Troughton era that the effects department proper got its first credit on the programme – Michealjohn Harris' work on *The Evil of the Daleks*. Up to this point all effects had been the responsibility of the set designer, with the actual execution of these effects going to a number of independent prop and model companies.

As time went by and trends in cinema produced more and more elaborate science fiction, *Doctor Who* always adapted to keep up, though with the arrival of *Star Wars* in 1977 it became obvious that the gap between what feature films could achieve and what was possible on a television budget was now an impossible one to bridge.

Rather than try to compete with Hollywood, the programme fell back on good stories with strong characterisation, keeping expensive effects to a minimum, or finding plausible reasons for having only one spacecraft or only six monsters. The introduction of K9 in the seventies ensured an almost constant effects presence since both design and operation fell within the responsibilities of the effects department.

My own involvement with the show began in 1985, but my relationship with the series goes back much further. Like so many of my generation, I dimly remember images of Hartnell and Troughton doing battle with Yeti, Daleks and Cybermen on grainy black and white television sets – the series having begun transmission six months before I was born.

With the arrival of Jon Pertwee, and colour, I was one of

Above: Two photographs showing the typical daily business of the BBC visual effects workshop.

Above: Mike Tucker with Richard Gauntlett as Urak the Tetrap from Time and the Rani.

millions watching from places of safety in the front room, avidly tuning in each week, growing up with the series as Pertwee regenerated and Tom Baker began his mammoth run.

It was at about this point that I happened to catch an edition of the BBC's magazine programme *Pebble Mill at One*. The guests were Jack Kine and Bernard Wilkie of the BBC special effects department, talking about their work on the series. The item struck a nerve and I confused careers teachers for months afterward by announcing that this was the job that I wanted to do. I managed to get a visit to the effects workshops in North Acton and got put on the books. In 1985 I was offered a temporary contract, two years later that contract was made permanent and I'm still there!

Rather than try to compete with the definitive reference works that are currently being written about *Doctor Who*, it seemed sensible to adopt a slightly different approach. A lot of the details of how and when and where the programme was put together are already accessible, but some of the fine detail is only known to the people who worked on the show. It is that sense of immediacy that I hope we've captured and I hope that this is an insight into how much fun it was to make. To those actually worked on this era of the show perhaps it will be a good reminder of those times and a bit of a memory jogger – it has been for me. **M**

Mike Tucker

Above: The Doctor (Colin Baker) attempts to uncover the secrets of the sleepers guarded by Drathro. Trial of a Time Lord.

Above: Joan Simms and visual effects assistant Paul McGuinness during rehearsals for Trial of a Time Lord.

Above: Paul McGuinness in the full Drathro costume, built by visual effects.

Above: The newly regenerated Doctor (Sylvester McCoy) makes his way back to the TARDIS with the Rani (Kate O'Mara) posing as Mel. Time and the Rani.

Above: The Time Lords' fibre glass collars. Trial of a Time Lord.

Below: An early design sketch by Colin Mapson of the Rani's citadel. Time and the Rani.

Below: A later design sketch by Colin Mapson, which is very close to its final appearance.

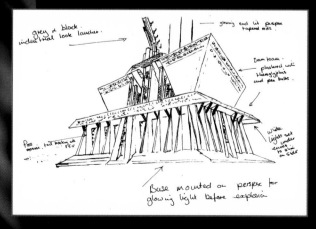

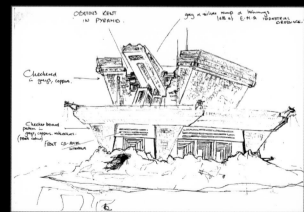

Life Before Ace

Left: A press cutting from The Sun newpaper, announcing Sylvester McCoy as the seventh Doctor. Mike Tucker was required to operate the TARDIS lamp whilst Bonnie Langford and Sylvester posed for pictures.

Above: Urak the Tetrap (Richard Gauntlett), with the partially animatronic head built by Stan Mitchell. Time and the Rani.

Above: Another of Colin Mapson's sketches showing the design detail for the mouth and tongue of the Tetrap.

Above: Side and back view of the Tetrap head.

Left: A sketch of the Tetrap head as viewed from the front, drawn by Colin Mapson.

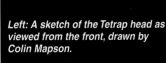

Below: The model of the citadel under construction in the visual effects workshop.

Below: The model is placed in its cliff edge setting on the model stage at North Acton, and is now ready for filming.

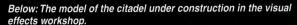

DOCTOR *W*HO WAS ONE OF THE FIRST PROGRAMMES THAT I WORKED ON when I joined the effects department. I was at college at the time, spending two terms on secondment before returning to complete my course. I was working under effects designer Mike Kelt on the first segment of *The Trial of a Time Lord – The Mysterious Planet –* scripted by the late Robert Holmes.

I was part of the effects crew responsible for the opening motion control shot of the TARDIS being dragged towards the Time Lord space station. My first job was to build two miniatures of the TARDIS, the existing models having vanished during the programme's 18 month hiatus. The larger of the two was eventually used in the shot, the smaller one not making its screen debut for several years.

The space station itself was a monstrosity of a thing. Built in several sections, the final fibreglass miniature was about five feet across and nearly six feet high. Filming for the sequence took place at Peerless motion control studios, the first time that this sort of computer controlled camera had been used on *Doctor Who*.

The following year I started work, as one of Colin Mapson's assistants, on the first story of the new Doctor. This started a run of working almost continuously on the show until 1989, and it is something I am very proud to have been associated with.

For me the era of the seventh Doctor actually began when I was dispatched by Colin to one of the many BBC offices that are scattered through central London, clutching the TARDIS lamp. The reason for this was to reach the press call announcing that Sylvester McCoy was the new Doctor. The TARDIS was there as set dressing and, due to the peculiarities of job responsibility in the BBC, the police box shell is always handled by the scenic department whereas the flashing light is the responsibility of the effects department!

With the press beginning to assemble, I had to climb up the rather unsteady prop, fit the light and run the leads to the flasher unit, run from a twelve volt car battery. Over the next few years I found myself doing this rather a lot, as I seemed constantly to be the one delegated to flash the light for all the materialisations and dematerialisations. Unlike its television image, the TARDIS is very cramped inside and I regularly spent scenes squeezed inside with Sylvester, Bonnie or Sophie, desperately trying to listen for my cue.

Sylvester McCoy is possessed of a boundless energy, and when he and Bonnie were brought out to meet the press I knew that they had found an actor who would bring his own unique signature to the rôle of the Doctor. During this session he was asked by one of the photographers if he would be keeping the hat that he was wearing as part of his costume. A nod from John Nathan-Turner meant that the first part of the seventh Doctor's

Right: The Time Lord's space station from The Trial of a Time Lord, *awaiting painting.*

Below: Mike Kelt adds fine detail to the space station model.

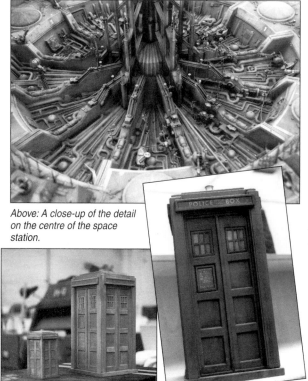
Above: A close-up of the detail on the centre of the space station.

Far left: The two wooden TARDIS models built by Mike to replace those lost during Doctor Who's 18-month hiatus.

Above: The larger TARDIS model undergoing painting, with the lamp flasher wiring attatched.

Left: The larger of the two models fully painted. This model was used for the filming of the space station sequence at the beginning of The Trial of a Time Lord.

apparel had been confirmed.

I remained as part of Colin's effects team for all the location and studio work for *Time and the Rani*, though for the bulk of its production the show was referred to as *Strange Matter*. Whereas on *The Mysterious Planet* I had been confined to the workshop building props while the rest of the crew went out on location, Colin gave me my first taste of what a real *Doctor Who* location was like – a wet, cold, quarry in almost constant driving rain! We had great fun.

Colin had chosen a team of four assistants. Two were old hands from the department: Roger Barham and the late Len Hutton, who had been a designer himself at one point. The others were Russell Pritchett and myself, neither of us having been in the department a year. This enabled us to learn a great deal from the 'old timers' whilst Colin had the security of knowing that if Russell and I turned out to be utterly hopeless he still had enough staff to get the job done.

Time and the Rani kept us very busy with miniatures, creatures, guns, communicators and pyrotechnics – in fact, the full range of effects that I would find myself working with regularly. I also found my niche as a miniature maker. I had always enjoyed model-making and my experiences on the motion control sequence the previous year had only served to fire my enthusiasm for more. Colin made use of that enthusiasm by giving me the job of constructing the Rani's citadel, a large scale miniature that would be used both on location and in the visual effects model stage at North Acton.

The elements of the story that attracted the most comments were the Rani's bubble traps, and these were my introduction to the world of video effects. The video effects department is completely different from visual effects. Whereas the bulk of our work is done as the show is being recorded, all of their work is done when recording is completed. As a result, they are referred to as a post production department, although a lot of their work overlaps ours.

A good example of this overlapping is seen in the way that the bubble traps were created. Although the actual bubble itself was created entirely on a Paintbox computer, the figures inside and the explosions that result from the bubble's impact were created by the effects department. Predetermined points were set on location as to where the bubble would bounce, and charges set. The camera then followed the path of an imaginary bubble and the charges were set off by Colin as they came into frame. The figures were six inch miniatures revolved against CSO blue and added to the scene in post production and the swirling bubble was added last. All the video effects for this era of the programme were handled by Dave Chapman, a veteran of *Doctor Who*, and someone that I ended up working a lot with over the next few years.

Each season featuring the seventh Doctor was split into two four-part stories and two three-part stories, with the two three-parters being shot back to back, using the same production and design teams. Because of the way that the stories overlapped in production it was impossible for one effects designer to handle the entire season. However, John Nathan-Turner was keen on having someone looking after regularly used props such as the TARDIS console, the lamp and several of the Doctor's gadgets.

John asked if I could be allocated to all the shows for the following two years. In the end it proved impossible to do four stories in a year, but I managed three, missing out on *Paradise Towers*, *Remembrance of the Daleks* and *Battlefield*.

With a new crew coming in, and a new era of the programme about to start, Bonnie decided that it was time for her to move on from the world of *Doctor Who*. The new companion was the creation of Ian Briggs, who came up with a character based on a trio of teenage girls he knew from drama classes, and Ace was born. Ace's debut was in the last story of Sylvester's first season – *Dragonfire* – and *Doctor Who* companions were never going to be the same again! Ⓜ

Left: Bonnie Langford and Sylvester McCoy stand in the doorway of the battered TARDIS prop, at the press photocall arranged to introduce the seventh Doctor.

Below: Colin Mapson's design drawing for the Tetrap's head. Time and the Rani.

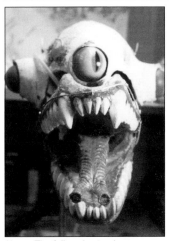

Above: The fully animatronic underskull for the Tetrap head.

Above: A unused version of the centre of leisure from Time and the Rani.

Below: Mike, busy constructing the Rani's citadel for Time and the Rani.

Season 24

Photo: Russell Pritchett

Above: The crab robot from Paradise Towers, *in the visual effects workshop.*

Above: Mike prepares the Bannermen space ship, from Delta and the Bannermen, *for filming against a CSO blue backdrop in the video effects workshop.*

Right: The Doctor and Glitz's plans for dragon hunting are interupted by the arrival of Kane's mercenaries. Dragonfire.

Season 24 had a lot to live up to. It was being closely scrutinised by the upper echelons of the BBC, following the dismissal of Colin Baker from the programme. It had to introduce the new Doctor, write out the existing companion and introduce a new one, all in fourteen weeks. On top of this, the season's first story, *Time and the Rani*, was commissioned before a new script editor had been appointed. As a result, Sylvester's debut story is the only one of his era that was scripted by writers who had written for the show before.

Andrew Cartmel brought a completely new team of writers to the show, all of them with fresh and unusual ideas. Rather than continue the trend of a run of four-part stories and a two-parter tacked on the end, Andrew and John Nathan-Turner structured the seasons around two four-part stories and two three-parters, one of the three-parters being studio based whilst the other was shot entirely on location. The four-part stories were shot with the usual traditional mix of studio and location recording. This pattern was to continue for the rest of the McCoy era.

With all the celebrations for the 25th anniversary of the show still a year away, season 24's milestone was the 150th story. This was *Dragonfire*, one of the three-part stories, twinned for production with Malcolm Kholl's quirky *Delta and the Bannermen*. With *Delta* obviously being the all location story, *Dragonfire* was confined to the studios of television centre, and was second in recording order.

Dragonfire

By Ian Briggs
Story 7G

3 Episodes – broadcast 23 November to 7 December 1987

The Cast

The Doctor	Sylvester McCoy
Melanie	Bonnie Langford
Kane	Edward Peel
Glitz	Tony Selby
Ace	Sophie Aldred
Belazs	Patricia Quinn
Kracauer	Tony Osoba
McLuhan	Stephanie Fayerman
Bazin	Stuart Organ
Customer	Shirin Taylor
Anderson	Ian Mackenzie
Archivist	Daphne Oxenford
Arnheim	Chris MacDonnell
Pudovkin	Nigel Miles Thomas
Zed	Sean Blowers
The Creature	Leslie Meadows
Announcer	Lynn Gardner
Stellar	Miranda Borman

The Production Team

Producer	John Nathan-Turner
Director	Chris Clough
Script editor	Andrew Cartmel
Production manager	Gary Downie
Production associate	Ann Faggetter
Production assistants	Rosemary Parsons
	Karen King
Assistant floor manager	Chris Sandeman
Producer's secretary	Kate Easteal
Designer	John Asbridge
Costume designer	Richard Croft
Make-up designer	Gillian Thomas
Make-up assistant	Petrona Winten
Visual effects designer	Andy McVean
Visual effects assistants	Paul Mann
	Jonathan Clarke
	Lindsey MacGowen
	Mike Tucker
Video effects designer	Dave Chapman
Technical co-ordinator	Richard Wilson
Camera supervisor	Alec Wheal
Vision mixer	Shirley Coward
Video tape editor	Hugh Parson
Film cameraman	William Dudman
Lighting director	Don Babbage
Sound	Brian Clarke
Incidental music	Dominic Glynn
Special sound	Dick Mills

MY FIRST TASK WAS TO MANUFACTURE THE BASIC SHAPE FOR THE Iceworld guard's guns. These were made in wood and then passed over to the BBC's plastic workshops to be moulded and the final fibreglass versions fabricated. This was to prove time consuming since the small guns had to be hollow to allow the insertion of firing mechanisms, while the bazooka-style guns had to be able to be taken apart and reassembled in vision as well as being able to fire several times.

One 'special' prop was the gun dropped into a vat of supposed liquid nitrogen. Once pulled out of the vat, the gun had to shatter on the floor when dropped. To achieve this a gun was made using PS2 resin, or sugar glass, usually used for breakable windows or bottles. The gun was then painted to resemble all the 'real' guns.

I then began work on the Nosferatu, Glitz's trading ship. Two versions of the ship were needed – the one I built was for all the establishing and take-off shots whilst another version was needed for its destruction. This was built by Alan Marshall, a massive amount of work going into something that made the screen for only one, albeit very spectacular, shot.

By this time Andy McVean and the rest of the effects crew had begun work on the rest of the *Dragonfire* requirements. Paul Mann began work on the mechanical Dragon head that would split open to reveal the treasure, and Jonathan Clarke concentrated on the treasure itself .

The sets featured two distinct control areas, the main control room and Kane's forbidden zone, the latter featuring the ice sculpture of his lover, Xana. The sculpture was to prove tricky since it had to be seen in several different stages, from ice block to final figure, and needed to be visibly chiselled by the actor playing the sculptor. Andy eventually opted for a clear vacuum-formed prop that could be dressed and frosted internally to give the illusion of ice. A genuine ice block was incorporated into the statue once in studio to enable the actor to work at it convincingly.

Subtle smoke effects were required for scenes where Kane clasped his hands onto his victims, freezing them to death. Tubes were run up Edward Peel's sleeves, stopping just under his cuffs. As his victims 'died' smoke was pumped down the tubes appearing from between his fingers. Similarly, when he places his coin on the console, meaning to tempt Ace into taking it, the director wanted smoke to rise around it, as if the coin was so cold that it was burning into the surface of the panel. For this effect two chemicals that smoke on contact were used, one on the back of the coin, the other on the set, the reaction starting as soon as the prop was put down.

Ace's Nitro cans were eventually made from spray cream cans – the paint and graphics removed with wire wool, a time consuming job. I speak from experience as the man who had to do it! Explosions in studio are always time consuming since the large scale effects that are possible on location are obviously not practical and other methods have to be employed. This usually entails using compressed air devices with actual pyrotechnics being used for dressing only.

As well as the nitro explosions there was a body hit on the barman in the milkshake bar and the dragon burning its way through a door in one of the Iceworld corridors. The barman is the only one actually seen to be shot in the story because of time restraints. Although body hits are relatively easy to set up they are time consuming since any pyrotechnic effect involving an actor has to be safe. A small pyrotechnic charge was rigged on the actor's chest, just under his shirt so that the fabric would burst open as the device was fired.

The Dragon burning through the door was achieved in stages. First a copy of the door was made, then a thin channel was cut all around the edge of it and a thin polystyrene sheet was pasted over the front. On the take, a pyrotechnic device was ignited behind the door, burning through the polystyrene and sending a shower of sparks

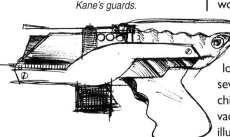

Below: One of the completed guns built for Dragonfire.

Below: Design sketch by Mike Tucker for the guns used by Kane's guards.

Above: A special prop gun made from PS2 resin, designed to shatter when dropped.

Below: Six completed guns awaiting use in the studio.

Right: Andy McVean's design sketch for the larger guns used on Dragonfire.

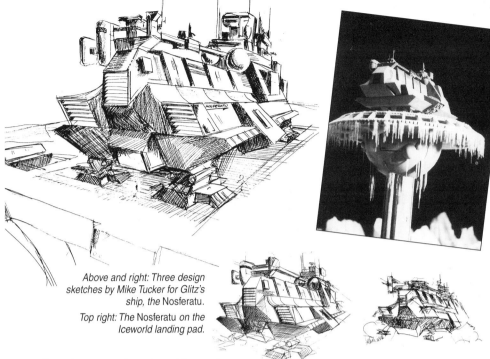

Above and right: Three design sketches by Mike Tucker for Glitz's ship, the Nosferatu.

Top right: The Nosferatu on the Iceworld landing pad.

into the set on the other side.

Perhaps the most memorable effect in the story is the destruction of Kane himself and for this Andy turned to Susan Moore and Stephen Mansfield.

Knowing that Stephen was an excellent portrait sculptor, Andy contracted him for the melting head of Kane. Working from a set of polaroids of Edward Peel in a suitably agonised pose, a clay bust was fashioned. From this, a plaster mould was made so that wax faces could be produced. Once this was done the bust was sculpted to a skull-like state and a fibreglass version made, plumbed up with various air bladders and tubes. The final effect was achieved by melting the wax faces off the fibreglass underskull with hot air guns, whilst coloured goo was fed through the tubes, and the bladders were pulsed. Although only on the screen for a few seconds the scene was horrific enough to cause a plethora of complaints to the BBC duty office.

As well as the melting head there was meant to be a shot of Kane's body withering. To achieve this Andy purchased a sex doll that would be dressed in the appropriate costume and suspended from a scenery hoist. The plan was that the dummy would be deflated as the hoist was lowered providing a simple way of effecting a collapsing body. Unfortunately, during recording the message to lower the hoist wasn't relayed and, in front of the entire crew, the dummy deflated until its trousers fell off – needless to say that shot isn't in the final programme!

With all studio work out of the way it was only the miniature work that was needed to complete the story. The main shots were the establishing shots of Svartos with its ice colony, the Nosferatu on its landing pad and the eventual take-off and destruction of the ship. Svartos itself had been built around a four foot diameter perspex sphere by an independent model-making company. The take-off of the ice colony was achieved in long shot using this miniature rather than using a close-up section. In contrast the take-off of the Nosferatu featured a large scale section of the door and the docking arm. The miniature was rigged with flashing lights and a steam jet that would vent just as the arm withdrew.

Finally, the other Nosferatu was rigged with explosives and attached to the ceiling. The camera was positioned directly below it and protected with a perspex screen. For all miniature explosions it is best to film at high speed so that the final shot has some weight to it. As soon as the camera was running, Andy set off the bang and the Nosferatu was destroyed.

With all filmed effects you never know quite what has been shot until you see the film. With explosions this can be quite nerve wracking, especially when you only have one model to blow up! Fortunately, the Nosferatu bang was perfect and the effects crew began to plan for the anniversary season. **M**

Writing Dragonfire

The idea was that my story was going to be last in transmission. Andrew had come up with a new companion called Alf, I think, because they wanted her to be a fairly normal person from Earth. Then it was decided that I wouldn't be writing the last story after all so I dumped the character that I'd been given and started afresh. I didn't like the idea of making someone tomboyish just by the name and I knew these teenagers that I was teaching at a drama group who were perfect, the perfect amalgam, from Perivale and Greenford. As I was writing different things for Ace I could hear these teenagers talking. I remember asking them what they said if something was good and got 'well good', 'mega' and 'ace'.

Glitz wasn't originally Glitz. He was originally a space pirate called Razorback in a story called *The Pyramid's Treasure* and when that started to become *Dragonfire* John Nathan-Turner said that he was very close to this character who had been very popular and asked if I was prepared to rewrite him as Glitz.

The description of Ace's bedroom said 'typical teenagers bedroom with discarded socks and knickers disappearing under the bed'. This came back from typing as 'discarded clothes'. When the set was being dressed I said to Kathy, the design assistant, that it should have been discarded knickers and from then on, every time she was dressing a set I would tell her that the original script had specified knickers as set dressing – Kane's ice chamber, Glitz's ship . . . On the final day of shooting we bumped into each other and she said, 'I've got a present for you,' and presented me with a large pair of women's bloomers which I tucked into my breast pocket. I can recall chatting to Bonnie and her eyes were fixed on this pocket. She eventually asked what it was in my pocket and I pulled them out saying 'It's a pair of women's knickers, Bonnie, what does it look like!'

We didn't know that Ace was the new companion until the very last minute. That final scene was written in a BBC tea bar on the morning that we shot it, on the back of a paper napkin. Sylvester wanted to use his audition script but that didn't work with what I was trying to do, so Andrew and I were trying to knit both ideas together. We found a speech with phrases that Sylvester liked and mixed them with the stuff I needed for storytelling purposes.

Andrew asked me to write up the background for Ace to be given to other writers in the series Bible, and the page on Ace was the page I'd given Andrew, just photocopied. I was very concerned about handing her over because she was my baby and I always feel attatched to my characters. I remember that when I sent the notes to Andrew there was a covering letter saying, 'Take good care of her'.

Ian Briggs
Writer

Above: The Nosferatu *before it received its final colouring.*

Above: The Nosferatu *under construction. Note the design drawing on the wall above the model.*

Right: Visual effects assistant Lindsay McGowan airbrushes detail on to the head of the Dragonfire *creature.*

Below: The completed head.

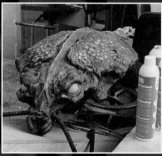

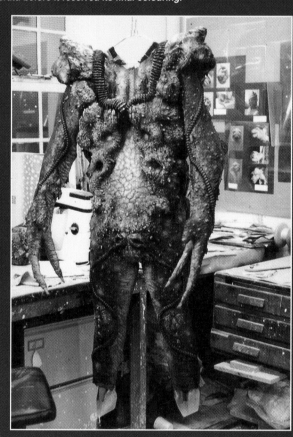

Right: The unpainted bodysuit for the Dragon creature.

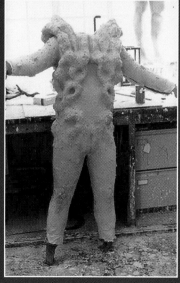

Above: *The completed Dragon bodysuit after painting.*

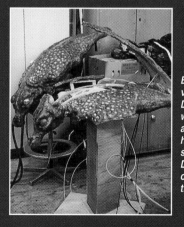

Below: The two versions of the Dragon's head: one worn by the actor and the mechanical head used for the scene when the Dragon's head opens revealing the treasure.

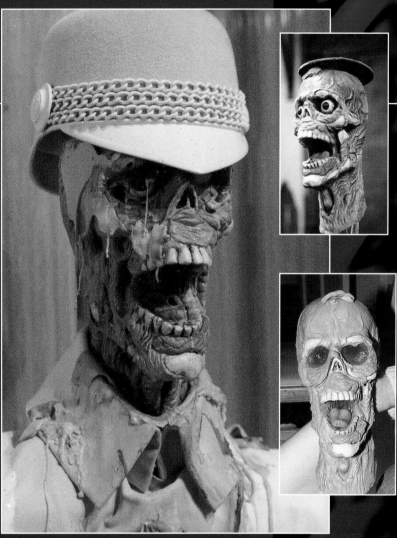

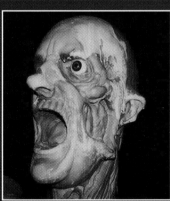

Above: Edward Peel poses with an agonised expression, for a reference photograph used by sculptor Stephen Mansfield to produce the clay bust used to make the wax heads for Kane's demise.

Right: The clay sculpture of the underskull which would be revealed by the melting wax faces.

Above: The underskull with helmet and collar fitted, after the sequence had been filmed. Top inset: The underskull set up in the studio with a circle of board for the helmet to sit on. Bottom inset: the underskull with inflatable rubber bladders which were used to push the melting wax away from the skull beneath.

Above: One of the wax casts of Kane's face being painted in the studio, prior to use.

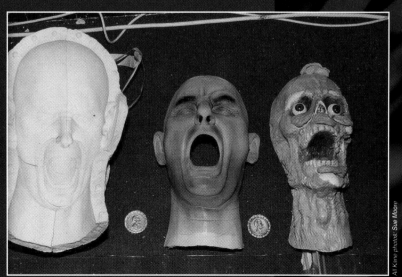

Above: Three elements used in creating the melting Kane. On the left is the mould used to make the wax faces, in the middle is a completed face and on the right is the underskull. In between the heads are two coins with Kane's head on them, used for the scene when Kane tries to get Ace to join his mercenaries.

All Kane photos: *Sue Moore*

I'LL NEVER FORGET THE MIXTURE OF EXCITEMENT AND NERVES AS I PUSHED open the door of room 202 at the BBC North Acton rehearsal rooms for the first time. There were a couple of tables pushed together at the far end and round them people were laughing and chatting. I recognised Sylvester McCoy from *Vision On*, and who could miss Bonnie Langford? I took a seat a little way off feeling nervous, and after introducing ourselves in turn, the read-through began.

I can't remember the historic moment Sylvester and I were introduced – I was probably too nervous – but I recall being surprised about Bonnie. I had only seen her in her 'I'll thrcream and thrcream until I'm sick!' persona on television and expected she'd be the same in real life, but I was delighted to meet a warm, generous person with a wicked sense of humour and a very trendy wardrobe.

Right: A letter from director Chris Clough's secretary informing me of the date of the first rehearsals for Dragonfire.

Andrew Cartmel introduced himself and said he really liked the way I was dressed. I was wearing a pair of army shorts dyed black, a stripy blue and white T-shirt and black Doc Marten shoes. Andrew suggested it might be a good look for Ace, and suddenly I knew exactly what she should wear. I had a copy of *The Face* magazine at home, which I promised to show the costume designer, Richard Croft. In it were a couple of photos of teenage girls out clubbing. They were wearing cycling shorts, stripy tights, and baggy army-style bomber jackets with badges and patches safety-pinned to them. Back in a Manchester club, I'd seen someone wearing a *Blue Peter* badge pinned to a black bomber jacket.

Below: The photograph printed in The Face *magazine, which inspired my costume, cycling shorts, stripey tights, jacket and all.*

A few days later, Richard Croft and I set off up the Kings Road, Chelsea, to find my costume. It was like shopping with my dad when I was little; I'd try on a jacket or a T-shirt, say yes or no, and Richard handed over the cash. We found some of the patches and badges there. Richard went to Oxford street for others, and I later contributed some of my own. My *Blue Peter* badges had to be checked out as the genuine article before I could wear them on TV. In the files for 1970 there was a mention of a little girl called Sophie Aldred who had written letters containing brilliant ideas including a rocket launcher ingeniously fashioned from a washing up liquid bottle and a garden hose!

Back at the rehearsal rooms, I was becoming very protective of Bonnie, just like the relationship between Mel and Ace in the script. She confided to me in the ladies' loos that she'd badly sprained her ankle jogging that morning and not to tell. I think she was worried that someone would stop her exercising – something which was so important to her. She was trying to decide whether or not to leave the series – in the

Right: postcard from a writer.

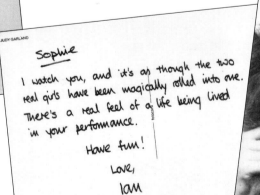

BRITISH BROADCASTING CORPORATION
TELEVISION CENTRE WOOD LANE LONDON W12 7RJ

15th June 1987

Dear Miss Aldred,

I enclose the script of our DR WHO 'Dragonfire'. We shall be rehearsing in Room 202 at the BBC Rehearsal Rooms at North Acton, starting on July 16th with a read-through of all the serial at 10.30am, and we look forward to seeing you then.

Yours sincerely,

Rosemary Parsons

(P.A. to Chris Clough)

Miss Sophie Aldred,

Sophie

I watch you, and it's as though the two real girls have been magically rolled into one. There's a real feel of a life being lived in your performance.

Have fun!

Love,
Ian

original script it's Ace who goes off with Glitz at the end.

Television rehearsals didn't seem that different from the theatre world I was used to. The cast swapped ideas, worked out characters, and we blocked through the first few scenes. Everyone was eager to help me with characterisation, including Pat Quinn, whose teenage son helped us with suitable expletives for Ace; 'Gordon Bennet, what a bunch of prats!' became 'a bunch of spots' at his suggestion, when we discovered 'prats' was not suitable BBC terminology. Each rehearsal period ended with a Producer's run with selected technicians watching the scenes in recording order to get an idea of each studio day. I was nervous and excited, wanting to give a good performance. It seemed strange to go through the action out of chronological order. I wrote the order of the scenes in which I appeared in a notebook to help me remember the continuity of the action and Ace's progression through the story. At the end of the producer's run we left the safety of the rehearsal room.

'See you at Television Centre!' shouted Gary Downie, the floor manager to cast and crew. I sidled up to him.

'Where actually is Television Centre?' I asked, turning crimson in front of Bonnie, who must have been given directions on how to get there in the womb.

Gillian Thomas, the make-up designer, had a look at my hair. She decided to give me a natural style, hair up and no make-up. I breathed a sigh of relief. I'd never liked or understood make-up, having been an Ace prototype tomboy.

A couple of days later I stepped out of White City tube station and found Television Centre. The truth hit me. I was actually going to be in *Doctor Who*. Even my grandparents knew *Doctor Who*.

My name was on the list at reception. So far so good. I was handed a key with a number tagged to it. I matched the key number with the door to my dressing room. There, hanging on a rail, neatly tied up in plastic, was my brand new costume. I couldn't wait to put it on – and I admired myself in the mirror. But what to do now? I wandered around until I found the studio. I was taken aback by the size of it – a mass of blazing lights and huge pieces of scenery. Suspended from the gantry were great powerful lamps, while the floor was covered with a spaghetti of cables, and there were people bustling about everywhere. It was bright and hot.

'Ah, Sophie, there you are. Have you been to make-up?'

'I don't think I'm having any.'

'Well, pop in for a check, anyway.'

I was propelled into a small room filled with lots of people I'd never seen before sitting in front of a long row of ▶

PROPOSAL FOR THE DOCTOR'S NEW COMPANION

ALF –

Alf is a teenage London girl who used to work on the till in a supermarket, until she was swept away from earth by a time storm. The Doctor finds her in a distant galaxy ... working on the till in a supermarket. Fed up with her routine job, determined to see the sights of the universe, Alf pours a drink into her talking till, quits and joins the Doctor on his adventures in the TARDIS.

Alf is uneducated but sharp, nobody's fool. She has a sense of wonder about their travels through time and space. She is smart and tough and protective of the Doctor. Can also be stroppy and sullen. She approaches her cosmic adventuring with a down-to-earth pragmatism and a somewhat off-beat sense of humour.

26th January 1987

Notes on the character ACE

Name: 'Ace' is her nickname. She's ashamed of her real name, and only told Mel in a moment of intimacy. (I feel that she would only ever tell another girl; not a man or a boy - probably not even the Doctor.) Her real name is Dorothy. I didn't specify a surname; it can be either the surname of Dorothy in *The Wizard of Oz*, or something that works in the context of the story it appears in - or, more likely, she'll just avoid the question and keep it secret.

Age: At the point of her appearance in *Dragonfire*, she was meant to be 16 years and 11 months. In fact, she's based on three girls I know, all of whom are 14, so she has the personality and maturity of a young (rather than middling) teenager.

Home: She comes from Perivale, which she regards as the pits of London. As far as she's concerned, the only good thing about Perivale is that it has two Tube stations! (One of the girls she's based on actually said this while watching a recording.)

Family: She doesn't have any brothers or sisters. If she did, she'd have mentioned them in her intimate speech with Mel. Besides, she's too much of a loner inside. She didn't get on with her parents, and she gets angry simply at the mention of them. Sometimes she refuses to accept that her 'real' parents - the kind, loving ones - are somewhere else, maybe on another planet. But however bad a picture she paints of them, the truth is that her parents are an ordinary middle-class couple who always kept their feelings hidden, and didn't know how to cope with their tearaway daughter.

School: She enjoyed chemistry and was taking it at A-Level - although she would probably have failed because she isn't the academic type. She got suspended from school when she blew up the Art Room.

History: While she was at school she also had a boring evening job working in a fast-food cafeteria. She also used to do experiments with explosives in her bedroom, and it was an accident with one of these that triggered a time storm and carried her to Iceworld - where she again found work as a waitress.

Speech: She uses phrases typical of London teenagers: 'Wicked!', 'Well worth!', 'Naff!', and of course 'Ace!'. I don't care if, technically, she left Perivale in early 1987, and so ought still to be using the phrases of that period; the more current and realistic her speech, the better. She coins nicknames for everybody, such as 'Doughnut' for Mel, and 'Bilgebag' for Glitz. And even though it irritates the Doctor, she can't help calling him 'Professor'. The only time she reverts to using real names is when she's frightened, as when Kane was holding her hostage in *Dragonfire*.

Personality: Typical teenager really. Bright and full of life one moment, spiky and argumentative the next. Even though she likes the Doctor, she's bound to come over all moody and complaining with him from time to time. A particular characteristic is her heightened sense of excitement, which sometimes overrides her sense of danger: her immediate reaction on first seeing the Creature in *Dragonfire* was to yell with delight, and only later did she think to run like hell!

/ October 1987

Far left: Andrew Cartmel's initial outline for the character of Alf, who was replaced by Ace when Ian Briggs wrote Dragonfire.

Left: A background sheet for Ace written by Ian Briggs for use in the programme's writer's bible.

Right: Kane's guards in the Iceworld control room. Note the final version of the large gun.

Foot Acting

Extensive use was made of the Paintbox graphics system, allowing director Chris Clough some freedom in his wide shots. Indeed, video effects designer Dave Chapman was eventually able to add several more levels to the central control area complete with guards on the gantries. He also provided the seemingly bottomless chasm that the Doctor hangs over at the climax of episode one, although the legs seen in that particular shot are not actually Sylvester McCoy's. During the video effects session it was decided that I was closest in build to Sylvester and so, donning the lower half of the costume, I lay across two chairs in front of a CSO blue screen and waved my legs in, what was hopefully, a convincingly agitated manner – foot acting directed by Chris Clough!

Mike Tucker

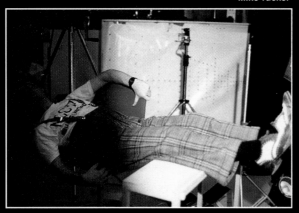

Above: Mike stands in for Sylvester McCoy. Wearing the lower part of the Doctor's costume, Mike is suspended above a blue screen to provide shots of the Doctor's legs for video effects.

Above: With the background added to the shot it appears that the Doctor is hanging over a deep chasm.

Above: Sylvester McCoy pleased as punch with his new umbrella which was first seen in Dragonfire. *It would quickly become one of his Doctor's trade marks.*

Above: The Doctor reads The Doctor's Dilemma *in the canteen on Iceworld. The book started a running gag with the Doctor's reading matter – the Doctor reads* Doctor in the House *in* Remembrance of the Daleks.

Above and left: Tony Selby, Bonnie and me. I never let on that I had a bad attack of scabies during filming, courtesy of a second-hand mattress in my house. I tried hard not to scratch and prayed that Bonnie wouldn't catch it.

Below: 'I was working as a waitress in a milkshake bar when I met you!' The weird and wonderful creatures inhabiting the bar were mostly supplied by freelancers Stephen Mansfield and Susan Moore using masks that they had to hand.

Dragonfire FX

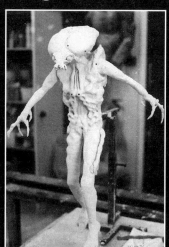

Above: The Dragon maquette.

The original maquette of the creature was very beautiful, very menacing, but the actor that they cast was short and fat and we ended up making blocked up shoes for him to try and get him to look taller. He really couldn't cope at all, because he had a complete rubber body suit on, which was uncomfortable, and because his hands needed to be free as he had to operate the smoke from the nostrils with a blow switch. This meant that when he blew into a mouthpiece it operated a solenoid but it also meant that you had to have a battery and a gas canister in the head, so the entire thing was quite top heavy.

When Kane was in his cryogenic chamber we had all these different gauges built into the back of the set and they had to indicate that things were going wrong and that the temperature was starting to go up. These consisted of bits of orange perspex inside clear tubes that you pushed up or down depending what was wanted. One of these got stuck and I can remember Gary Downie asking if anything was wrong and Jonathan, my assistant, saying, 'No, no, I'm pretty sure that the electronic feed to the linear interositer had a fault to it but we've sorted it out and it should be all right next time'. All it was was him pushing these rods up and down by hand and he'd forgotten to push this one up, but he managed to convince everyone that there was something very technical.

Andy McVean
Visual Effects Designer

Right: A letter sent to Sophie by one of the girls Ian Brigg's used as the basis for Ace.

► mirrors. Gillian motioned me to an empty chair and asked me questions I didn't understand.

'I didn't think I was having make-up,' I offered.

'But everyone has to have make-up.'

Pat Quinn rescued me as the light dawned, 'This is Sophie's first telly, isn't it darling?'

'Ooh, I see!' exclaimed the world at large.

In the theatre, I'd always spent tedious hours in front of the make-up mirror and now a professional did it for me. It was like being at the hairdresser's being pampered and cared for and I liked it! Gary Downie came to find me. They wanted to check my costume on camera, he said. I followed him onto the studio floor towards Kane's control room. I stood quivering as a hundred eyes studied me. Richard Croft stood by reassuringly.

'The tights are strobing – can we change them?' asked Gary. Richard beetled off to have a look. The only pair he had to hand were bright red – not half as nice, I thought, as the yellow and black stripes we'd chosen, but as those were sending the cameras wild, I changed quickly.

My first scene was Kane tempting Ace with a coin and Ace feeling scared – no acting required! Eddie Peel pointed up to the monitors round the studio so that I could see myself on camera. The shot was a huge close up of my face, and I almost wished I hadn't looked. It was so odd to see five or six Sophies gazing back at me.

We ran through the scene for a camera rehearsal and I got used to the geography, ignoring cameras and people standing around the studio. I saw that they weren't concerned with my performance, but with their particular area of work – was my hair sticking up, or was my costume tucked in. We recorded the scene and in a flash it was gone – a strange feeling after theatre when you do the same thing over and over.

That evening, John Nathan-Turner came down from the gallery and strode towards me, beaming. I smiled nervously back.

'Well,' he said, 'I've come to ask you if you'd like to join us next year as the new companion – we're on if you're on!' I looked at him incredulously and then realised he was deadly serious about the offer. My stomach looped the loop with excitement, and a grin spread itself effortlessly across my astonished face. I wanted to shout and jump up and down, but instead I mouthed a breathless, 'Yes please!' and hurried home on a cloud of pure happiness to ring family, friends, and anyone else who'd listen to me.

Throughout rehearsals writer Ian Briggs was very much in evidence. We talked at length about the character of Ace, who was based on two teenagers with whom he'd worked at Questor's youth theatre in Ealing. On the day of the first studio, he gave me a card bearing a picture of Judy Garland in *The Wizard of Oz*, for obvious reasons, with the inscription:

'I watch you, and it's as though the two real girls have been magically rolled into one. There's a real feel of a life being lived in your performance.'

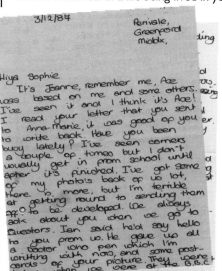

During the first studio, I was introduced to the concept of visual effects. I'd never realised that there was a whole department devoted to making models and then blowing them up. I was hooked, and watched with fascination as explosive charges were laid for the scene where Ace blows a hole in the docking bay door. Bonnie and I were told just how close we could get to the charges, the cameras rolled and BANG! The debris showered down on our heads, and Ace's delighted 'Wicked!' contained a lot of real Sophie Aldred.

One of the most nerve wracking scenes turned out to be one I'd loved rehearsing. It was set in the refreshment bar where Ace argues with a customer, Shirin Taylor, and then pours a milkshake over her head. I'd rehearsed with gusto, though not with liquid. In studio, Shirin was dressed in an ostrich feather gown and I had one chance to get the milkshake in the right place for the camera – there was no way the dress could be cleaned should I miss. It sounds quite simple, but I was so nervous about hitting the right spot that my hand was shaking and it was more of a throw than a pour. However, it looked fine on camera.

By the time we returned to the studio after the second block of rehearsals, I felt like an old hand. We still had to decide on a definitive version of the final scene. Ian Briggs was delighted that his creation, Ace, was to stay on in the TARDIS, and he and Andrew Cartmell sat in the tea bar outside the studio poring over a napkin on which they scribbled the Doctor and Mel's parting scene. Several cups of BBC coffee later they handed the dialogue, still on the napkin, to Bonnie and Sylvester, who learned it just before the cameras rolled.

I was amazed that the TARDIS interior scenes consisted of a few 'flats' and the famous TARDIS console, which looked pretty battered up close. In contrast, the Iceworld scenery was massive with metal gangways, huge sheets of plastic and polystyrene and clever lighting. We'd decided in rehearsals that the Iceworld corridors would be slippery and we should slide around as though walking on ice. When it came to the studio, everyone save Sylv and I seemed to have forgotten, so it looks as though the Doctor and Ace are wearing slippery shoes!

Another misunderstanding was with props. When I'd suggested in rehearsals that I carry a rucksack, I'd imagined a small brightly coloured bag – the equivalent of a bum bag which is what I'd have had if they'd been around at the time. I wanted it to be like Batman's utility belt. In studio I was handed a monstrous rucksack from a camping shop, and it was too late to get anything smaller. I became the packhorse of the show. For two years the writers loved giving me heavy props to cart around. I asked for a large pocket to be sewn into the inside of my jacket so that I could carry Nitro 9 canisters in there, plus things like hankies and lip salve!

My favourite scene was Ace confiding in Mel – after all it did have significance for me, being the speech which got me the job. We did about three takes of the scene and I was aware of nothing save the camera and Bonnie. I'd developed a good relationship with 'Doughnut' – probably the most inappropriate name Bonnie has ever been given. But ... that scream proves she's not such a delicate flower. It was late evening when we came to the scene where we see the Dragon for the first time and I'd developed a slight headache after a long day. We rehearsed a couple of times so that Leslie Meadows inside the costume didn't bump into the set, and then went for a take. Bonnie turned to me.

'I'm sorry about this, Soph,' she said, and on 'action', let out a piercing scream which reverberated round my ear drum.

'Cut!' shouted Gary, and then to my horror, he added, 'Technical problem, we'll have to go again.' Luckily, it was the final shot of the day and I could go home and lie down!

During the final studio block, John asked Sylv and me to come to television Centre early one morning and pose for press photos. This was for the big announcement that I was to be joining the Doctor in the TARDIS in the next series. Richard Croft and I had trudged up and down Oxford Street on another shopping mission until we found the perfect skirt and top in a little shop in St Christopher's Place.

I stood in front of the TARDIS with dozens of cameras trained on me. Each photographer jostled to get the best shot for their paper.

We stood in the drizzle for about half an hour. Luckily, Sylv was great at making me laugh – I thought my cheeks were going to seize up with so much smiling for the cameras.

After the final day's studio, cast and crew gathered in room B209 in the basement of Television Centre for celebratory drinks. We toasted Bonnie, who received a bouquet of flowers nearly as big as herself, and said our goodbyes. As I wandered off to the multistorey car park, I looked up at the stars through the gaps in the clouds and whispered 'Thanks!' **S**

Photo: Steve Cook

Above: My first brush with the press. 'Sophie, look this way for the Daily Mirror... *over here a sec – it's the* Sun... *Sophie, Sophie...*

Designing the Sets

The sets by designer John Asbridge featured two distinct control areas: the main control room and Kane's forbidden zone. Both these sets required functional switches and lights that would be provided by the effects department.

Andy McVean had some panels custom made for the story, others were salvaged from the now redundant 'Delta' spacecraft set and reworked to suit the Iceworld control rooms.

John's sets similarly made use of vacuum-formed plastic, particularly in the lower levels of Iceworld. Three distinct looks were given to the sets. The more populated areas were rife with gantries and railings that became less evident the lower down the action moved.

Andy's effects team also provided the ever-present icy mist from a number of dry ice machines concealed within John's sets. The freezer centre similarly had effects involvement with each chest freezer being filled with smoke prior to each take so that vapour billowed out as they were opened.

Mike Tucker

Season 25

Right: The Gods of Ragnarok: Janet Hargreaves, Kathryn Ludlow and David Ashford. The Greatest Show in the Galaxy.

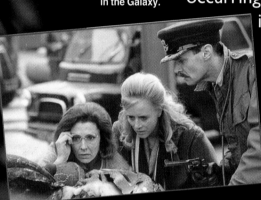

Above: Rachel (Pamela Salem), Allison (Karen Gledhill) and Group Captain Gilmore (Simon Williams) examine Dalek innards in the Totters Lane junkyard. Remembrance of the Daleks.

Photo: Andrew Cartmel

Above: Sylvester McCoy, Mary Reynolds, writer Kevin Clarke and Sophie Aldred pose for publicity photos during the recording of Silver Nemesis.

Right: The Kandyman (David John Pope). The Happiness Patrol.

Season 25 – the anniversary season. If this season of *Doctor Who* had a theme then it was 'unfinished business', a phrase that kept occurring in several of the stories and in the publicity material.

During the filming of *Silver Nemesis* a trailer was shot with the Doctor and Ace sitting on the riverbank outside the TARDIS, the location from the beginning of the story. The Doctor is telling Ace that it is twenty five years – Earth time – since he first visited the planet and that he has made a lot of enemies along the way. There was then a series of clips of all the stories that had been made in the season, before a short scene with the Doctor telling Ace that he has a lot of unfinished business.

All the stories followed this idea of the Doctor returning to deal with some threat that he has faced before, though it is only *The Greatest Show in the Galaxy* where the Doctor is unaware at the story's outset that he has old enemies to deal with.

Although *Silver Nemesis* was officially the anniversary story, *Remembrance of the Daleks* managed to fit in a few continuity references as well, tying up as it did with the very first episode *An Unearthly Child*. Cast and crew watched many old episodes to ensure that history was followed and even though small touches – such as Ace picking up a copy of *The French Revolution* – were put in, errors occurred, such as I.M. Foreman being spelt wrong on the junkyard gates!

Remembrance of the Daleks

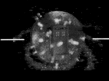

By Ben Aaronivitch   Story 7H

4 Episodes – broadcast 5 October to 26 October 1988

The Cast

The Doctor	Sylvester McCoy
Ace	Sophie Aldred
Gilmore	Simon Williams
Mike	Dursley McLinden
Rachel	Pamela Salem
Allison	Karen Gledhill
Ratcliff	George Sewell
Headmaster	Michael Sheard
Harry	Harry Fowler
The girl	Jasmine Breaks
Embery	Peter Hamilton Dyer
Vicar	Peter Halliday
John	Joseph Marcell
Martin	William Thomas
Kaufman	Derek Keller
Emperor/Davros	Terry Molloy
Black Dalek operator	Hugh Spight
Dalek operators	John Scott Martin
	Tony Starr
	Cy Town
Voices	Roy Skelton
	John Leeson
	Brian Miller
	Royce Mills

The Production Team

Producer	John Nathan-Turner
Director	Andrew Morgan
Script editor	Andrew Cartmel
Production managers	Ian Fraser
	Michael McDermott

Production associate	June Collins
Production assistant	Rosemary Parsons
Assistant floor managers	Val McCrimmon
	Lynne Grant
Lighting engineering manager	Ian Dow
EM2	Brian Jones
Outside broadcast sound	Doug Whitaker
Outside broadcast Cameramen	Les Mowbray
	Robin Sutherland
	Barry Chaston
Designer	Martin Collins
Costume designer	Ken Trew
Make up designer	Christine Greenwood
Visual effects designer	Stuart Brisdon
Visual effects assistants	Micky Edwards
	Andrew David
	Tony Auger
	Martin Geeson
	Dave Becker
Stunt arranger	Tip Tipping
Video effects designer	Dave Chapman
Vision mixers	Shirley Coward
	Fred Law
Technical co-ordinator	Richard Wilson
Studio camera supervisor	Alec Wheal
Videotape editor	Hugh Parson
Properties buyer	Chris Ferndby
Studio lighting	Henry Barber
Studio sound	Scott Talbot
Incidental music	Keff McCulloch
Special sound	Dick Mills

REMEMBRANCE OF THE DALEKS IS A GREAT REGRET FOR ME. OF ALL THE Sylvester McCoy stories it is the only one that I would really like to have done, and one of the ones that I had almost no involvement in whatsoever.

It was at one of Andrew Cartmel's lunchtime brainstorming sessions that I learned that a Dalek story was under way, and was introduced to Ben Aaronovitch – a man who likes his special effects. It was obvious that Ben had a lot of really spectacular ideas, all of them well outside the realms of a normal *Doctor Who* budget, though I think that even Ben was surprised at what was achieved on *Remembrance*.

The effects designer for the story was Stuart Brisdon, a long serving member of the effects department and a man who specialised in pyrotechnics. The *Remembrance* script was a delight to him, with barely a scene going by without some explosion or other.

For the effects crew, however, there was far more than just pyrotechnic work. The Dalek props themselves needed extensive work, not just refurbishment. A complete new set of Daleks was called for, as well as two special props, the special weapons Dalek and the Emperor Dalek.

Stuart had all the existing Dalek props shipped over to the effects department from the store where they had resided since their last appearance. Although many of the fibreglass Daleks had lasted quite well, some of the older, wooden props were beginning to show their age. Stuart decided that the Imperial Daleks would all be constructed as new whilst the existing shells would all be repainted in the grey and black livery of the renegade Daleks. Whilst refurbishing these existing Daleks he also had all the mesh removed from the shoulder section, replacing it with a soft foam, vacuum-formed in a mesh pattern, making the props slightly more user friendly.

The new Imperial Daleks had all the slats moulded in with the shoulders, and the mesh was dispensed with altogether. Similarly, the neck section, that had previously been constructed from timber and clad in mesh, was now a single fibreglass piece, as was the eye stalk. The redesigned 'ears' of the Daleks were created by Paul McGuinness who, fed up with the car indicator lights that had been used for several years, made up a set in his own time and showed them to Stuart, who liked them. The domes were also made anew, giving the Imperial Daleks a very crisp, clean look.

Stuart's final update was to remove the much mocked sink plunger, replacing it with a similarly shaped probe that would locate into a socket. These sockets were reproduced in fibreglass and handed over to the set designer to fit to all the Dalek control panels in place of buttons and dials. The result of this was that the Dalek sets all had a very austere, functional look.

The two new design Daleks were quite unlike anything ever seen in *Doctor Who* before. Stuart designed the special weapons Dalek as little more than a mobile cannon, with no eye stalk and no probe arm. The prop, built by effects assistant Dave Becker, ended up almost identical to Stuart's original design drawing. The final touch was to weather it quite severely, making the Dalek look as though it had seen a lot of action.

The special weapons Dalek evolved from two ideas in the original script that were dropped for cost reasons. The Imperial Daleks were to stalk through the streets of London with a large floating gun emplacement. The special weapons Dalek as such was merely a normal Dalek with a gun capable of firing around corners. When these ideas were dropped, the 'mobile tank' was a good alternative. The Emperor was described in the script as being spherical, and a large perspex sphere left over from the *Bodymatters* programme formed the basic shape of the prop.

The Emperor evolved from one of Andrew's lunchtime ideas meetings. I ran the idea of Davros being inside the Emperor past Ben and he jumped at it. The idea itself had been something that I had discussed with costume maker

Above: Andrew David touches up the paintwork of one of the imperial Daleks.

Writing Remembrance

When I wrote *Remembrance* I didn't know if we were going out at 5.15 pm or 7.30 pm. I'd have had more violence in it if I'd known that we were going out at 7.30 pm.

Ken Trew came up to me to say that he'd sent someone down to the Imperial War Museum in order to determine exactly what sort of cap badge an RAF soldier would have been wearing in 1963. What type of gun, what type of helmet, it all had to be right, yet if you set something ten years in the future all that happens is that someone sticks a flashing light on it.

We all knew that there was a mystery as to who exactly the Doctor was but we all had different ideas about what it was so that it remained a mystery. I remember that Kevin Clarke had a completely different idea as to who the Doctor was, and he wasn't telling! So there were two objectives for me; to get more mystery back and to get the kids back behind the sofa.

Drama goes through cycles of light and shade, light and shade and it just seemed right that the Doctor became slightly darker. The whole business about the Doctor knowing what was going on was simply because I thought it would be nice if the Doctor knew what was going on right from the start for a change, so that he is manipulating everyone else. It's a self limiting factor though, if he becomes totally omnipotent. You can't start every adventure with him knowing what is going on. We had a whole spectrum of ideas so that you could have a darker Doctor and a lighter Doctor for a whole series of stories, so some stories would be slightly more surreal.

Ben Aaronovitch Writer

Right: The special weapons Dalek designed by Stuart Brisdon, nicknamed 'Punk Dalek' by Sylvester.

Photos: John Freeman

Robert Allsopp and I still regret not having had the opportunity to build that particular prop.

The original ending of the show was also changed quite considerably from the original script, though not for cost reasons. The Doctor's final confrontation with the black Dalek saw him armed with Omega's flare gun, used to send interstellar distress signals. This was to be referred to as the Finger of Omega. The story's climax was to be a showdown in true spaghetti western style, with the Doctor out-drawing the Dalek and blowing it to pieces. It was Sylvester who turned the idea down, pointing out, with some validity, that the Doctor wielding a gun was not really in character.

Although very ambitious with his ideas, Ben was always very conscious of the limitations of a television budget and his script notes constantly showed an awareness of the way that the programme would be put together. For the scene of the Dalek ship landing in the school yard he indicated that it could probably be achieved using miniatures and the Paintbox graphics system and yet, upon arriving on location in Hammersmith he was confronted with a full size imperial assault shuttle being lowered into the yard on the end of a crane, achieving the shot for real!

The shuttle design was governed by the fact that it had to be big enough to hold about six Daleks and yet not be too complex to construct. The basic framework of the modular design was made by the scenic construction department whilst the originals for the fibreglass panels that clad it were made by effects assistant Melvyn Friend, who also manufactured the miniature of the shuttle.

Melvyn was also responsible for the other miniatures in the show, both representing the Dalek mothership. The main miniature was about five feet long, with an hexagonal basis to the design, done at Stuart's request. A close-up section of the docking bay was also constructed, and my only involvement with the show was the surface detailing of this close-up section. In the final transmitted shot, however, the back lighting is so harsh that none of the surface detail is visible!

In a break with tradition, the Daleks fired pulses of energy, as opposed to a beam, and Ben had specified that the soldier was to be hurled backwards by the impact. Stunt man Tip Tipping was rigged to a jerk harness by the effects crew and, on cue, pulled backwards into a specially prepared, corrugated iron wall. In post production Dave Chapman and Paintbox artist Jim McCarthy animated a skeleton, frame by frame onto the actor, also adding the now familiar 'negative' glow.

Of the all the set pieces in *Remembrance*, the battle between Ace and the Dalek in the school lab was one of the most effects intensive. Stuart and his team rigged the science lab so that as gas taps were blown off, the gas would ignite, and water pipes were made to spew water when fractured. They also built up the resin glass window that Ace jumps through. The entire sequence was edited very tightly and most of the effects work is only visible fleetingly. Indeed, the gas jets are only visible reflected in the glass of the cupboards on the back wall but it is this attention to detail throughout *Remembrance* that give it such an epic feel. **M**

Above left: The special weapons Dalek awaits its operator.

Above: Sophie and Sylvester and the imperial Daleks waiting for the start of recording.

The Doctor's character

There was no definite game plan about Sylvester's character. It was more like the writers fell into place and it naturally happened that we developed the Doctor. Ben and Marc had quite clear cut ideas although Marc was the only one who came from the background of being a fan.

My basic idea was that I wanted the show to be quite dark and scary. When I went in to talk to the Head of Drama one of the first things that he asked me was 'Who is *Doctor Who* for ?' and I said that it was for everyone – a diplomats answer – but he said 'no, it's for children' and I nodded but thought 'no it isn't'. I never thought that it should be a show that children shouldn't be able to watch but I thought it should be an adult programme that was accessible to children.

I think kids can watch adult programmes and I wanted it to be more macabre, certainly darker and scarier because the Colin Baker era, even though it tried to be scary, never got to me in the way that some of the better McCoy stories did. There was a lot of the Colin Baker years where there would be endless bickering in the TARDIS, a bit like *Neighbours* with roundels on the walls.

We certainly did want to build up the mystery. Having said that we had no agenda, I think that we did say on several occasions that we wanted the Doctor to be more mysterious and also more powerful because he didn't seem to be this huge, dangerous, interesting alien, and I think we managed to recapture some of that with Sylvester.

Andrew Cartmel
Script Editor

Above: The full size Dalek shuttle under construction.

Right: The full size Dalek shuttle is attached to a crane to film the scenes where the ship lands in the school yard.

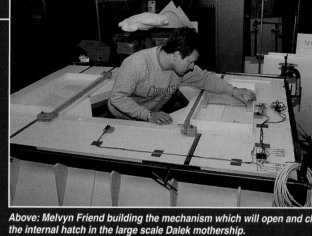

Above: Melvyn Friend building the mechanism which will open and clos the internal hatch in the large scale Dalek mothership.

Above: The shuttle takes to the air.

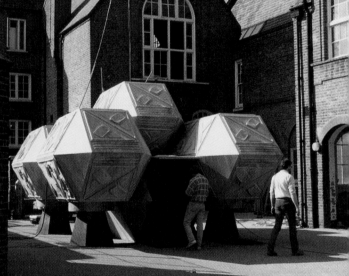

Above: The completed Dalek shuttle stands ready for action in the school yard.

Above: Liquid nitrogen is rigged to escape from the shuttle's thruster ports.

Photos: Melvyn Friend and Ian Dow

Playing the Doctor

Originally, I went Chaplinesque, with the hat and the umbrella I had a profile that I thought looked good. My Doctor developed slowly. I came to it with distant memories of Troughton and Pertwee, and the early days of Tom Baker and so that was the baggage that I brought with me.

The dark side I was enjoying playing. My grandmother had led a very long life and she once said to me, when she was about one hundred years old, that she was still fit and bright but fed up and bored, she'd lived so long and seen so many people die and I thought that it would be nice to bring that to the Doctor, that weariness of time. He's been around 950 years and has lost so many companions and I wanted to bring that on, every now and then bring this incredible sadness at the length of it all, but never losing the comedy. Having that as a front and every now and then letting bits slip and seeing sadness, or anger or bewilderment.

It was also discussed that too much was known about the Doctor and that it would be great to bring back the mystery, of not being sure who he was. The writers were working towards the idea that he was part of a triumvirate that created Gallifrey but I don't know how it was going to develop.

I was very sad that it came off when it did because I had a feeling that it was beginning to work. We'd got it right and the feedback was saying, 'You've got it, you're on the right track.'

Sylvester McCoy
Actor, the seventh Doctor

Above: Mike's only work on Remembrance of the Daleks *was detailing the large section of the Dalek spacecraft.*

Above: The effects crew hard at work rigging the Dalek shuttle with tanks of liquid nitrogen to provide exhaust gases when the ship took off and landed.

Photos: Melvyn Friend and Ian Dow

Above: An Imperial Dalek and the special weapons Dalek are filmed in front of the shuttle.

Right: The miniature of the shuttlecraft.

Above: Close-up of the detailing on the underside of the Dalek mothership.

Right: The spacecraft on the North Acton model stage.

Who is the Doctor?

There was a time when I felt that, probably because the writers had met Sophie, that they were focussing too heavily on Ace at the expense of the Doctor and I did have to curtail and soften the writers' obsession because I felt that there was a time when the balance of the series was wrong. If the title of the show is *Doctor Who* then the companion, whilst important, shouldn't overshadow the Doctor.

Andrew and the writers had all sorts of sensational revelations as to who the Doctor was, none of which I was prepared to entertain. I was prepared to accept the odd hint, but originally it was spelt out. I think that you have to be very careful with what you say to an audience, especially an impressionable one, and I felt that what Andrew and the writers were going to do went totally against making the Doctor more mysterious.

**John Nathan-Turner
Producer**

Below: The Remembrance *twins! My stunt double Tracey Ebbon and me in costume. I'd gone off cycling shorts having looked like a black pudding in* Dragonfire – *in fact, JNT had asked me to lose half a stone, which I had conveniently forgotten. The leggings and skirt were inspired by a trendy friend, and Ken Trew bought new Doctor Marten boots as my own still shed polystyrene balls from Iceworld's fake ice and snow. I also added my own badges which caused continuity agro later.*

Right: Simon 'Sam' Williams and John Nathan-Turner in the schoolroom.

Never let Sylvester McCoy drive!

We were shooting in an old Bedford Dormobile around Old Oak Common. When you are shooting on vehicles you can do it in one of two ways. You can put the vehicle on a trailer and tow it around, but it always looks unnatural. Ideally, the vehicle should actually be travelling and you mount a camera on the bonnet or on the door, in which case it sticks out of the side of the vehicle and you must remember not to go too near lamp posts. Now, when actors are doing this it's not very easy for them, because as well as delivering their lines they have to concentrate on driving, remembering that the vehicle is two feet wider on one side than usual. The advice I would give anyone who works in television is this: never let Sylvester McCoy drive!

Ian Dow
Outside broadcast manager

WEDNESDAY, JANUARY 13TH, 1988. I'M HOLDING FORTH IN A DINGY cafe in Shepherd's Bush, extolling the virtues of motorbike riding and football to a handful of writers and script editor, Andrew Cartmel. His idea is for the writers of this season to meet me and check out my personality for Ace's characterisation.

'Fine,' I thought, 'free lunch.'

So here was Ben Aaronovitch analysing my Dalek bashing potential and Graeme Curry making sure I couldn't tap dance for the Happiness Patrol auditions. I assured him that my tap dancing ability matches Bonnie Langford's to play centre forward for Charlton Athletic, and Graeme breathed a sigh of relief.

We discussed Ace's vocabulary; Ben came up with some choice 'street' words and I promised to suss out some 'yoof' phrases.

Several weeks later we gathered for a read-through at North Acton. We rehearsed Totters Lane where pandemonium breaks loose; soldiers run about shooting everything in sight, the Doctor grows steadily more irritated with the futility of human lust for power, and Ace has a great time doling out Nitro 9 and watching explosions. I stood to one side and looked round the room. Grown men charged around holding pieces of wood to their shoulders and making machine gun noises, Sylvester stood in the middle waving his script and shouting, and over in the corner, Cy Town stuck his arm out in front of him at eye level, shuffling round the side of an old cupboard firing pretend laser beams.

I was overjoyed to be working with Daleks. I wouldn't have felt like a kosher *Doctor Who* girl without having confronted the 'pepper pots.' With the experienced Dalek operator team of John Scott Martin, Cy Town and Tony Starr, we were in good hands. New-boy Hugh Spight, a dancer, moved faster than his more sedate companions, and was often seen storming ahead, while the others shook their eye-pieces at the little upstart.

My first day on location was a chilly April morning and not for the last time I was glad of my warm Ace jacket as I sat nursing a cup of tea in make up. Technical problems included wobbly Daleks and a massive visual effects explosion under Waterloo station which set off car alarms for miles around.

The Totters Lane scenes took two days at Kew Bridge steam museum. I'd met stunt director Tip Tipping during rehearsals, and now watched as he showed Sylv how to dive onto a crash mat so he could look heroic on camera without breaking any bones. Tip doubled as the soldier who comes under Dalek laser fire. He positioned a sheet of corrugated iron, harnessed himself up, and was snatched backwards on cue. Tip had a

busy couple of days, even doubling for me, donning my Ace jacket and driving the old Bedford van out of Totters Yard, smashing into an oil drum as he went.

I was disappointed at not being allowed to drive, but got my chance the next day when Sylvester and I were let loose on the unsuspecting North Acton streets. In the back of the van crouched a nervous sound and camera crew, plus JNT who was directing these scenes while Andrew Morgan was a few miles up the road filming Mike's struggle with the dastardly headmaster.

The camera was mounted securely to the passenger window and I drove first. It was an interesting challenge to drive, act and remember my lines at the same time, but not as interesting as when we swapped and it was Sylvester's turn. He leant towards me and confided, 'I'm completely blind without my glasses; let me know when I'm driving too near the kerb, and whether there's any on-coming traffic'. I gulped, and had visions of thousands of pounds worth of television camera hitting a lamp post as we veered towards the pavement. In the end we had to dub a large chunk of the dialogue in post production. I think the sound man must have been terrified to deafness by Sylvester's blind driving.

The next day a cab picked me up at some unearthly hour and took me to Hammersmith to a disused school in the forebodingly named Macbeth Street. It was a big day for me – my first big stunt sequence – and I was excited and scared too. My stunt double was Tracey Ebbon. Make up were delighted that she had a similar hair line, costume were relieved that she was roughly the same size as me, and I was secretly jealous that she was going through the window and not me. Tip had previously explained that although I could do most of the stunt, jumping through a sheet of sugar glass and balsa wood is not as easy as it sounds. Tracey would have to jump with enough force to break the window, while being careful not to smack into the opposite wall.

Tip had choreographed all my moves with me in the rehearsal room, and we walked through the stunt several times. I slid under the school desks, worked out a neat way of jumping up on top of them, and after a couple of camera rehearsals, we were ready for action. My adrenalin was pumping. I only had one bash at this so I had to get it right first time.

'Action!' Andrew shouted, and my first surprise was the jar of metal upon metal as I smashed my baseball bat down on the Dalek. My second shock was the spurting water, fire, and resulting smoke courtesy of the visual effects which made it quite hard to see. I slid under the desks, commando style, leapt up on top, breaking test tubes as I jumped, ran hell for leather for the window, and remembered not to jump through it.

I climbed down from the benches, adrenalin pumping through my body – I was hooked on stunts. Tracey took my place and charged at the window, burst through, and landed safely on the crash mats the other side.

Location filming over, it was back to North Acton for studio rehearsals. In the original script, it was the Doctor who fires the ATR at the Dalek. Sylvester pointed out that this was out of character, and that Ace should do it. When I practised, Doug Needham warned me of the kickback, and of the alarming flame which shot out of the back. I took a deep breath, pulled the trigger, and even though I was prepared, bruised my shoulder from the kickback. When I fired at the Dalek on the take, I didn't realise that I'd positioned myself so near the wall behind me, so Sylvester was somewhat surprised to see a huge flame shoot out of the back of the gun scorching the paintwork behind him.

The transmat scenes were my initiation into the ancient *Doctor Who* girl ritual of reacting to monsters that aren't there. I was told that the materialising Dalek effect would be added in post production and to pretend to look horrified. At least I didn't have to scream. **S**

The most expensive earring

*R*emembrance of the Daleks must feature the most expensive earring in the annals of the BBC. We were coming up to do the close-ups of Sophie in the laboratory. We'd been shooting the night before and the girl who was dressing her that night wasn't there the next day. Anyway, the following morning we couldn't find these Batman earrings and there was a mad panic. I tried to make one but that wasn't very successful. Eventually I told my assistant, Andrew Duckett, to just get a cab and go to Covent Garden, find the same earrings and get back.

I never forgave that jacket because bits kept flying off it and I was always cursing poor old Richard Croft like nobody's business.

Because we'd already done the Army and the Navy somebody had the bright idea that we should use the RAF regiments, which threw me completely because I know nothing about the RAF at all. So I spent a couple of days down at the Imperial War Museum looking up what things ought to look like because I'd had a sticky incident a few years before on another programme. It was a drama set in the 1940s but the costumes were from 1956 – they are regularly changing jackets and that sort of thing. *Remembrance* wasn't really that adventurous from our side.

Ken Trew
Costume designer

Bottom left: The Doctor's Dalek jamming device.

Below: Sylvester takes a practice dive on to a crash mat in preparation for the scene where a Dalek explodes behind him.

Photo: Russell Pritchett

Above: The big bang!

Photo: Russell Pritchett

The day the Daleks blew up Waterloo

It was Easter Monday, the anniversary of the Easter Rebellion in Dublin and we were filming under the arches of Waterloo station. Now, normally when you're filming the police are told. The Dalek factions are fighting each other and so the effects guys set up these explosions and battle commences. And wow, what a battle! It was wonderful. Then this explosion went off that was so large that all the car alarms for miles went off and suddenly, in the distance, we heard sirens and it was reported on the news that the IRA had blown up Waterloo station! Someone had forgotten to tell the ambulance service or the fire department or the railway police - and they were really panicking - and there was smoke everywhere and I was standing watching all this. Then an ambulance arrived and the driver stopped and looked out of his windscreen and his mouth just dropped open because out of the smoke came all these Daleks. I'll never forget the look on his face!

On the same story, we were filming in a building owned by Independent Television. There was this big gate and the Daleks were all outside. The Rambo Dalek was going to blow up the gate and all the Daleks would come marching in. The cameras are all set up and then 'Bang!', the gate disappears, all the windows break around us and the Daleks melt!

Sylvester McCoy
Actor, the seventh Doctor

Above left: Chunky and me at attention outside the church. During rehearsals 'Sam' had earned the nickname 'Chunky'. Our juvenile and hilarious (at the time) humour meant that he would pull out his gun and say, 'I've got a big one here.' You had to be there, I suppose. The nickname even made it into a couple of scenes.

Above: Extras waiting for action in the junkyard.

Left: Me hoping to drive Sylv round the bend!

Above: Sophie sprints into action during a camera rehearsal in Totters Lane.

Building the Imperial Daleks. Far left: Two newly cast domes. Middle: Casting the neck section. Left: Two body sections awaiting finishing touches including the half spheres around their sides.

The Greatest Show in the Galaxy

By Stephen Wyatt   Story 7J

4 Episodes – broadcast 14 December 1988 to 4 January 1989

The Cast

The Doctor	Sylvester McCoy
Ace	Sophie Aldred
The Captain	T P McKenna
Mags	Jessica Martin
Ringmaster	Ricco Ross
Stalls lady	Peggy Mount
Chief clown	Ian Reddington
Morgana	Deborah Manship
Bellboy	Christopher Guard
Whizzkid	Gian Sammarco
Nord	Daniel Peacock
Flowerchild	Dee Sadler
Bus conductor	Dean Hollingsworth
Deadbeat	Chris Jury
Dad	David Ashford
Mum	Janet Hargreaves
Little girl	Kathryn Ludlow
Tumbler	Alan Heap
Clowns	Paul Sadler
	Philip Sadler
	Patricia Ford

The Production Team

Producer	John Nathan-Turner
Director	Alan Wareing
Script editor	Andrew Cartmel
Production managers	Ian Fraser
	Gary Downie
Production associate	June Collins
Production Assistant	Alexandra Todd
Assistant floor managers	David Tilley
	Duncan McAlpine
Outside broadcast lighting	Ian Dow
EM2	Brian Jones
Outside broadcast sound	Doug Whitaker
Outside broadcast cameramen	Barry Chaston
	Alan Jessop
Designer	David Laskey
Costume designer	Rosalind Ebbutt
Make-up designer	Denise Baron
Visual effects designer	Steve Bowman
Visual effects assistants	Dave Wells
	Dave Becker
	Jim Lancaster
	Mike Tucker
	Biddy Palmer
Video effects designer	Dave Chapman
Vision mixers	Barbara Gainsley
	Dinah Long
	Julie Mann
	Fred Law
Technical co-ordinators	Michael Langley-Evans
	Richard Wilson
Studio camera supervisor	Alec Wheal
Video tape editor	Hugh Parson
Properties buyer	Bob Blanks
Studio lighting	Don Babbage
	Henry Barber
Studio Sound	Scott Talbot
Incidental music	Mark Ayres
Special sound	Dick Mills

MY FIRST WORK ON THE ANNIVERSARY SEASON WAS AS STEVE BOWMAN'S assistant on *The Greatest Show in the Galaxy*. Because of my commitments to *Silver Nemesis* I would have to leave the show early, before the studio block took place, but for a two week period I was working on both shows for two different designers – one of the busiest periods of my life and I have to say that I can't recommend it!

Robots made up the bulk of the work for us. Biddy Palmer started by manufacturing the panel that could be fitted to an actor's back and opened, revealing circuit boards. She was also responsible for the complete robot suit seen in the circus workshop. The face mask for this 'unclothed' robot was vacuum-formed from a metallic plastic whereas the bulk of the clown masks were made from soft foam with only the eyes metalised.

The other 'worn' robot costume was the bus conductor. Two versions were required by the script – one battered and one new. The conductor destroyed by the Doctor on the bus was based around a shop window mannequin, jointed in such a way that it would collapse like a person, albeit a rather stiff person! The neck was dressed with various pipes and tubes, the plan being to reveal spurting hydraulics once the head had been blown off. The dummy was suspended from a single wire to the top of the head, and at the same time that the explosive charge was set off, the wire was cut, allowing the robot to fall to the ground.

The other robot, destroyed by Ace, was to be completely blown apart and so complete bodies were made from plastic and rigid polyurethane foam. Two dummy robots were made in case of retakes and both were quite extensively detailed. None of this is visible, however, since the explosion was so quick and so devastatingly effective!

All the other robots were completely non-human. The 'junk mail' robot was built as a full size prop and as two sizes of miniature – the live action prop built by Tony McKillop and the miniatures by me. Originally scripted to scuttle around the console like a metallic spider, Steve eventually opted for a far simpler wheeled mechanism with the legs merely as dressing, though they could extend and retract. Lights and motors were dressed onto the basic shape, everything being operated by radio control. The probe plugging itself into the console was done in the time honoured tradition of pulling the plug off the console and reversing the tape.

The miniatures were built for a lengthy sequence of the probe approaching the TARDIS, slowly deactivating its defences as it gets closer and closer. The sequence was shot several weeks before the rest of the production was under way, an unusual state of affairs, as model filming is usually done after the main shoot. The two TARDIS miniatures that I had built for *The Trial of a Time Lord* were used. All of the shots were eventually considered to be lit too moodily and the entire sequence was trimmed from the show.

The final robot was the huge buried killer. Jim Lancaster constructed a steel framework fitted with air rams that would lift the robot from a lying to a sitting position. The arms were operated by Jim, sitting inside the torso of the robot, while the head and mouth were controlled remotely. The frame was clad in plastic and wood and detailed to look as though it had been buried for a very long time.

Much discussion had gone on about how to do the tent. The earliest, and most obvious, suggestion was to hire a real big top but this proved to be far too expensive. In the end, set designer David Lasky opted to build the vestibule full size

The producer directs

I was going to direct some *Doctor Who*. We used to do enough episodes for there to be a two-parter and that would mean that you were only away from the office for a short time. There were two stories that I was going to do, but one clashed with leave and the other happened when we were writing out K9 and I had to do the spin-off. Because of that I didn't feel that I could do the two-parter, because we were doing 26 episodes and a special.

Later on, there was a scene in *The Greatest Show in the Galaxy* where I got totally wrapped up in the love story. Alan Wareing had asked me to film the scene between Bellboy and Flowerchild and I told them to do it as they felt naturally – there was no pressure because we had plenty of time to shoot it. Anyway, we played around with the scene the way that you should and it was lovely. It's such a sweet scene because it was done without any of the pressure that normally surrounds making *Doctor Who*.

**John Nathan-Turner
Producer**

Below right: Jim Lancaster at work on the large killer robot.

Below: The almost-finished robot being painted.

whilst the rest of the tent would be a miniature that fell to me to construct.

With the skeleton of the model tent complete I could begin applying the fabric. This was done in sections to help with the collapse, and all the guy ropes were made from thin elastic.

The final detail was to make a miniature replica of David's full size vestibule, complete with graphics, and I worked directly from his construction plans to ensure that set and miniature matched exactly. The model was shot on location to ensure that the lighting conditions were the same on both miniature and full size section.

My task once on location was setting up the big top miniature and dressing it to match the real one. In order to stop the model getting damaged, a small canvas tent was erected over the top of it for the days prior to it being shot. The model was dirtied down with dust from the quarry and a rough landscape built around it.

For the destruction of the clown robots Steve and Jim had devised a dummy that had every joint as a small mortar, so that by placing small charges then assembling the limbs and torso, the robots could be blown apart in a variety of ways. Because there was only one dummy, however, it did mean redressing it in a different costume for each take and the old problem of not having enough time meant that the exploding dummy never got shot.

We did get enough time for the bus conductor explosions. When the bang went off inside the bus, the dummy left shot so quickly that it was barely on screen for more than a few frames. Rather than reset for another try it was decided to slow the sequence down in post production.

The second bang was outside the bus and has to be one of the loudest explosions that I have ever been involved with. All the sand for several metres around leapt into the air as it went off. Needless to say there was nothing left of the robot except a few scraps of shredded uniform that Ros Ebbut collected to see what the costumer store would say when she tried to hand it back in!

The most memorable explosion of the show has to be the one that goes off behind Sylvester as he calmly walks out of the vestibule of the tent. Steve had originally planned this to be an air mortar explosion, as if a huge raging wind was ripping through the tent. We had hired several large air mortars from an independent effects facility but when we came to assemble them we found that we had been given the hoses and fittings for a different set of mortars.

As an alternative we arranged several steel pan mortars inside the vestibule, intending to achieve a similar effect with pyrotechnics. Unfortunately, this information was never conveyed to Sylvester who was still expecting the 'rushing wind' effect and was more than a little surprised to feel the heat of a fairly sizeable explosion behind him! Ⓜ

Above: Steve Bowman's design sketch for the junk mail satellite which invades the TARDIS.

Above: Dean Hollingsworth tries on the conductor head at a fitting session in the visual effects workshop.

Designing the bus conductor

Alan Wareing didn't want the bus conductor looking too jokey. It went through several phases. It started as a more traditional square jawed head with very angular features, but he wanted something different. We had different views aesthetically as to how it looked in the end but what we got was quite amusing and quite different.

For the big top, a model seemed to be the logical way to go about the problem. The cost of constructing a big top in the middle of a sand pit would have been quite astronomical, especially since we had to make it collapse and catch fire and everything.

The auditorium was done in two phases. There was a model that Jim Lancaster built which was a table top model about two or three feet across with rows of amphitheatre-like seating. The model was made of plaster and had wires that would pull it apart whereas the main set was constructed from jabolite sections with a collapsing trap in the centre where the three gods were sitting. They went through the trap door and everything else, columns, pillars, lintels – all lightweight stuff – collapsed.

The model was shot but they had a problem with the tape, I think. It was done on a second unit and we only had one go at it, but in the last minute rush the machine wasn't running so it never made it into the show. It's unfortunate, but these things happen every now and again.

Steve Bowman
Visual effects designer

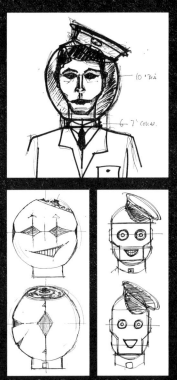

Above: Steve Bowman's design sketches for the bus conductor's head.

Making the conductor's head

Steve and director Alan Wareing had discussed the bus conductor at some length and had originally arrived at the idea of a grinning, spherical head. Steve had reservations about the design and had me make a mock-up to show Alan before we started on the actual prop. I found a polystyrene sphere in the workshop and made the mock-up from that, cutting in the eye and mouth holes. Once he had seen it, Alan agreed that it wasn't quite right and so Steve came up with the more streamlined design that eventually made it to the screen.

One problem that we encountered was that the heat build-up inside the mask caused the eyes to mist over quickly, making vision very difficult. The problem was solved by one of the effects crew who rode a motorbike. He provided us with a gel that motorcyclists use on the inside of their visors and it worked perfectly.

Mike Tucker

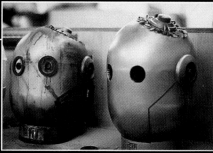

Above: The clean and dirty versions of the bus conductor robot's head.

Left: The dummy version of the bus conductor robot is set-up ready to be blown-up.

Below: The demise of the bus conductor. You can spot his eyes top left of picture! I wondered how Mike felt about his weeks of patient model work being blown to smithereens at the touch of a button.

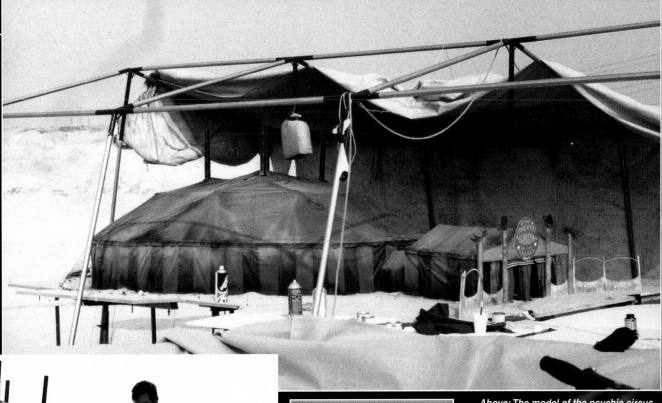

Above: The model of the psychic circus tent protected by its own full size tent, on location at Warmwell quarry.

Far left: The miniature tent being rigged.

Left: How the model appeared in the finished story.

Above: Sophie's make up man Mark works whilst Sylvester rests his feet.

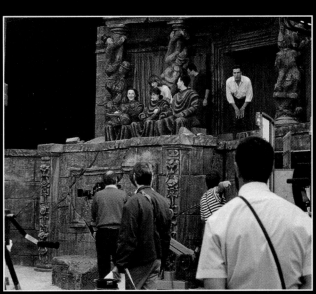

Photo: Sue Moore

Above: Setting up for the destruction of the dark circus with the gods of ragnarok minus their heads while the actors take a breather.

Lying in the back of a hearse

For *The Greatest Show in the Galaxy* we had a hearse driven by a clown. We also had to get a camera inside the hearse. Now, in those days you got a better result if you had an engineer controlling the iris of the camera. With it being very bright outside but you're trying to expose for inside, and with the sun constantly changing direction as you're driving, you get a better picture if you've got an engineer watching the picture on a high quality monitor and tweaking the colour and adjusting the iris. Now, what you may not know about hearses is that in order to save money they often carry a second body underneath the main coffin – you can actually slide a second coffin underneath – and that's where we put the engineer. We opened the back door, two people picked him up and stuffed him head first under the floor with a monitor.

Ian Dow
Outside broadcast manager

REFRESHED BUT SADDLESORE AFTER A CHARITY BIKE RIDE FROM LONDON TO Oxford, and a week of walking, sailing and eating in Norfolk, I returned to the delights of North Acton's stewed BBC coffee. Most of the new cast were around my age, and judging by the atmosphere during the read-through, this looked like being fun.

We had a few days to rehearse the location sequences before travelling to Dorset to my first *Doctor Who* quarry – another milestone in the life of a burgeoning *Doctor Who* girl. As for the script, Stephen Wyatt explored Ace's vulnerability with her fear of clowns. Childhood memories of circuses came flooding back. I was holding a warm grown-up hand as I stumped, red wellied, across Blackheath towards the lit up fairy palace that was Billy Smart's circus at night. Bundled up in a snug anorak and mittens on a string to guard against the chilly Autumn air, I was fascinated by my breath puffing out in front of me. I pulled my parents impatiently through the canvas corridor, clambering to my seat on a wooden bench, nostrils twitching with that heady circus smell of sawdust and warm animals, mingled with popcorn and candy floss. But I could never see the point of clowns. My first idols were the trapeze artists, who climbed nerve janglingly high up to the eaves of the big top, who swooped and dived way over our heads in their sequinned tights and tunics. Yes, that's what I wanted to be. My parents had invested in a small trapeze which hung next to the swing in our garden and I spent happy hours hanging upside down and planning my act. I never gave a second thought to those silly painted men who fell over for no apparent reason, feet stuck in buckets and smacking each other with planks of wood. Now where's the romance in that? I didn't find clowns scary, but neither did I laugh.

Ian Reddington had a blank canvas to work on for the Chief Clown. His hand gesture, like a French fop, and his chilling laugh exploited Ace's fear and made it easy to act scared.

The other clowns were played by street performers, circus folk and tumblers, who taught Sylvester and me to juggle with clubs in our spare moments. In between juggling and tumbling lessons, we blocked the location scenes. The director, Alan Wareing, was new to *Doctor Who*. I liked his style immediately. He was willing to work on our suggestions, but gave it to us straight when we were self indulgent or if something wasn't working. Our Doctor and Ace characters were wearing in together like a pair of comfy shoes, so Sylv and I had a good idea of what our characters would and wouldn't say or do.

Sylvester's one man showmanship was explored in the closing stages of the script and The Great Suprendo was booked to help him create a magic show to appease the Gods of Ragnorok. The AFM taped paper over the glass part of the rehearsal room doors: Keep out – Magic Circle in progress. I felt left out, like a kid who has been told to go away and play because the grown-ups are doing grown-up stuff.

We gathered early one morning at Television Centre for our trip to Dorset. It was like a school journey, with the advantage that we weren't going to have to write homework about the trip when we returned. I sat at the front with Jessica Martin. Unlike one memorable childhood coach journey when my best friend Zoe was sick into her school hat, Jessica kept us entertained with her impressions – notably Anthony Newly. We all joined in:

'You were maaayde for meee!'

The boys sang through the obligatory repertoire of rugby songs, then we dozed off into silence and contemplated our location lunch while the coach trundled past sun drenched fields.

As we arrived, the TARDIS was being eased into position on the edge of a sand cliff which Sylvester immediately included in the action, opening the door and stepping out over the cliff edge, me saving him just in time. There was one problem before we could start. For some reason the props crew were having problems coaxing the TARDIS roof into place. It was a shock to see the TARDIS flat packed – it seemed so undignified

Flat heels for Sophie

Ros Ebbut, costume designer, liked the skirt and T-shirt from *Remembrance* and suggested we look for patterned tights instead of leggings, with lace-up boots. After the read-through, we'd met up at Liberty's in Regent Street, and rummaged through the hosiery department. The tights I chose, with an embroidered scarlet zig-zag pattern down each leg, happened to be the most expensive in the shop, so Ros had extra pairs painted up by the costume department. We found the perfect boots in Hobbs in Covent Garden, flat heeled and good for running around strange planets. The last thing I wanted was high heels. As a child I'd often wondered why so many of the companions insisted on running around quarries in ridiculous footwear. No wonder they were always falling over and spraining their ankles. My heels were to be as flat as a Dalek's vowel sounds.

Sophie Aldred

Below: Ricco and me rehearsing

for the 'old girl'.

Sylvester and I crammed ourselves into the famous blue box. It was musty and cramped, with black felt drapes hanging from the roof, peeling paint work and spiders who must have had a nodding acquaintance with William Hartnell. With my childhood illusions in tatters, I stepped from the TARDIS for my first materialisation. One small step for Ace, one giant leap for Sophie.

Being a firm believer in equal opportunities, I was happy to acquire the services of a male make-up assistant, Mark, who loved heavy metal and drove a huge motor bike. He had such a gentle touch, that sometimes I had to ask him whether he'd actually put the make-up on my face. Mark loathed creating hairstyles – I pitied him with my fine flyaway stuff – so I fixed my own pony-tail. Mark was in charge of hair spray and gave my locks a liberal dousing every take to stop it wisping into my eyes.

Luckily for Mark, I'm the kind of gal who doesn't break out into a sweat until melting point. Even after a tough aerobics class I'm red-faced as a tomato with no sign of having sweat glands. However, make-up designer Dee Baron had problems enticing Ian Reddington's Chief Clown make-up to stay on his face. It melted down his cheeks in long white rivulets while Dee stemmed the flow with copious amounts of powder.

My worst moment was food related. We arrived at the quarry early on Sunday morning as the sun was warming up the sand dunes. We had to complete the stall holder scenes that we hadn't finished the previous night, where the Doctor and Ace are forced to eat some disgusting looking fruit. I had foregone breakfast and was looking forward to some nice fruity concoction cooked up by the props team. Little did I realise that they had taken the script literally and I stared in horror at a large dollop of custard and sweetcorn which I realised I had to eat. I cannot recommend it as a gourmet dish. The look of disgust on my face required no acting.

As a biker, I was intrigued to find out what kind of vehicle would be booked for Nord the Vandal. I was not disappointed. Bootsy, Ferret and their motley crew were a band of local bike enthusiasts who had enough tattoos and hair among them to people a race of Nords. They were interested enough in the filming to hang around and help out, and to my delight allowed Sylvester and me to take the bike off for a spin.

One good thing about filming away from home is that everyone is thrown together in a hotel for a few nights and gets to know each other. The Rembrandt Hotel, Weymouth had the added attraction of an outdoor swimming pool which proved just the job after a day in the dusty quarry. Drinks were served round the pool before supper, which we ate together round a long table in the dining room. One evening, TP McKenna was in mid theatrical anecdote when a woman dragging a small child approached our table.

'Ooh, it's you!' she exclaimed, 'I'm so glad. I wonder if you'd mind signing this for my son, he loves watching you on the telly.' She handed TP an autograph book, he smiled smugly round at us, signed his name, and handed back the book.

'What's this?' the woman shrilled, 'TP who?'

'Well who did you think I was?' asked TP humbly.

'That nice bloke what does the kiddies' art programmes – Tony Hart!' We stifled our laughter behind our table napkins!

We all liked the golden pond location for the hippy bus scenes. By now the sun was blazing hot and the make up and costume teams tanned happily. I found it hard not to squint as the sand acted like a sheet of foil, and I couldn't wear sun glasses between takes because of the mark they left on the ridge of my nose. Sylvester and I had decided by this time that Ace's annoying habit of calling the Doctor 'Professor' was an affectionate term to get up his nose; when faced with any kind of danger, Ace would revert to the more serious 'Doctor'. And we stuck to this pretty ▶

Above: Sylv and me relaxing around the pool at our hotel after a day at the quarry.

The TARDIS key

It was during this story that I designed and built a new-look TARDIS key and although it never actually got used in this story – JNT only saw the prop at a production party – it was adopted as one of Sylvester's continuity props from this point on.

Mike Tucker

Below: Shoot the writer! Stephen Wyatt gets some grief from myself, Sylvester and TP McKenna.

In the robot workshop

Apart from the arena, the set with the most involvement from the effects department was the robot workshop, which required both full body and partial robot corpses. One of the effects crew was concealed inside the workbench in order to play the part of the robot arm that grabs at Ace, while Jim operated his small-scale robot toy.

Mike Tucker

The clown workshop scenes contained my most satisfying acting. Chris Guard, who played Bellboy, is an intense, serious actor, and we knew the scenes would work well, given the right atmosphere. Alan gave us as much time as he could, and we did a couple of takes, knowing after the first that we'd got it better in rehearsals.

The extra take did the trick.

Sophie Aldred

Top right: Ian Reddington (the chief clown) keeps out of the sun to try to stop his make up from melting.

Right: Chris Jury as Deadbeat, practising being mad.

Right: Script editor Andrew Cartmel receives a friendly hug from Jessica Martin (Mags).

Above: I enjoyed my scenes grappling with the conductor (Dean Hollingsworth) who suggested that pulling my hair would look painful and indeed it was, although I was holding his hands down with mine and he wasn't pulling. I got my own back by mistake as Alan suggested I kick Dean's leg and I forgot it was flesh and bone and not metal alloy!

Above: Daniel Peacock (Nord) gets a few instructions on riding the bike.

Right: Charge! Daniel takes Sylvester and Sophie for a ride.

Above: More tea anyone? The Captain (TP McKenna) and the Doctor glare at each other over a spot of light refreshment.

A game of skittles and a drink

One evening we were invited to play skittles at a country pub against members of the *Crimesquad* crew who were filming in the area. I had ulterior motives for my participation. JNT was on our team, and after the game I settled myself down at the bar to get to know him better, and to confront my fear that he didn't like me. A couple of hours chatting and liquid refreshment later, we emerged from the pub arm in arm and have remained firm friends ever since.

Sophie Aldred

Right: Back to the North Acton rehearsals rooms, and Sylvester is caught in mid creation...

Above: ... Meanwhile TP gets stuck into a good book.

Below: Having lunch with the two baddies in the canteen at Elstree.

well throughout the following stories. Here was an occasion for a 'Doctor', though due to time in the edit my final line was cut. The script goes:

THE DOCTOR: [IN PLEASED SURPRISE] Doctor eh? So you can remember if you want to.
ACE: [NODDING CHEERFULLY] Seems so, Professor.
[THE DOCTOR ROLLS HIS EYES IN DESPAIR.]

A couple of scenes later, I looked down at my jacket and discovered to my dismay that one of my *Blue Peter* badges had fallen off into the sand. I alerted the costume team, and we scrabbled around sifting sand with our fingers, until it became obvious that this was a needle in a haystack job. Unfortunately, the lost badge happened to be the rarer of the two, and when

we contacted the *Blue Peter* office to send out another as soon as possible, they were unable to oblige with an exact replica as my own dark blue badge, acquired in 1970-something, had become obsolete long ago. They eventually sent us a light blue badge, which explains the colour change in subsequent episodes.

Another continuity conundrum was due to the final transmission order. The original plan was to air *Greatest Show* before *Silver Nemesis* and *Happiness Patrol* so the amazing appearance of Flowerchild's earring on my jacket two stories early has to be put down to the well-known Time Lord's affliction – time lag.

On the final day, the weather deteriorated. Shorts and T-shirts were exchanged for wellies and anoraks. Jim Lancaster climbed inside his robot creation which was like something from *Star Wars*. Pretty impressive, especially when it reared upright. I derived great satisfaction from hitting it on the head with a spade, though I'm sure Jim must have gone home with a headache after the mighty thwack I delivered. I was glad of my Ace jacket, and managed to sneak a thermal vest and cardigan underneath.

After a day off, it was back to rehearsals. I loved the TARDIS interior scenes, which turned out to be rare in my assistantship. Even this time we had to make cuts. Originally, there was a second scene where Ace was searching for her rucksack and the Doctor professed innocence. Sylvester borrowed his sons' Klutz' guide to juggling and we worked out how he could make the juggling ball disappear. A crew member had to stand out of shot with a large shrimping net on a pole and catch the ball as Sylvester threw it in the air. Paul Daniels, eat your heart out!

For once, it wasn't me who committed the continuity clanger: Dee Baron had designed Nord the Vandal's salon hairdo so that extensions could be woven into the ends of Daniel Peacock's hair. However, after filming his location sequences, Daniel had his curly locks trimmed at the back by mistake, and Dee had to practically stick the extensions to the ends of his shorn hair with super glue.

During rehearsals, a spot of redecorating at Television Centre unearthed a plague of asbestos, which prompted an immediate shutdown of all facilities, including our planned five studio days. I never realised the scale of the problem until recently when I gathered that it was lucky we didn't have to pack it in altogether. The only possibility of *Greatest Show* making it to the screen meant setting up camp – or rather Big Top – in the BBC Elstree Studios car park. There was one big problem, however. . . Noise!

The silence needed for filming was almost impossible to achieve. We'd go for a take, Gary Downie would shout 'Quiet, please!' and a light aircraft from a nearby airfield would chose to circle overhead, showing passengers an airborne view of the *East Enders* lot. Or a lorry delivering beer to the BBC bar would be chugging up the driveway. The atmosphere grew more fraught. My beloved TARDIS scenes, tricky to direct at the best of times due to a lack of reference points for the cameras and the Jalopeder obscuring the centre of shot, became rushed and tense. I stopped speaking halfway through a take when I thought I heard that stupid beer lorry again. Gary, who by this time was tearing his hair out because we were so far behind schedule, lost his temper, and I was the unhappy recipient of his anger. Biting back tears, I continued with the scene, and was relieved when it was over and I could run off to the toilets for a quick cry. Highly embarrassed by my over sensitivity, I visited make up for a repair job on my eyes and Gary apologised profusely.

Another tense moment was the result of an unaccustomed and highly justified wobbly thrown by Sylvester. He and Jessica were creeping round tented corridors and reacting to a voice-over which would be dubbed in post production. Our floor manager was reading in the lines, but hadn't corrected her script, which we'd changed substantially during rehearsals. She read the lines wrongly, so another take started. She read them wrongly once more. After another couple of takes, Sylvester lost it. I've never seen anyone actually jump up and down with rage before, but Sylv's explosion of Scottish anger was spectacular, and luckily, over very quickly.

At long last, against all the odds, we completed *Greatest Show*. Everyone breathed a sigh of relief, especially John Nathan-Turner who had been looking more harassed each day and was keeping the British tobacco industry in business. **S**

And the rest . . .

Most of the remainder of the effects involvement was with props – kites, clown's batons, lightweight dumbbells, some double-headed coins for Captain Cook (which although never clearly seen depicted the head of Alpha Centauri from *The Curse of Peladon*) and the crystal ball. This was plumbed up with smoke so that it could mist over on cue. A lightweight vacuum-formed sphere was also made for the scene in which the crystal ball blows up.

Mike Tucker

Above: Mike, Dean Hollingsworth as the conductor and Andrew Cartmel on location.

Below: Sylvester and me battling with the noise outside the makeshift studio in the Elstree car park.

Photo: Sue Moore

Far left: Sylvester rehearses for the final battle with the gods.

Left: The Captain and Mags take a ride in the jeep.

Below: Sylvester shows his cool as he walks unflinchingly from the largest explosion Warmwell Quarry had seen for years. And he thought it was going to be a wind effect!

facilities, including our planned five studio days. I never realised the scale of the problem until recently when I gathered that it was lucky we didn't have to pack it in altogether. The only possibility of *Greatest Show* making it to the screen meant setting up camp – or rather Big Top – in the BBC Elstree Studios car park. There was one big problem, however. . . Noise!

The silence needed for filming was almost impossible to achieve. We'd go for a take, Gary Downie would shout 'Quiet, please!' and a light aircraft from a nearby airfield would chose to circle overhead, showing passengers an airborne view of the *East Enders* lot. Or a lorry delivering beer to the BBC bar would be chugging up the driveway. The atmosphere grew more fraught. My beloved TARDIS scenes, tricky to direct at the best of times due to a lack of reference points for the cameras and the Jalopeder obscuring the centre of shot, became rushed and tense. I stopped speaking halfway through a take when I thought I heard that stupid beer lorry again. Gary, who by this time was tearing his hair out because we were so far behind schedule, lost his temper, and I was the unhappy recipient of his anger. Biting back tears, I continued with the scene, and was relieved when it was over and I could run off to the toilets for a quick cry. Highly embarrassed by my over sensitivity, I visited make up for a repair job on my eyes and Gary apologised profusely.

Another tense moment was the result of an unaccustomed and highly justified wobbly thrown by Sylvester. He and Jessica were creeping round tented corridors and reacting to a voice-over which would be dubbed in post production. Our floor manager was reading in the lines, but hadn't corrected her script, which we'd changed substantially during rehearsals. She read the lines wrongly, so another take started. She read them wrongly once more. After another couple of takes, Sylvester lost it. I've never seen anyone actually jump up and down with rage before, but Sylv's explosion of Scottish anger was spectacular, and luckily, over very quickly.

At long last, against all the odds, we completed *Greatest Show*. Everyone breathed a sigh of relief, especially John Nathan-Turner who had been looking more harassed each day and was keeping the British tobacco industry in business. **S**

And the rest . . .

Most of the remainder of the effects involvement was with props – kites, clown's batons, lightweight dumbbells, some double-headed coins for Captain Cook (which although never clearly seen depicted the head of Alpha Centauri from *The Curse of Peladon*) and the crystal ball. This was plumbed up with smoke so that it could mist over on cue. A lightweight vacuum-formed sphere was also made for the scene in which the crystal ball blows up.

Mike Tucker

Above: Mike, Dean Hollingsworth as the conductor and Andrew Cartmel on location.

Below: Sylvester and me battling with the noise outside the makeshift studio in the Elstree car park.

Photo: Sue Moore

Far left: Sylvester rehearses for the final battle with the gods.

Left: The Captain and Mags take a ride in the jeep.

Below: Sylvester shows his cool as he walks unflinchingly from the largest explosion Warmwell Quarry had seen for years. And he thought it was going to be a wind effect!

Silver Nemesis

By Kevin Clarke

Story 7K

3 Episodes – broadcast 23 November to 7 December 1988

The Cast

The Doctor	Sylvester McCoy
Ace	Sophie Aldred
Mrs Remmington	Dolores Gray
Lady Peinfort	Fiona Walker
De Flores	Anton Diffring
Richard	Gerard Murphy
Karl	Metin Yenal
Cyber leader	David Banks
Cyber lieutentant	Mark Hardy
Mathematician	Leslie French
Security man	Martyn Read
First Cyberman	Brian Orrell
First skinhead	Chris Chering
Second skinhead	Symond Lawes
Cybermen	Danny Boyd
	Scott Mitchell
	Bill Malin
	Tony Carlton
	Paul Barrass
Walkmen	Dave Ould
	John Ould
Queen	Mary Reynolds

The Production Team

Producer	John Nathan-Turner
Director	Chris Clough
Script editor	Andrew Cartmel
Production manager	Gary Downie
Production associate	June Collins
Production assistant	Jane Wellesley
Assistant floor manager	Lynne Grant
Producer's secretary	Lorraine Godding
Trainee Runner	Jeremy Fry
Finance assistant	Hilary Barratt
Lighting EM	Ian Dow
Planning EM	Brian Jones
Sound supervisor	John Nottage
Sound operative	Ken Osborne
Camera supervisor	Barry Chaston
Cameraman	Alan Jessop
Senior vision engineer	Roger Neal
Vision engineers	Dave Thwaits
	Mark Robinson
Rigger supervisor	Peter Whitchurch
Chief electrician	Pete Webb
Vision mixer	Barbara Gainsley
Designer	John Asbridge
Design assistant	Phillip Harvey
Properties buyer	John Charles
Visual effects designer	Perry Brahan
Visual effects assistants	Paul McGuinness
	Mike Tucker
	Russell Pritchett
	Alan Marshall
Video effects designer	Dave Chapman
Armourer	Doug Needham
Costume designer	Richard Croft
Costume assistant	Leah Archer
Make-up designer	Dorka Nieradzik
Make-up assistants	Jayne Buxton
	Sara Ellis
Senior dresser	Riley Clark
Dressers	Michael Johnson
	Debbie Roberts
Production operatives supervisor	Les Runham
Production operatives	Derek Waite
	Ken Robins
	Mickey Cox
Incidental music	Keff McKulloch
Special sound	Dick Mills

AS WITH THE **D**ALEKS, THE **C**YBERMEN WERE TO BE SUBTLY UPDATED. Although there were minor modifications to the head and chest units, the main difference was that all the fibreglass parts were given a highly reflective silver finish. Although very impressive, this did cause quite a few problems during the filming. The lacquer used to seal the finish tended to 'yellow' in daylight and the Cybermen turned slowly gold – not a good thing for them!

The Cybermen needed new weaponry, several new spacecraft and a communications console. Visual effects designer Perry Brahan opted for a pyrotechnic device in the guns, a circuit capable of firing up to a dozen individual charges, either singly or in rapid succession. A magazine containing all the charges could be screwed to the front of the gun, making reshoots very quick, though many evenings were spent recharging them for the following day's shooting.

The Cyber assault shuttle was built by me, and the exploding version by Alan Marshall – the same arrangement that we had on *Dragonfire*, the previous year. The model used for the bulk of the scenes was about two feet long, a timber and plastic construction around a metal frame. The exploding version was about twice the size to help scale the explosion. The ship was composited into the live action scenes in post production, the model mounted on a gimbal so that it could be rotated as the image was manipulated.

A helicopter was hired on location to fly the route supposedly taken by the Cybership. This ensured that foliage was disturbed by its passage and, when it landed, the grass was flattened. The helicopter was simply replaced with the model in the transmitted shots.

The communications console went through several variations before the final version was arrived at. The earliest concept was that it was a creature adapted to the Cybermen's needs, capable of independent movement. This evolved into a communications Cyberman, but with the special weapons Dalek in the same season, it was decided that the ideas were too similar. The final idea was a console, and knowing that a similar device had been constructed for *Earthshock,* whilst not slavishly copying the design, I hoped that the similarities were obvious enough for people to make the connection. The only other bit of Cybertechnology that nearly made it to the story were the Cybermats. Upon seeing the scene where the policemen were overcome by gas, I suggested to Andrew that it was a good point to reintroduce them. Andrew said that he had never found them remotely convincing and we stuck with the tubes emerging from the earth. The tubes were rigged and operated entirely on location. A large trench was dug and a board, pre-cut with slots, was placed over the top. On cue I had to push the tubes through. The gas was, in fact, talc, blown out under pressure. The subsequent shots of the policemen enveloped by gas were achieved with a smoke gun.

Filming began at Greenwich when the Nemesis asteroid arrived. Several pits were dug for the mortars and a large petrol explosion rigged up. When everyone was at a safe distance, and the cameras recording, Perry set off the charge. The arriving comet was

Ace's ghettoblaster

One of my main contributions to the story was the design of Ace's ghettoblaster. Perry's original idea had been to buy a modern portable entertainment centre and modify it, but it became obvious that Kevin Clarke and Andrew Cartmel had envisioned something a bit more quirky. I came up with a number of design sketches for Perry to look at, nearly all of them based around an old radio. Once a design was chosen I began building the prop, basing it around a small tape recorder – the ghettoblaster having to be practical.

One early version of the prop had Zygon-style nodules as speakers and a funnel at the back with a small sign that read 'For best results please water regularly' but neither of these features was kept, it being decided that they were too silly. A slightly more technological speaker grille was added in place of the nodules.

Although everyone was very pleased with the look of the prop, they were slightly concerned about the weight, particularly Sophie, who had to spend the whole show carting it about!

Mike Tucker

Below: Two designs for the Cybermen's console by Mike (below left) and Paul McGuinness (below centre), with the finished prop in the visual effects workshop.

subsequently added in post production.

With the arrival of the Cybermen the pyrotechnic work increased. Charges were set at various points all over the waste ground, cars were rigged with ricochet effects and the Cybermen themselves were wired up with spark emitting charges appropriately called Robotics.

Rather than use petrol for these ground charges – all of them occurred around the actors playing the mercenaries – cement bags were placed on top of the charges, giving grey clouds. The result of this was that at the end of the sequence everyone was covered in a thin layer of cement dust.

The arrows hitting chest units were simply achieved by setting the arrows in place in specially prepared sections of the chest panel and pulling them out very fast using fine fishing line. The shot was then reversed for transmission. The arrow hitting the TARDIS was achieved in exactly the same way, a door with removable foam panels having been provided.

Above and left: Three design drawings for the Cyber shuttle by Mike and Paul McGuinness.

One major sequence never got shot due to the enormous amount of material that was left out featured Ace runing through the deserted buildings, a Cyberman firing shots at her every step of the way. A steadicam operator was hired for the day to stay in front of Sophie, filming as the Cyberman gained on her. We set dozens of charges into the walls and floor so that we would be able to go straight for a take when the moment came. As we approached the end of the day, however, we still hadn't shot the climax of the story and that took priority.

That day also saw the destruction of the Cyberman on the gantry, the burning of two Cybertroopers and the take-off of the asteroid. The falling Cyberman was an old *Earthshock* Cybersuit fitted to a dummy which was, in turn, attached to a prop dropping device and wired with several charges. These charges were rigged in such a way that they would go off at different points during the fall, before a final explosion as the Cyberman hit the ground.

Below: Mike's design sketches for Ace's new ghettoblaster.

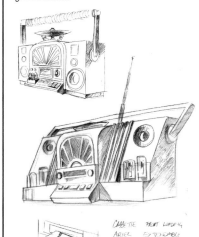

The two Cybermen destroyed by the Nemesis engines were played by two actors positioned behind a sheet of heat resistant glass. On cue the engines of the asteroid – three powerful gas jets – were cranked up to full power and the effect of the two Cybermen being engulfed in flame was thus achieved with the actual artistes.

As the asteroid lifts off the jets were fired up again along with a powerful air jet rigged underneath the prop to stir the dust up. The bulk of the movement was provided by fitting the asteroid to a fork lift truck and although the asteroid clearing the hangar was done in post production, the explosion of dust was achieved live. Two air mortars were set just inside the hangar door and filled with several bags of cement. Compressed air blasted a huge cloud of cement dust into the air and the miniature Nemesis was subsequently shown emerging from the cloud.

The rest of the effects took place at Arundel, the two major ones being the Nemesis coming to life and the destruction of the Cybership. All the elements of the Nemesis statue, including the bow and the arrow, were coated with front axial projection material, a highly reflective material usually found on road signs

The exploding Cybership was to be achieved as a miniature, but a large explosion on location was also needed, the smoke from it alerting the mercenaries to the Cybermen's position. Once again, a large petrol explosion was set up, though we couldn't dig very large holes since a condition of our filming on the Arundel estate was that we caused no damage. The amount of petrol used in this explosion was carefully measured so that it all burnt off as a fireball and no burning petrol fell back to earth. Ⓜ

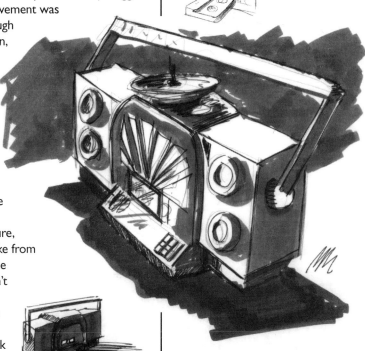

A tale of glowing props and Dolores Gray's missing luggage!

On *Silver Nemesis* everything had to glow and throb and so we got ourselves involved with FAP (Front Axial Projection). Now, this is basically the kind of effect that you get on road signs with headlamps. If you shine your headlamps at a road sign at night then it glows but if you're off axis – say, at the side of the road – then it doesn't glow quite as brightly. It's a special cloth or paint that throws the light back directly at the light source, a bit like a radar reflector on sailing boats.

We had to have Lady Peinforte in a glowing dress, a glowing arrow and a bow that glowed when it was pointed in the right direction, and this was quite a challenge. What I had to do was put a light on the axis of the camera, as near the lens as I could, and point it at what the camera was looking at. If it worked, then whatever the camera was looking at would appear to glow. You could, therefore, put a coloured gel in front of the light and the item would glow that colour. Also, with a dimmer I could make the bow throb as Sylvester turned it and eventually pointed it in the right direction.

We had to use a different technique depending on how far the item was from the camera. If Sylvester was only three feet away then we couldn't use a light so bright that it would light his face, so we could get away with a reverse auto cue. An auto cue is a bit of semi silvered glass, held at 45 degrees to the lens. We shone a light from underneath the camera and reflected it through the glass and onto the bow and the camera saw the reflection coming right back at it.

The next technique was making a circular plate that clipped onto the front of the lens and held six 12 volt, 50 Watt bulbs – the kind that you get in shop window displays. I would sometimes gel half the bulbs blue and half orange, so that I could throb something from blue to orange. Surprisingly, even on a sunny day, you could get about 200 yards away and still get a strong reflection.

If we were half a mile away then we could do it with a two and a half kilowatt lamp and it was surprising what you could get away with, even at that distance.

The only time that we blew it was when we attempted the glowing effect at Arundel Castle – in mist. That didn't work because there was so much light coming from so many directions that we couldn't stop it glowing. We ended up holding a sheet of black polystyrene behind the camera so that it stopped the light from the mist behind the camera hitting it. We didn't win there.

We were also trailed by a camera crew who came over from America to shoot how we made *Doctor Who*. We shot on a two camera unit which looks very big – there's cables and generators and all the gear that goes with it but we were pretty quick at moving it and we were very pleased on this shoot that we actually beat a single camera film crew who were simply in a car. We'd moved site and started recording before

▶

Top row: Building Ace's ghettoblaster, including the prop with its Zygon-like speakers, which were later changed to a more traditional speaker style.

Above: As the prop appeared in the programme, incorporating Dave Chapman's paintbox effects.

Left: The finished prop in the visual effects workshop.

Left: The visual effects crew for Silver Nemesis standing in front of the Nemesis comet with its flame jets on.

Below: Paul McGuinness' design for the Cybership, and as the model appeared on screen, many times over, courtesy of the video effects dept.

Above top: The Cybershuttle under construction.

Above: The finished model in position for filming.

Right: The shuttle landing as it appeared in the finished story.

Right: Visual effects assistant Paul McGuinness dons a Cyberman costume to stand in for the actor in a scene featuring an exploding chest panel.

Far right: The panel explodes safely.

Below: Paul McGuinness prepares the model of the folly for its explosive demise.

Below right: The destruction of the folly is filmed in the Elstree car park for safety reasons.

they'd packed up and caught us up. They were quite amazed by this.

We had a Hollywood star with us for this story – Dolores Gray. Now Dolores had very specific ideas about what she wanted to look like – very young, with no wrinkles – which was a problem! She demanded an 'inky-dinky', a light right beside the camera lens that blasted straight into her face and took all the wrinkles out. Whether you used it or not, whether it was faded down or not, it had to be there.

She also wanted a better method of travelling from her flat in Putney to the location. The normal way of getting people to a location was to give them a rail timetable, and if they are really important then you meet them at the station! Dolores wanted to come in a limo. Now, we actually had a limo for the show – a stretch Lincoln Continental – and because it was Dolores, the owner of the company that was supplying it decided that he would drive it himself.

When he turned up at her flat and went in, she was treating him like a chauffeur, whereas he was acting like a managing director. She appeared and dumped her cases and walked away from them, expecting him to carry them. He took the cases to the boot and she stood by the car door, very obviously waiting for him to open it for her, so he rushed round to let her in and they set off for the wilds of Arundel.

Dolores had brought a great many changes of clothing and a lot of jewellery so that we could choose what best suited the script. When she arrived she demanded her cases only to discover that the boot was empty – the 'chauffeur' had left the cases on the footpath in Putney. As I recollect, they contained nearly £25,000 worth of jewellery, so this was not a good start to the lady's day out on *Doctor Who*. Luckily, the caretaker of her flat had spotted them and taken them back inside, so they were quite safe. The Lincoln continued to be a problem because, having set it up with lights and cameras, we discovered that it didn't have enough fuel to do the shot. We couldn't drive through Arundel with all this paraphernalia on the car (VT machines in the boot, lamps tied to the bonnet and cameras stuck to the door), so we had to strip the whole lot off while the driver went off to fill up with fuel. Then, on the first take, with the camera looking back at Dolores and out of the back window, there was a click and the boot popped up!

As an outside broadcast manager I look after Royal events from Windsor – Royal banquets, state events and so on – and John Nathan-Turner was never one to miss out on chances, so he asked if I would go to the controller of the castle and ask if we could film *Doctor Who* there. I have to say we did get close, but the Buckingham Palace press office turned it down. No-one has ever managed to shoot a drama there but we were as close as you're ever going to get. As a result we filmed at Arundel Castle. We had explosions there and the woman who owned the estate came to watch. As they went off, her dog took off at a rate of knots, so the entire production ground to a halt as the great dog hunt began!

Ian Dow
Outside broadcast manager

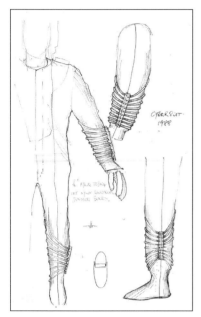

Above: Richard Croft's re-design for the Cybermen's bodysuits.

Right: The Cybermen as they appeared on screen.

Right: I found Jessica Martin's fake fur she used to keep warm during The Greatest Show in the Galaxy, and posed unashamedly outside the costume trailer.

Below: So that's what's underneath. Three cyber-actors take a break from their costumes.

STILL REELING FROM *GREATEST SHOW*, SYLVESTER AND I HAD THE disadvantage that we'd missed the first few days of rehearsal. We had one day to block the entire show before the producer's run the following afternoon – no time for luxuries like learning lines. I was working on scenes when I hadn't even had time to read the script, but it was good to be working with Chris Clough again.

John Nathan-Turner had managed to coax the famous Anton Diffring from Germany to play De Flores. As Anton was a huge tennis fan, he agreed to the rôle because filming coincided with Wimbledon fortnight, which he watched on his hotel television. He had no idea what *Doctor Who* was and borrowed a tape of *Dragonfire* to see what he'd let himself in for. I'll never forget one lunchtime conversation.

'Who vas zat screaming girl viz ze red hair? And Sophie – mein Got – you vere so fat!' Thanks, Anton.

Cybermen were turning out not to be scary. Experienced Cyber Leader David Banks, and his fellow speaking Cybermen who rehearsed with us were all tall, deep voiced and unthreatening in jeans and T-shirts. They perfected cyber walks and brandished plastic coat hangers as prop guns. On location the Cybermen extras were all six foot plus male models and when I knew the secret lurking beneath those shiny silver head pieces, I was rather keen on making their acquaintance!

Location number one was a derelict gas works in Greenwich. As it was within easy cycling distance of my house, I arrived on my bike. The hangar was huge and foreboding, and dominated the industrial landscape round the entrance to the Blackwall Tunnel. It was a favourite with film crews; the Pet Shop Boys shot a video there, but it has since been demolished.

I can cope with most things. I can pick up spiders with my bare hands, share my kitchen with a mouse and Cybermen are now no threat to me. But heights… It's like that old joke about aeroplanes - I'm not afraid of flying, I'm frightened of crashing! I feel the same way about tall buildings and cliff edges. When Chris asked me in rehearsals how I was with heights, I'd said it depended how high. I could have sworn he looked up to judge the height of the ceiling and muttered

'Hmm, not that high; twenty or thirty feet.'

'Fine!' I answered boldly, 'no problem.'

So my first move was to ask about the gantry scenes. Designer John Asbridge didn't seem to have built the walkway yet, and I went to ask him where it was going to be. He pointed upwards into the rooftop. I followed his finger, my stomach turning cartwheels. Way up was a rickety rusty string of metal slung from one end of the hangar to the other. I gulped, and waited with growing anxiety for the moment when I would have to mount the hundreds of concrete steps into the roof. Talk about 'nemesis.' On reaching the gantry, I knew I had to look down. Below me through the criss-cross metal floor was the TARDIS, looking like a tiny blue money box. I took a deep breath and stepped forwards. At that moment, Ace took over, and suddenly my fear went – even when I had to duck down from a Cyberman's bolt of fire, and realised that there was nothing on my right hand side stopping me tumbling a hundred feet to the hangar floor. How did the Cybermen cope up there with restricted helmet vision and thick boots and gloves? I'd never seen a steadycam up close before, and was amazed at this heavy contraption strapped to the operator's body, weighted in order to balance while the cameraman leapt around. He darted forwards, and mainly backwards, with no apparent fear, as though he was running along a pavement on terra firma.

I loved the action sequences. I had to run into the hangar skidding to a halt when I saw two angry Cybermen in front of me.

On the take I ran too hard, fell over, and slid to a giggling halt on my bum at the feet of two bewildered Cybermen.

The visual effects team set up a series of explosive charges all along an outside hangar wall to simulate cyberfire. The camera crew positioned a long track in order to run the camera alongside me as I ran, ducking from the blasts. On the camera rehearsal, I ran too fast and the crew couldn't keep up with me, so on the actual take, I ducked and dived to slow myself down. I could almost hear the *Starsky and Hutch* theme tune in my ears.

We filmed the final Greenwich scenes in the echoing gloom of the hangar under great pressure of time. The precious minutes before wrap was called were ticking away and Chris decided to set up several cameras, position us in a group, and film whatever happened. With no time for rehearsal, and with Sylvester and me still pretty wobbly on the lines, the tension was enormous, which luckily fitted in perfectly with the atmosphere of the scene. None of us were quite sure who had the next speech, and we looked round at each other for signals as to who was going to speak next - a sort of improvisation from hell. On screen, it seems to work well - the tension certainly comes across, and the dialogue even makes sense!

We then set off for the south coast, arriving for lunch on location. All afternoon, Sylv and I tramped through the undergrowth, walked for miles, and squatted in bushes. This was not helped by Mike Tucker who'd redesigned my *Remembrance* ghetto blaster. It was a wonderful looking prop, but incredibly heavy especially the batteries, before I took them out! I should have known not to moan about it in Sylv's presence, because he decided it would be hilarious if I was carrying everything including his umbrella. I couldn't get out of the TARDIS door, and felt like a packhorse but yes, it was funny.

Chris chose the location for our listening to cybersignals on the ghettoblaster without thinking how difficult it might be to perch on the side of a steep hillside and look comfortable. On the first take Sylvester went to get up and slid gracefully out of shot to the bottom of the hill. Everyone was in high spirits; Sylvester decided that I looked good in his Panama hat and that he should wear an English holidaymaker's knotted hanky. We improvised a scene with no dialogue with some cheerful if tuneless whistling as we walked towards the crypt to deliver the glowing bow into the hands of the enemy.

We recorded inside the castle on a staircase hung with several genuine Gainsborough portraits of the aristocracy and one fake portrait of yours truly. Several weeks ►

Above: John Nathan-Turner kindly let me choose this as my publicity photo from a shoot during Silver Nemesis *because I hated the previous photocard from* Dragonfire.

Exploding the Cybership

I wanted to do the explosion of the Cybership on film, away from video, to try and ensure that it had a feeling of scale to it. It was one of the most gratifying pieces of the whole story really, because there were always the constraints of time and money. The fact that we did it outside, with a real sky, livened it up no end. If we'd tried to do that in the model stage I don't think that we'd have got quite the same effect. Considering the rush it was done in and where it was done, it wasn't bad at all.

John Nathan-Turner insisted that the guns actually fired and we had to get a mechanism that could be re-used in *The Happiness Patrol* guns, albeit in a different guise. They had to be operated by the artistes and the gloves on the costumes didn't help matters much! Le Maitre made the charges for us, repacking fuses so that they emitted a red glow and gave a bit of a crack. It was a problem knowing what to use that would be a little different from a normal pyro fuse.

Perry Brahan
Visual effects designer

Far left: A Cyberman operates the cyber-console.

Left: Sylvester explores the folly at Arundel whilst trying not to fall through the floor.

Below: "Excellent." David Banks leads his cyber-troops.

The Nemesis comes to life . . . with a little help

Once the explosion at Greenwich had been recorded, checks were made that all the explosive charges had gone off and the prop asteroid was set into place. For the sequence where the rocks roll off the surface as the statue becomes active Alan Marshall was crammed inside the prop, operating the rocks by removing rods from underneath. He remained inside the asteroid, along with several of the lighting deparment's lamps, for the bulk of the scenes, losing several pounds in weight in the heat of the day.

For the scene where the Nemesis comes to life, the crypt was wired up with a number of pyrotechnic charges. The four pillars at the corners of the tomb were also plumbed up with electrically operated gas valves so that they would burst into flame simultaneously. The Cyberman seen amidst the chaos was, again, Paul McGuinness, Perry having decided that he would prefer one of his crew to be in the costume, rather than one of the supporting artistes.

Mike Tucker

Above: Jazz saxophoniost Courtney Pine gains two new members for his band.

Above top: John Nathan-Turner supervises Cybermen while they rehearse the scene where they arrive to claim the Nemesis statue.

Left: 'Strike a pose'. The scene featuring the picture was eventually dropped.

Below: The photograph used by the BBC artist to produce the painting.

Above: The Cyber leader, David Banks, with silver make-up round his eyes and mouth.

Right: Sylvester poses for a photograph with Dolores Gray, looking much happier after being reunited with her case containing her 'rocks' and a corset, on top of the Lincoln Continental limo.

Below left: Sylvester tries to look relaxed while perched half-way up a hill.

Below centre: Also trying to perch on the hillside, while laughing at you know who!

Below right: Sylvester tries a spot of Cyber-cross-dressing.

Time travel courtesy of the video effects dept.

An added complication for this story was that some of it was set in the present day, some in the past, and some in South America. Video effects supervisor Dave Chapman was on hand to lend his expertise to the proceedings, adding palm trees and cloud-shrouded mountains to some shots, whilst removing anachronistic architectural details from others.

One particularly time-consuming sequence was the time travel scene where Lady Peinfort and Richard travel to the twentieth century. Once all the scenes in the house – in its period form – had been recorded, a camera was set up, locked off, and a shot of the entire room taken. The designer, John Asbridge, then completely re-dressed the room to resemble a modern day tea room, and the second half of the scene was recorded. The two sequences were eventually combined by Dave in post production, a flawless effect reliant on the camera being in exactly the same place for both parts of the scene.

Mike Tucker

Top right: Sylvester and me posing (as usual) outside Lady Peinforte's house, which in this dimension was in the village of Bramber.

Above: Mike and myself at Black Jack's in Harefield.

Below: The old girl in the bowels of Arundel Castle, surrounded by prop junk.

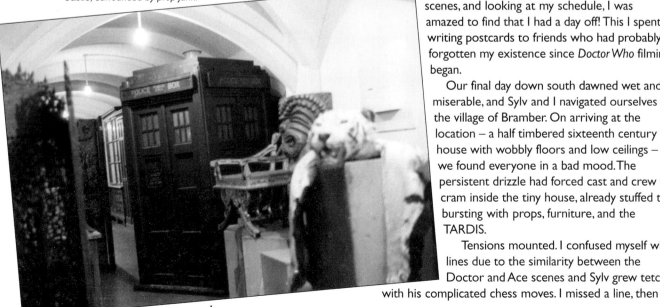

▶ previously I was called to Television Centre, where I posed for my portrait. Actually, we cheated. There was no way I had time to sit still for hours for an artist, so I sat for a photographer instead. I was relieved, as I had memories of sitting for a portrait when I was a child, getting bored as my patient mother read me endless stories and fielded my younger brother, who crawled round my feet and annoyed me. This photo business was much better. The most suitable print was taken to a BBC artist, who came up with a very good likeness without ever having seen me in the flesh. And here was the result, hanging in splendour on the staircase at Arundel Castle.

In the end, the scene was never used in the transmitted version of the story. The Doctor and Ace are running away from two of the Queen's security guards when Ace notices her portrait. The Doctor mutters confusingly that it hasn't happened yet, and they hurry on. We finished the scene, then moved to another location in the castle basement. A couple of hours later, Lynne our AFM, said she'd spotted tourists stopping beneath my portrait and flicking through their guidebooks to find the name! I asked whether I could keep the painting, as it could never be reused, because it was recognisably me. So, it now hangs in my living room and puzzles visitors; 'My ancestor,' I say vaguely, when asked.

For the next couple of days we set up by a crumbling architectural folly. Sylv and I were curious and sneaked off to explore. We had been warned not to go up the tower, because of rotting beams and mouldy floorboards, but Sylvester was undeterred and I wanted to take some photos. We startled pigeons, dislodged spiders, and managed to avoid the holes in the floor. It was a shame it was unsafe – it would have made a great set.

In the cybercamp, a new threat to survival had been discovered by the costume department: cybercrotch! The suits had been given a heavy paint job as they were originally too light in colour, and by the time we reached Arundel, the dried layers of paint caused the material to tear in embarrassing places. It was amusing to watch the dressers repairing the crotch damage with sticky tape and spray paint, which gave rise to much banter and joking. The cybermen extras were very patient, sometimes having to sit around for many hours, bolted into their claustrophobic helmets, or eating large quantities of their silver face paint along with their lunch.

As usual, my favourite scenes were the more emotional. Sylv and I were building up the idea of the Doctor as a father figure, and we liked the touching scenes where Ace owns up to being frightened of the Cybermen, and the Doctor suggests she could go back to the TARDIS. These were our last Arundel scenes, and looking at my schedule, I was amazed to find that I had a day off! This I spent writing postcards to friends who had probably forgotten my existence since *Doctor Who* filming began.

Our final day down south dawned wet and miserable, and Sylv and I navigated ourselves to the village of Bramber. On arriving at the location – a half timbered sixteenth century house with wobbly floors and low ceilings – we found everyone in a bad mood. The persistent drizzle had forced cast and crew to cram inside the tiny house, already stuffed to bursting with props, furniture, and the TARDIS.

Tensions mounted. I confused myself with lines due to the similarity between the Doctor and Ace scenes and Sylv grew tetchy with his complicated chess moves. I missed a line, then made another silly mistake, and uncharacteristically, Sylvester snapped at me. I couldn't stop the tears rolling down my cheeks. Luckily, this broke the tension; Sylv gave me a big hug, and we laughed at our bad tempers.

After wrap was called, Sylv and I dashed off to a public appearance which had been organised for us at an army camp by John Nathan-Turner – several hours drive away, during which my tummy started to behave in the most curious manner. As we arrived at the camp, I was feeling definitely below par, but soldiered on. I lasted until the first plate of food was brought to the table, excused myself rapidly and ran for the nearest toilet. The ball gowned officers' wives were surprised to see a small figure in black bomber jacket and Doc Marten shoes push past the queue for the ladies just in time to be hideously sick. It turned out I should have shunned the delights of the avocado prawn cocktail at lunchtime – I had a nasty attack of food poisoning.

After a couple of much needed days off, I had fully recovered, but Sylvester had managed to catch a nasty cold. We met at Television Centre at some ungodly hour, make-up and costumes were applied to our semi-conscious bodies, and we set off on another coach journey to Black Jack's Mill Restaurant in Harefield. Courtney Pine and his jazzmen had just stepped off a plane from America and were jet lagged and rather bewildered, but quite brilliant.

I hadn't done a stunt for a while, and was looking forward to getting my teeth stuck into today's menu, which meant leaping into a fast flowing river. Paul Heasman stunt coordinated the story, and much to Sylvester's frustration, doubled for him. Paul was worried about me doing the stunt, and was ready to call Tracey Ebbon, but I was determined. The problem was the river, which was shallow with jagged rocks near the surface. I wanted to dive in headfirst, but Paul insisted that I clutched onto the handrail and flopped in, so as not to split my head open. In retrospect it was a good idea, though at the time I felt cross, and tried to persuade him otherwise! I changed into my half wet suit which would be covered by the costume. This involved covering myself in talc and giggling with my dresser, until I managed to squeeze myself in. The river was freezing; the wet suit would keep out the cold, and protect me from the rocks.

Then came the take. The water was indeed cold, and we were swept quickly downstream. The visual effects crew had rigged up a rope across the river which we could grab as we floated past. Paul was hanging on to me, unnecessarily I felt, in case I was swept away, and when later I had to dub a line over the action, I could hear 'I can do it on my own, thanks!' Refusing to be helped, as usual!

After lunch, we found an intruder. A duck had wandered in to have a nose round the TARDIS and Sylv, who was feeling better by this time, was determined to have the newcomer included in the story. He took such a shine to it, I thought we would have a new companion on our travels! ⑤

Silly poses for the paparazzi

I was self-conscious in rehearsals due to the presence of an American film crew, who were taping a documentary – *The Making of Dr Who* for their Public Broadcasting Station in New Jersey, in honour of the 25th Anniversary. Eric and his team were polite and unobtrusive, and understood our sense of humour, having been raised on a diet of *Monty Python* and *Doctor Who.*

Similarly the paparazzi came down in droves from London, and the Cybermen patiently posed with us in the various ridiculous positions required by the tabloids. One photographer even asked me to drape myself over a car bonnet for a classic girlie shot and I thought that it was so funny and out of character, for both myself and Ace, that I agreed.

Sylv and I had previously posed for some pics with our Queen lookalike, and with some corgis who had been hired in for the filming. Unfortunately, they were feeling a little frisky, and had to be forcibly separated at one point.

Sophie Aldred

Above: Rehearsing the river stunt with Paul Heasman, while Sylvester looked on jealously.

Above: Mike to the rescue as we use the safety rope to scramble to the river bank.

Finishing touches

With a tremendous amount of material to shoot in a very short space of time, we had to be quite flexible about where some of the material was shot. On the day that we shot the climax of the story at Greenwich we were unable to shoot a close-up of the statue in the asteroid, or the Cyberleader's death. Once at Arundel we discovered that we had a little more time, and so decided to 'pick up' these two scenes.

Whereas at Greenwich we had the gloom of the hangar to film in, here we had no such luxury, the crypt being far too small to accommodate the asteroid. We ended up making our own studio by borrowing several large black drapes from the design department and hanging them between two of the visual effects trucks. We were eventually able to make a temporary studio big enough to set up and film the asteroid shot.

David Banks had been very disappointed that he hadn't been able to have an explosive finale and so was delighted to have the chance to shoot his death scene. Here we were able to use the crypt since we only needed a patch of ground and, suitably wired with Robotics, got the death that he wanted.

The shot of the Cybership exploding was done several weeks after the end of the OB shoot in the car park at Elstee Studios. Alan's large-scale miniature of the Cybership was wired with about twenty individual charges, set so that they would go off in a ripple starting at the doorway. This session was also used to shoot the explosion of energy from the window of Lady Peinforte's tomb. Having been banned from setting any explosives on the crypt itself, we had to make a large-scale miniature. Only one side of the tower was made since it was only needed for this one shot.

Mike Tucker

Out-takes and bloopers

We ended up with so much free time at Arundel that we were even able to help the OB crew compile an out-takes tape, adding comic touches like a dancing Cyberman that subsequently explodes, and a singing Cyberman, accompanied by me playing the communications console as if it was a music hall piano! Thankfully, even though the story has been released in an extended form by BBC Video, it has not been extended enough to include that!

Mike Tucker

The Doctor and Ace made a dash from the TARDIS across some scrub to meet the gang of soldiers. On the first take we ended up in the wrong spot, so we put stones as markers. Second take, we still ended up in the wrong place – after all, one stone looks much like another. Third take, we charged out of the TARDIS, Sylvester tripped over a bush and fell flat on his face. To everyone's delight he jumped up and waged war on the bush using his umbrella as a sword, then, since he was exhausted by his gallant efforts, I gave him a piggy-back back home to the TARDIS.

Sophie Aldred

Above: I had to be careful not to get rain splashes on my sunglasses, which I was determined to wear.

Left: Writers Kevin Clarke, Stephen Wyatt and Graeme Curry came down with a group of Doctor Who 'old boys' from the BBC to act as the tour party.

Below: I was star struck and asked Courtney if he'd mind posing for a photo with me.

Les bows out as the Timelord marches on

PRODUCTION of the Doctor Who Silver Anniversary Story was briefly interrupted to mark another milestone in the programme's history — the retirement of one of its longest serving associates.

Production operative supervisor Les Runham worked on the show on-and-off virtually from the day it started in November 1963, in addition to assignments on countless other BBC programmes.

He set up and took down props for all the Doctors, from William Hartnell to Sylverser McCoy, and probably travelled with the Tardis more often than any of them.

Doctor Who producer John Watton-Turner presented him with a silver bow and arrow as a parting shot to thank him for his long, loyal service.

Les is seen here flanked by the latest Dr Who, Sylvester McCoy and his assistant Ace, played by Sophie Aldred. Surrounding the Tardis are the rest of the production team.

The Happiness Patrol

By Graeme Curry   Story 7L

3 Episodes – broadcast 2 November to 16 November 1988

The Cast

The Doctor	Sylvester McCoy
Ace	Sophie Aldred
Helen A	Sheila Hancock
Joseph C	Ronald Fraser
Daisy K	Georgina Hale
Susan Q	Lesley Dunlop
Gilbert M	Harold Innocent
Trevor Sigma	John Normington
Earl Sigma	Richard Sharp
The Kandyman	David John Pope
Silas P	Jonathan Burn
Wences	Philip Neve
Wulfric	Ryan Freedman
Newscaster	Annie Hulley
Priscilla P	Rachel Bell
Harold V	Tim Barker
Killjoy	Mary Healey
Execution victim	Cy Town
Snipers	Steve Swinscoe
	Mark Carroll
Forum Doorman	Tim Scott

The Production Team

Producer	John Nathan-Turner
Director	Chris Clough
Script editor	Andrew Cartmel
Production manager	Gary Downie
Production associate	June Collins
Production assistant	Jane Wellesley
Assistant floor manager	Lynne Grant
Producer's secretary	Lorraine Godding
Finance assistant	Hilary Barratt
Lighting Director	Don Babbage
Technical co-ordinator	Richard Wilson
Sound supervisor	Scott Talbot
Gramophone operative	Mike Weaver
Camera supervisor	Alec Wheal
Vision mixer	Shirley Coward
Floor assistant	Alex Starr
Designer	John Asbridge
Design assistant	Phillip Harvey
Properties buyer	John Charles
Costume designer	Richard Croft
Costume assistant	Leah Archer
Make-up designer	Dorka Nieradzik
Make-up assistants	Jayne Buxton
	Sara Ellis
	Anna Lubbock
	Françoise Cresson
	Mark Phillips
Visual effects designer	Perry Brahan
Visual effects assistants	Paul McGuinness
	Mike Tucker
	Russell Pritchet
	Alan Marshall
Video effects designer	Dave Chapman
Production operatives	
Supervisor	Tony Sargent
Dressers	Michael Johnson
	Debbie Roberts
	Robin Smith
Incidental music	Dominic Glynn
Special sound	Dick Mills

Right: An early design sketch for Fifi by sculptor Sue Moore.

The Happiness sets

*T*he Happiness Patrol set was a façade – it was phony. It was meant to look as if the whole thing was a pretence and it was only when we got into the studio that I realised that it would look, to the viewer, like we'd run out of money. It looked like stuck on frontispieces, which is exactly what we wanted, but the audience saw it in a different way and that saddened me. I thought that the whole idea was so good, but it looked cheap. We put in some extra lines about it looking false, not to justify it, but to try and explain that we weren't doing cardboard sets, that this was the style. I thought that the design was very good but we'd underestimated how it would look.

I think that the show needs the sort of cash injection that a Spielberg production has, and which the BBC doesn't, but I think that too much money would destroy the essence of what *Doctor Who* is. We did it for so long on a shoestring! We used people who knew the situation and still made a good stab at professional science fiction and made it look good. There has been no wobbly scenery or yoghurt pot spacecraft, that's all part of a mythos that people like Danny Baker have invented.

I don't think that mega millions is the answer, because it will turn *Doctor Who* into something that it never was. It needs investment with a hard eye on what its roots were so that it will be a natural progression and not an Americanisation. There is a homely feel to it that has nothing to do with the size of the sets or the quality of the costumes – there is a somewhat cosy feeling about it and that should be preserved.

John Nathan-Turner
Producer

Above: The clay sculpture of Fifi's head used to make the moulds for the latex foam skin.

Above right: Stephen Mansfield and Mike check out the puppet version of Fifi.

Right: The finished head with fur and colouring added.

IF THERE IS EVER A PRIZE FOR THE ODDEST *DOCTOR WHO* STORY MADE THEN *The Happiness Patrol* has to be one of the front runners. From script to final screened version, it was always challenging the design teams to come up with something new and original while remaining within budget. From very early on, however, it was obvious that not all of the ideas would make it to the screen intact.

One early plan was to have all of Helen A's victims incarcerated in an area known as the arcade, with hundreds of fruit machines that the unfortunate inmates had to play continuously until their execution, or 'routine disappearance', orders came through. The cost of hiring the fruit machines alone was prohibitive and so the waiting zone was born, which only required one solitary fruit machine.

The sets had a deliberately theatrical feel, in keeping with the feeling of enforced jollity that the script specified. They were dirtied down quite considerably, giving the impression of a vaudeville show gone to seed. The only parts of the city that retained their bright colours were Helen A's office and the kandy kitchen.

The upper part of the kitchen was a mass of cogs, wheels and pipes, all designed to carry the fondant surprise to the doom pipe in forum square. Although some of this had been constructed full size, the bulk of it fell to visual effects designer Perry Brahan, who had it constructed in miniature and subsequently added to the set in the post production sessions.

Both full size set and miniature needed to have practical pumps to carry the strawberry coloured goo through the pipes. The goo itself also fell to the effects department. Made from an industrial food thickener and coloured with non-staining dyes, the mixing of the gunge was always the first task that greeted us on the studio days – not a good way of starting the morning. Several large bins on wheels were filled so that they could be positioned behind whichever set was going to need fondant surprise.

For the kandy kitchen pumps were submerged into the bins and the slime pumped into the perspex pipes that were built into the set. As soon as the slime cleared shot it was channelled back into the bins so that the system was enclosed. A similar system was

made for the miniature, though on a much smaller scale, the entire process being quite mess-free. The execution sequence in Forum Square was quite a different matter!

The script called for the unfortunate prisoner to have the doom pipe lowered over him, filled with fondant surprise and kept there until he drowned. Actor Cy Town was the unlucky one chosen for the sequence and it was decided that it could best be shot by splitting it into two sections. The first part involved the firing squad leaving the square and the doom pipe being lowered. Once this was recorded the pipe was raised again and Cy removed. Perry had several large dropping devices filled with gunge suspended just above the pipe. As soon as everything was set Cy was submerged into a vat of gunge until he was thoroughly saturated and repositioned inside the tube. On action the dropping tanks were triggered and the tube raised. Cy and several gallons of red slime were deposited on the studio floor. This was the last sequence to be recorded for the story.

We did, of course, have more involvement with the show than just the gunge. The fun guns evolved from sketches that Paul McGuinness had done and were built from a combination of aluminium and fibreglass, in bright primary

colours, giving them a toy look. The firing mechanisms were stripped from the cyberguns, although the aluminium nozzles were redressed in more cheerful colours. They were also capable of firing either single or multiple shots.

The other guns required by the story are good examples of how the effects department is forced to be inventive under pressure. A late request was made for a small hand gun version of the fun guns, and for a sniper's rifle that could be assembled in vision. Both these props were eventually manufactured entirely from plumbing fittings from the local DIY store, though assembled in such a way that it is unlikely that they could be spotted as such, especially on a television screen.

The effect of bullet hits was achieved by wiring the set with a number of small charges that were set off by Perry. For the scenes where the 'musak' speakers are shot off the wall the speakers were duplicated in lightweight materials so that they could safely be blown apart with the actors close by. Similar small charges were rigged to the fruit machine for Harold V's death.

The other major piece of hardware used by the women of the Happiness Patrol was the buggy. The governing factor on the look was budget and a small company specialising in custom built vehicles adapted a buggy that they had in stock, adding grilles, extra running boards and the 'happy/sad' theatrical masks on the front. They also provided the waiting zone go-kart.

The main villain of the piece, the Kandyman, was handled by make-up designer Dorka Nieradzik. As originally conceived, the Kandyman was to be a rather rotund man in a white lab coat, with black teeth and a pasty complexion. It was Dorka who came up with the idea that he would look as though he was made of sweets, the script merely hinting at his internal composition.

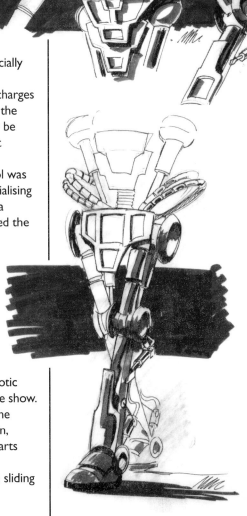

Although the effects department didn't have any involvement with the costume itself, we did have to come up with the robotic skeleton seen in the closing moments of the show. Paul McGuinness sculpted the skull while the body was made from a poseable mannequin, dressed with various mechanical looking parts and given a coat of silver paint.

When we came to record the skeleton sliding down the doom pipe it travelled at such speed that it shot off the end of the rostrum and slid across the studio floor into the adjoining set! The final version of the shot has the prop on a thin nylon line so that it stops at just the right point.

The Pipe People were made by Sue Moore, who sculpted a simple slip-on mask. Sue was also involved in the construction of the final monster of the story, Helen A's vicious pet Fifi.

Three puppets were eventually needed, a fully animatronic version for all the close-up scenes, one with minimal movement for all the shots where Fifi is being carried across the room, and the 'run along', a version based around the mechanism of a child's toy, the legs of which made running movements when the prop was pulled along the floor.

For the scenes where Fifi is stalking through the pipes we used a section of pipe raised about three feet off the ground, so that we could get underneath and operate Fifi through a slot.

There were very few requirements for model work, in fact the script only called for two shots of Helen A's escape shuttle. Perry constructed it from a number of *Star Wars* models that were commercially available at the time. Ⓜ

Above: Two early design sketches for the skeleton of the Kandyman.

Right: The completed skeleton with its skull sitting next to it on the filing cabinet.

Below: The kandy kitchen set, with its pipes of fondant surprise, in studio.

Above: An unpainted latex foam skin for Fifi's head.

Right: Two design drawings by Stephen Mansfield, showing Fifi's ability to change from docile pet to vicious killer.

Above: Sophie and Lesley Dunlop pose for publicity photographs under the doom pipe.

Above: The Happiness Patrol take the weight off their heels during a break in recording.

Left: Sue Moore's early design drawing for the Pipe People.

Below: Make-up assistant Sara Ellis checks the prosthetic make-up for the Pipe People.

Below: A Pipe Person in its natural habitat.

Designing Fifi and the Pipe People

Perry Brahan contacted us about Fifi and we were brought in at a very early stage to discuss it. John Nathan-Turner and Chris Clough were very concerned about it, probably because if it had looked silly then it would have detracted from Helen A. Also they'd never really had a puppet like this in the show before. Nothing that tiny, anyway. John originally said that he wanted it to be the size of a cat, but that would have been so incredibly difficult to do, because you wouldn't be able to get your hand inside the head to operate it.

Half of the time it had to look fearsome enough for everyone to be scared of it and the rest of the time it had to look lovable. There was a point where it was discussed as being like a hairy snake. It had to be really quick.

We wanted to do the Pipe People as half-masks, utilising the bottom of the actors' faces. Dorka said that if they couldn't get them done for the money then they were going to use masks left over from the BBC production of Alice in Wonderland. She showed me the ones that they were going to use and they were the mouse masks. I had to do six or seven. Dorka did head casts of the two lead characters and the others were just multiples. Since they had to be rodent-like we gave them pointed ears and because they lived in the sewers we made them albino looking, with big eyes.

Sue Moore and Stephen Mansfield Sculptors

Photo: Sue Moore

Above top: The various Fifi puppets. From the left: the walking model, the hand puppet, the rod puppet and the animatronic head which could snarl and raise its spikes.

Above: Sue Moore and Stephen Mansfield operate Fifi in the studio.

Right: Sheila Hancock (Helen A) with Fifi and Ronald Fraser (Joseph C).

Above: A close-up of the detail on the back of the Kandyman costume.

Left: Gilbert M (Harold Innocent) with his bizarre creation the Kandyman.

Above: Sue Moore and Stephen Mansfield operate the animatronic Fifi from behind Helen A's chair.

Above: The fun guns under construction.

Designing the Kandyman

Robert Allsopp came up with the final shape of the Kandyman: each part of the costume manufactured from different materials to try and convey the feel of different types of sweet. Effects company Artem provided the spinning eyes and the pumps that pushed coloured liquid through transparent veins. Dorka added the silver chin-brace to the costume after it was decided that he needed to look a little more robotic.

Fifi had to have two distinct looks: almost lovable when being cuddled by Helen A, and a vicious predator when hunting the people in the pipes. Stephen Mansfield came up with a series of colour drawings of both moods of the Stigorax that were approved by the production team.

Mike Tucker

An alternative location

The main restriction on designer John Asbridge was that this was the studio-bound story for the year, and yet the script required the streets of the city of Terra Alpha. Quite early on, video effects designer Dave Chapman had voiced the opinion that the story could be ideally filmed at the village of Portmeirion in North Wales, preferably at night, but the costs involved made this idea a non starter. It is interesting to speculate on what the story might have looked like if the idea had been taken up, and whether it would have been more popular with the audience as a result.

Mike Tucker

A GATHERING OF FAMOUS FACES GREETED ME AS I PUSHED OPEN THE DOOR to room 503. Sheila Hancock looked tall, elegant and actressy, Ronald Frazer was a familiar face from countless British movies, and Georgina Hale was kissing everyone on the cheek and asking their star signs. In the midst of the luvvie-ness, a voice of normality introduced herself as Lesley Dunlop saying that her husband, Chris Guard, had thoroughly enjoyed himself in *Greatest Show* and that this was her second *Doctor Who*. We started chatting and never stopped throughout the following weeks. Lesley and I were constantly being told to be quiet as we sat at the side of the room talking, giggling, and enjoying ourselves. I thought it would be funny if Ace was trying to emulate the Doctor by playing the spoons in one of our scenes rather than twirl a baton, as the script suggested. I discovered that Sylv's musical dexterity on cutlery isn't as easy as it looks.

Richard Sharp playing Earl Sigma also had a musical instrument problem, being scripted to play the trumpet. Although Richard is a fantastic singer and has appeared in musicals both in this country and round the world, playing an instrument is not his scene. Chris decided a harmonica would be easier to cart around than a trumpet, and Richard practised miming the mouth organ.

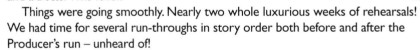

Never work with children or animals, the saying goes. Fifi, our animal star was animatronic and, therefore, reasonably controllable; our children weren't! Luckily, Phillip, who played Wences, was professional, grown up, and a *Doctor Who* lover.

Above: Lesley Dunlop (Susan Q), costume designer Richard Croft and I demonstrate some fabulous creations from the BBC wardrobe dept.

Right: What's cooking? Sylvester and Richard D. Sharpe in the kandy kitchen.

Things were going smoothly. Nearly two whole luxurious weeks of rehearsals! We had time for several run-throughs in story order both before and after the Producer's run – unheard of!

I was called for the three day recording at lunchtime on the first day. It was good to be back at Television Centre after all this time, now thankfully free from the terrors of asbestos. Richard Croft had enough on his plate with designs for the Happiness Patrol uniforms without thinking up something new for yours truly, and I kept the skirt, boots and T-shirt combination. It was dark enough in colour to contrast nicely with all the pink!

I renewed my acquaintance with Bootsy and Ferret, the tattooed bikers from Dorset, whom John Nathan-Turner had hired again to make outlandish motorised vehicles. Sylv and I liked the go kart and purred sedately round the corridors at every available opportunity. Sylv grew attached to a small pencil-like device handed to him by visual effects, and called it his sonic screwdriver. I had my eye on the fun guns, but to my disappointment I wasn't allowed to touch!

Rachel Bell's humour and Tim Barker's giggling had led to total breakdown in waiting zone rehearsals. We kept straight faces now as Rachel looked so awesome in her huge pink wig. I was relieved that Richard had decided to keep me in Ace gear so I didn't have a Happiness Patrol uniform – I haven't got the legs for it!

Shop Assistance

The Terrence Higgins AIDS charity organised a day of fundraising in Covent Garden called 'Shop Assistance'. The shops were manned by celebrities and a large percentage of the day's takings donated to the charity. Sylvester and I crammed ourselves into a tiny shop and worked behind the counter and then performed a not-so-musical interlude in the piazza, with Sylv on spoons and me on trumpet. I can't say I recommend the combination, and I'm not surprised that no-one signed us up for a record deal. But I was pleased to do something useful for a charity which I had supported in various ways for some time.

Sophie Aldred

Right: Pipe Person Phillip Neve (Wences). His proud mum and sister can be seen in the background.

Day two began with street scenes, and Wences was called in for manhole cover acting. I chatted with Phillip as he sat patiently in a make up chair having prosthetic rubber stuck to his face and nose. It looked hot and suffocating, but the boys were stars and never complained. They loved their costumes, which were quilted duvet type material. The boys soon became unrecognisable. Their dressers

carried battery powered plastic fans with which they cooled them off between takes. Luckily, they didn't have many scenes on their first day and got used to the claustrophobia. Phillip was quite happy, however, chatting away merrily to whoever would listen.

More gaps for me, and I purloined a couple of 'Ace at the Forum' posters. The photo was taken during the *Nemesis* portrait session before I'd read *The Happiness Patrol* script. Richard Croft briefed me on the action; Ace was not happy about having her photo taken and I should look bewildered. Not hard!

Back to the studio for more marching round corridors with the fearsome Georgina Hale, who loved her fun gun, and who looked fabulous in her uniform. These scenes were originally to be the end of episode one and beginning of episode two, the opening of which was cut in the edit. A sniper fires at the marching patrol, Ace and Susan Q try to escape, but run slap bang into Daisy K, who is hiding in a doorway.

Next were the second waiting zone scenes with Lesley and Rachel and then we jumped to the end of the story in the street where the Doctor meets Helen A, who breaks down when she sees the dying Fifi. This proved complicated, hiding Fifi's wires and operators while coordinating a complicated camera shot that Chris was determined to use. A crane camera was wheeled in, like the ones they use on *Top of the Pops* for those whizzing overhead shots. Chris wanted to end the scene with a long swoop out. It was difficult in the confined space of the corridor, but he got it eventually.

The final studio day for this block began with the last scene of the story. I was going to use a can of spray paint to repaint a pink patch on the TARDIS and I can't remember why I ended up using a paint brush! I felt nervous about slapping paint on to my childhood icon – it didn't seem right to be tampering. I wondered how it had felt to the scene painters who had painted it pink. It was a relief to have our true blue TARDIS back.

The rest of the day took place mainly down the pipes, which were cleverly designed to look much bigger and longer than they actually were. The lighting crew fiddled for hours to throw light on our faces while giving the effect of being underground. I stood in the cramped pipe with a crowd of people for what seemed like hours and was glad to leave the pipes behind for a while and go to the execution yard!

The Kandyman made his debut, running down the pipes pursued by his own fondant creation. We'd been curious about the finished Kandyman design. David John Pope had rehearsed a sinister aggressive character, which would play against the audience's expectations. We were all surprised to see the finished effect. Bertie Bassett was not what we'd imagined, and David was a bit disappointed that a lot of his movements and mannerisms weren't possible. Now he knew what he was up against, he could adapt his performance in the next rehearsal block.

My final *Happiness Patrol* day began with a pipe ride with Phillip, just like a ride on a short fast helter skelter. I asked whether I should shout anything – it seemed unlikely we'd whizz along silently. Gary passed on advice from the gallery: 'Just scream or something!' Scream? Ace? Not on your life! **S**

Left: The picture taken of me for the 'Ace at the Forum' poster.

A recipe for fondant surprise

Above: Cy Town is gunged in fondant surprise in preparation for his ordeal in the doom pipe.

Although my contribution to *The Happiness Patrol* was complete, the Vis FX team had a trick up their sleeves which I wanted to stick around and watch. Cy Town, better known to us as Dalek innards, drew the short straw. It was he who was to be Helen A's first fondant surprise victim, splodged from head to toe in thick red goo.

Cy looked understandably concerned as a huge cylindrical tube was lowered over his head and body. The Vis FX team tipped a mighty vat of gunge into the top of the cylinder and Cy fell in a crumpled heap on the floor, trying hard not to open his eyes or, worse, to swallow. The successful take was greeted with a round of applause for brave Mr Town.

Red slime spread over the studio floor, and while the actors changed into party frocks for the now legendary gathering in room B209, the Vis FX team were left to clear up the mess. I was concerned they'd miss the fun, and put aside a few cans. The Tina Turner tape had been round several times and they still hadn't appeared. I went to investigate. Poking my head round the studio door I saw the entire Vis FX team brandishing fire extinguishers and hoses in mid water fight. If I'd not had my party gear on I would have joined in! Instead I retrieved my party tapes from my car and rejoined the party. Eventually a damp and happy visual effects team appeared. We boogied til the early hours and as I made the familiar journey back to the car park I hoped that Season 25 would be well received and we'd be back together again next year.

Sophie Aldred

Above: I suffer a savage attack by Sylvester and Paul McGuinness whilst sitting on Helen A's throne.

Above: Richard D. sharpe and Georgina Hale wait for their next scene.

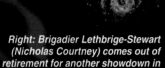

Season 26

Right: Brigadier Lethbrige-Stewart (Nicholas Courtney) comes out of retirement for another showdown in Battlefield.

Above: The Haemovores rise from the depths of the ocean in The Curse of Fenric.

Below: One of the Cheetah people from Survival.

Right: Sophie makes a friend on the set of Ghost Light.

If season 25 had concentrated on the Doctor's past, then season 26 certainly concentrated on Ace, with the so-called 'Ace trilogy'. *The Curse of Fenric*, *Ghost Light* and *Survival* all made use of the companion as a major plot device. The order in which the shows were eventually transmitted was not the way that they had been written, hence Ace's comment about not liking haunted houses coming after her experiences in *Ghost Light* rather than before. The original plan was that it is this comment – made during *The Curse of Fenric* – that gives the Doctor the idea of returning to Gabriel Chase.

Season 26 also delves into the darker side of the Doctor. Sylvester had liked the way that his character had progressed and suggested that he wore a darker jacket to emphasise this change. *The Curse of Fenric* was the first to be filmed and so, again at Sylvester's suggestion, the new jacket was hidden under a duffel coat for the opening scenes of the story so that it would be a surprise. (The fact that the locations were freezing cold had no bearing on his decision, of course!)

Once again, the change of transmission order meant that this idea was lost, the jacket already having been seen in *Battlefield* and *Ghost Light*.

Season 26 also has the dubious honour of being the last series of *Doctor Who* ever made by the BBC and, as this book is written, there seems to be no indication that this situation will ever change.

The Curse of Fenric

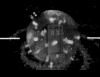

By Ian Briggs

Story 7M

4 Episodes – broadcast 25 October to 15 November 1989

The Cast

The Doctor	Sylvester McCoy
Ace	Sophie Aldred
Dr Judson	Dinsdale Landen
Millington	Alfred Lynch
Sorin	Tomek Bork
Jean	Joann Kenny
Phyllis	Joanne Bell
Sergeant Prozorov	Peter Czajkowski
Mr Wainwright	Nicholas Parsons
Kathleen Dudman	Cory Pulman
Vershinin	Marek Anton
Captain Bates	Stevan Rimkus
Sergeant Leigh	Marcus Hutton
Mrs Hardaker	Janet Henfrey
Nurse Crane	Anne Reid
Petrossian	Mark Conrad
Perkins	Christien Anholt
Ancient Haemovore	Raymond Trickett

The Production Team

Producer	John Nathan-Turner
Director	Nicholas Mallett
Script editor	Andrew Cartmel
Production manager	Ian Fraser
Production associate	June Collins
Production assistant	Winifred Hopkins
Assistant floor manager	Judy Corry
Vision mixer	Dinah Long
Designer	David Laskey
Assistant designer	Julia Gresty
Costume designer	Ken Trew
Costume assistant	Andrew Duckett
Make up designer	Denise Baron
Make up assistants	Helen Johnson
	Wendy Harrison
	Lynn Sommerville
	Kathy Harris
Visual effects designer	Graham Brown
Visual effects assistants	Mike Tucker
	Alan Marshall
	John Van Der Pool
	Russell Pritchett
	Steve Bland
	Dave Vialls
Video effects designer	Dave Chapman
Properties buyer	Yvonne Alfert
Costume dressers	Michael Percell
	Ray Greenhill
	Cathy George
	Sara Wilkinson
	Denis Addoo
Lighting engineering manager	Ian Dow
EM2	Brian Jones
Sound supervisor	John Nottage
Sound assistants	Peter Hales
	Ken Osborne
Camera supervisor	Paul Harding
Cameraman	Alan Jessop
Vision supervisor	Dave Jennings
Vision assistants	Dave Thwaites
	Anthony Kemp
Video tape editor	Dave Potter
Production operatives supervisor	Vic Young
Production operatives	Stan Cresswell
	Alan Bennett
	Neville Quhne
Armourer	Ken Bond
Safety officer	Des Stewart
Incidental music	Mark Ayres
Special sound	Dick Mills

Below and opposite: Mike's original storyboard for the destruction of Jean and Phyllis.

1: JEAN LIFTS CLAWED HAND TO STRIKE ACE, BUT...

3: REACTION OF ACE

4: JEAN GOES DOWNHILL QUICKLY FROM HERE...

5: ...AND MAKES A MESS ON THE GRASS!

6: ACE SPINS TOWARDS OTHER SIDE TO SEE...

Right: The original Haemovore design by Graham Brown. Andy Fraser drew up Graham's idea and, with Mike, did a full-size plasticine mock-up.

EARLY PLANNING FOR *DOCTOR WHO* ALWAYS INVOLVED A LOT OF WORK ensuring that the locations chosen were suitable for all parties, particularly the technical departments who needed adequate arrangements for the scanner and generator trucks. The *Fenric* production team spent several days in the south of England checking on the various locations that had been found for the story – the army camp at Crowborough, the church at Hawkhurst and so on.

It was during this recce that it was decided that it would be far easier to record the show entirely on location than to try and replicate some of the settings in studio and so *The Curse of Fenric* joined *The Greatest Show in the Galaxy* as a four-part story that had avoided the confines of Television Centre.

Another major change that happened on the recce was a change in the location that was to double for the Yorkshire coast. Originally, the scenes were to have been recorded at Hastings, but on the day that we visited the weather swiftly convinced cameraman Alan Jessop that the underwater scenes would be almost impossible to record unless it was a completely calm day. As an alternative, both Alan and effects designer Graham Brown suggested Lulworth Cove in Dorset, somewhere that they had both dived before. The natural cove meant that even in less than perfect weather conditions the underwater shots would be possible to shoot. Production manager Ian Fraser and director Nick Mallet were happy with this and work could begin on the props needed for the show. Apart from the physical effects that were required there were several effects-heavy sequences required by the story.

The destruction of the two vampire girls, Jean and Phyllis, was something that we had very clear ideas about. I manufactured an animatronic skull capable of jaw and general head movements, the idea being to fit it with a brittle skin that would crack off as the head thrashed around, smoke being piped up through the neck at the same time. Needless to say, this version of the effect never made it to the screen. A planning meeting held specifically to discuss the girls' transformation into vampires decided that teenagers were likely to identify with them and that it was, therefore, not such a good idea to show their deaths in quite such a graphic way.

The final version of the effect was substantially toned down. Face casts were taken of the two girls by make up designer Dee Baron and passed on to the effects department. I took silicon moulds from these plaster positives and manufactured a number of latex and foam heads. Rather than try to dissolve the skin to reveal a skull, the intent was now to dissolve to nothing.

Areas were carved away from the latex heads and thin, polythene pipes set in. These carved areas were then covered with a thin polystyrene skin, carved to follow the curve of the face. Acetone was then passed along the tubes, melting the polystyrene areas. Ironically, this effect looked far more gruesome than the animatronic head, since the features of the two girls were quite recognisable. The transmitted shot was substantially treated in video effects and an additional shot of a skull collapsing into a pile of dust was also shot, the dust eventually being blown away by the wind in true vampire tradition.

The gas grenades used by Millington's forces were adapted from a fake grenade that I found in a nearby shop. A mould was taken from this fake and hollow fibreglass copies were made. A screw cap was fitted to the bottom and a tube set inside that would take a phial of green liquid. Other versions of the props were adapted to take actual gas canisters that would emit green smoke. The green liquid itself was fluoroscene, a chemical that glows under ultra violet light.

The flask was sculpted by Andy Fraser, who

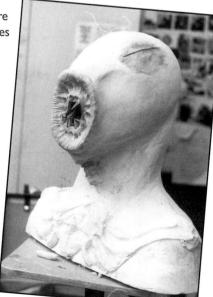

came up with a suitably oriental design with Graham. Cast in green, translucent fibreglass, the prop was heavily weathered and encrusted with plaster so that the green was only visible when the internal light source was switched on. Three flasks were eventually made in case of breakages.

For the sequence where the runes burn themselves into the church wall, Graham and I did several tests with a fast burning fuse and gunpowder set into boards pre-cut with the runic symbols. Having come up with a successful technique, John Van Der Pool made up three boards with the complete inscription for transportation to location. Although shot successfully, the amount of smoke generated was so great that the shot was not sufficiently clear and the entire effect was re-done electronically in the video effects workshop.

For the entire three week location the effects crew expanded to seven with our daily routine including almost constant rain, smoke and explosions. Doing effects rain is a cold job at the best of time, but the weather turned against us and we were having to provide fake rain while it was actually raining! (Real rain rarely shows up on camera so effects rain is substantially heavier.)

With all the huts in the camp looking the same, Graham was able to be a bit more adventurous with some of the explosions than might have otherwise been possible. Rather than do the explosion of Millington's office with the dressed hut, we found a hut that was empty and rigged the explosives to that – some in the windows, one on the door, and a petrol explosion at the far end, to give the impression that the end wall had been blown out. As usual with stunts, Sophie and Sylvester could not be dissuaded from doing the scene themselves and stunt coordinator Tip Tipping rehearsed with them while we wired up the charges. When everyone was happy, the two positioned themselves in the doorway, running out on cue. When they had reached a predetermined safe distance Graham fired the charges and they hurled themselves into the sandbag emplacement. By now I think that Sophie and Sylvester were getting quite used to effects explosions.

Dinsdale Landen also did his own 'stunt' for the scene where the decrypt room window blows in. Rather than use pyrotechnics, Graham positioned a large air mortar outside the window, which was replaced with resin glass. The mortar itself was also filled with resin glass and when fired, the impact shattered the window and blew debris across the room. Because Dinsdale was facing away from the blast it was perfectly safe for him to be standing quite close to it.

Several of the concepts in the script were simply impossible to achieve. From our point of view, one major change was the fog effects. As scripted, the Haemovores were to arrive in a black fog, and a reference to this still survives in the show, but black smoke is invariably toxic and we ended up using far more common, but far safer, white smoke.

Fenric is one of my favourite stories that I worked on. One magic moment for me was when the graveyard was suddenly filled with hoards of children, all crowding around Sophie and Sylvester, demanding autographs. That image of the two of them surrounded by kids confirmed that we were making a programme that was still as popular then as when I was at school, and I found that a very satisfying feeling. Ⓜ

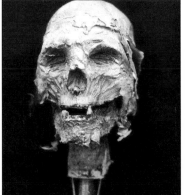

Above: The animatronic skull which was created for Jean and Phyllis' death scenes but never used.

Above: The latex heads, made from the head casts of the actresses, that were used instead of the skull.

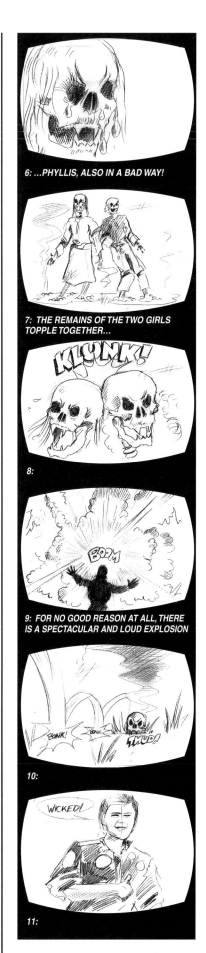

6: ...PHYLLIS, ALSO IN A BAD WAY!

7: THE REMAINS OF THE TWO GIRLS TOPPLE TOGETHER...

8:

9: FOR NO GOOD REASON AT ALL, THERE IS A SPECTACULAR AND LOUD EXPLOSION

10:

11:

Right: The Ancient Haemovore (Raymond Trickett).

Far right: The clay sculpture of the Ancient Haemovore head, with lentils added to the clay to add some fine detail.

Photos: Sue Moore

Writing Fenric

Fenric had a long gestation period because we never knew until commissioning time came around whether there was going to be another season. It was going to be recorded second, but Ben and I started writing at the same time and they worked out that I was going to finish my scripts first. I had quite a run up to it and Andrew and I started bashing ideas around. Andrew had wanted a period story and my initial thought was the seventies but he didn't think that was far back enough so I thought 'war'. We set it in the Second World War and had titles like *Powerplay* and *Black Rain* – images of all these bombs falling out of the sky. I had the idea of the Doctor and this old nemesis meeting up again and playing this huge, macabre game of three dimensional chess amid the Blitz, with bombs falling everywhere, these two madmen fighting with each other. It's a moot point as to which is the more insane of the two, the Doctor or the nemesis, playing chess with a war going on. I wanted this insane laughter ringing out through the bombed out shell of a building as they played chess, but all that mellowed.

My idea was for summer storms, the heat building up and up and sweat beginning to pour down people's faces, clothes sticking to bodies, and that was feeding into Ace's seduction scene, the steaminess of it all. That was the first scene that had to be rewritten, of course, because by this time there were biting winds and snow!

I hadn't been long back from Sweden and seeing these runestones, and so Vikings and things like that came into it. I'm the only writer who has had to provide six pages of explanatory notes for the crew! All through rehearsals I was explaining the mythological background.

I added even more to the novelisation. It was a chance to tie up some loose ends and complete the circle and take it back to where it started, which was tremendously satisfying from my point of view. I particularly liked doing the epilogue to the book and putting the icing on the cake by finishing off the Ace story. It was a pig to write and there were several drafts before I got it right.

I would like to have done another story. I can remember that I did have another idea for finishing Ace off. The final scene had Ace, now known as Dee, or something like that, aged about thirty, putting her new baby to bed. In the mirror she sees the doorway of the bedroom and there is the Doctor, just standing there watching her. She turns around and he's gone and she doesn't know if he was really there or if she was just imagining it. From the idea that she creates her own future and the baby in *Fenric* was her mother, I wanted to take that one generation further and get another reflection that in some obscure, convoluted way tied it up in an even neater package than it did.

Ian Briggs
Writer

Left: Two of the visual effects team donned haemovore garb to break through the vestry door and grab me. Graham Brown swore that his clutching a personal part of my anatomy was a mistake as he couldn't see through the mask.

Left: The various types of Haemovore masks created by Sue Moore and Stephen Mansfield. The top most masks were for the oldest Haemovores, showing that the creatures became less human in appearance as time passed.

Below left: The clay sculpture for one of the Haemovore masks. Below middle: The completed mask. Below right: With the costume and make-up departments co-operating on the story, the two jobs merged. Here, dressers Sara and Cathy practise make-up techniques on location at Lulworth.

Far left: Costume designer Ken Trew is surrounded by his own creations.

Above: Tip Tipping supplies the Haemovores with rocks to help them stay under the water.

Left: The Haemovores rise from the deep.

Above: Make-up designer Denise Baron tries out the make up for the decomposing vampires on herself.

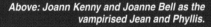

Above: Joann Kenny and Joanne Bell as the vampirised Jean and Phyllis.

Right: Dinsdale Landen had a problem with his red eyed contact lenses, so an optician was always on site to help him put them in and take them out.

Below: Setting up Millington's office.

Below right: John Nathan Turner discusses the weather with writer Ian Briggs, whilst Nicholas Parsons looks on.

Flying lead and the Ultima machine

Silvester and Dinsdale Landen stand by the ultima machine.

Bullet hits always look better if you can indicate that there is some kind of wound behind, but with *Doctor Who* we were never allowed to show blood, so we relied on blasting a hole in the cloth. Now, unless the lighting is particularly good, or it's a light coloured cloth you can't see them. They came out all right, though. We did them on Jean and Phyllis, and on Tip Tipping as a Haemovore who, needless to say, presses on in the tried and tested tradition of *Doctor Who* monsters, despite a hail of lead.

In the ultima machine there was a nice personal touch, because I used the insides of my old family television set, the very television that I had watched *Doctor Who* on for the first time as a kid.

Graham Brown
Visual effects designer

Underwater filming

Ideally, I'd like to go back and do all of my *Doctor Who* shows again and make them better in every way. There's an old axiom that if you get thirty per cent of what you want onto the screen then you're doing pretty well. *Fenric* is probably my favourite, but I'm fond of so many of them. I liked the Dalek one but *Fenric* was such an ambitious script.

I hadn't been on the underwater recce, either at Hastings or Lulworth Cove and I think that the estimation of it being half a day's work was wrong. We didn't have ideal weather and Nick Mallet got very behind, so at one of the meetings that we used to have at the end of every day's shoot, he asked if I would shoot the underwater scenes for him, so I went out in the boat.

John Van Der Pool, one of the effects guys, agreed to be the dead Russian body so we got make-up to 'white him up' since I didn't think there were any Russians his colour in 1944. People who watch it think that it's the spookiest thing because the make-up makes him look grey-green, that awful pallor.

John Nathan-Turner
Producer

Right: Ken Trew found this suit among the forest of clothes racks at the BBC's costume store in Wales Farm Road. He ordered two suits to be made up in a grey pinstripe material.

Below left: My hair test at Television Centre. Dee Baron had two crotcheted snoods which an industrious relation had run up. My fine hair didn't have enough weight or volume to fill the net which we nicknamed my sprout bag. Dee found two hairpieces and pinned them invisibly to my hair.

When I turned up at John Nathan Turner's office sometime the next spring, I thought he was going to throw a wobbly. A fortnight's holiday in Barbados meant that my hair was plaited in hundreds of dreadlocks, with multi-coloured beads jangling around my shoulders. Not suitable for a story set in the 1940s. I reassured him and Ken Trew, who was back in charge of costume design, that normal service would be resumed as soon as rehearsals started.

The read-through was held unusually in a Union House conference room. There was Tomek Bork talking non stop with his excitable Polish accent, Pete Czajkowski who'd been in the year above me at Manchester University, Cory Pulman, who was wearing a combat jacket which Ace would have killed for, and with whom I struck up an immediate friendship and Steven Rimkus, who I'd met a few years back through a mutual friend while working for a children's theatre company. Then, of course, the two Jos, who were looking forward to their long nails and designer vampire teeth, and Janet Henfrey, who had been at school with my mum. Then the famous faces: I was in awe of Nicholas Parsons, the immortal words, 'And now, from Norwich...' having heralded many a happy evening of family viewing, I'm also an avid listener to the classic *Just a Minute*; Dinsdale Landen, with his sharp wit and dry sense of humour, and the quiet gentle Alfred Lynch enjoying his power mad fascist character!

During the rehearsal week came a name change. The original script title had been *Wolftime*: it now became *The Wolves of Fenric*. One of my favourite scenes was Ace reading Kathleen's letter informing her of her husband's death. We shed tears, and hoped that we could achieve the same intensity in the location atmosphere. By the Producer's run, we were a pretty close bunch, and were all looking forward to filming an entire four episodes on location.

A disused army training camp was to be our home for the next week in some of the oddest weather I've ever known. I ventured out into the cold and braved my first scene – a TARDIS materialisation. No mention was made in the script of Ace's new look and surely the Doctor would make some derogatory comment. So he did! Another instant script change occurred a few scenes later outside the guardhouse where Ace chats up one of the soldiers. Ian Briggs must have had a weather consultation with Michael Fish when he wrote *Fenric*. It was meant to get hotter throughout the story, and to be fair, we were going to film much later in the season. Marcus Hutton and I stood shaking with cold outside the guardhouse. His cheeks wobbled as he tried to stop his teeth chattering. My lines seemed redundant:

ACE: Too hot. Clothes sticking to me. Is it this hot everywhere?

Cue ironic laughter from the crew. We altered the lines to fit in with current conditions. Snowflakes drifted through the air in agreement as Ian and Andrew parleyed. The new line arrived:

Above: The wardrobe room was an empty nissan hut where racks of soldier's uniforms rubbed shoulders with Haemovore rags, WREN's uniforms and extra hats, scarves and wellies with which to combat the elements.

A normal day on the beach

The production crew at Lulworth cove.

Once you have been shooting *Doctor Who* for a few weeks you lose any sense of normality, and are only brought down to Earth when you notice worried expressions on the faces of members of the public, who happen to be passing by.

This was brought home to me at Lulworth Cove while shooting a scene with a group of Haemovores during a very cold April. Haemovores appear to be victims of a nuclear explosion, with faces covered in blue latex, clothes of sacking, and a walk reminiscent of Charles Laughton playing the Hunchback of Notre Dame. The story called for them to rise from under the waves and walk ashore, splitting each side of the camera. The director explained that they should walk into the sea up to their chests and on the command 'Action' should duck under the water, remain for a count of three to let the water settle, and then rise and march ashore.

At this point, a bus load of geology students arrived to chip away at the stone which makes Lulworth Cove so famous. They stood there in coats, scarves and gloves and looked on in amazement as the Haemovores, without a word of protest, marched into the icy water and ducked under. Not for long, however!

Covered in latex and swirling clothes they floated to the surface, with bottoms sticking out and arms and legs thrashing, trying to stay under. The director was not one to give up easily, so he gave the ►

ACE: There's a wind whipping up. I can feel it through my clothes.

Cue nods of approval from shivering crew.

On the third day, we awoke to a white world. Snow on any other day would have aroused my feelings of nostalgia. Not, however, on location, wearing a thin, short sleeved suit and stockings and suspenders. Luckily, most of the scenes were interiors. Sylvester found a duffle coat to keep him warm between takes, and it looked so good, it became part of his costume. Scenes intended for the warmth of the bunk room were transferred for time reasons, to exteriors. The Doctor's umbrella became fully functional as Sylv, Nicholas and I slipped and slithered our way through the scenes. The sound of rain on umbrella drowned out the dialogue, and the sound crew told us to keep our volume up.

My hairstyle was suffering in the downpour. Dee battled with my sprouts, armed with cans of ozone friendly hair spray and a long comb. I was dragged away to the make-up hut at every opportunity and hairdyers were pointed at my steaming head in an attempt to dry my sodden locks. My lacquer filled hair set solidly, like a concrete monument to the 1940s. At least it was tidy.

Friday was lab day, where the showdown with Fenric took place. It was a relief to spend the whole day in one warm location, and I enjoyed my scenes with Tomek, uncharacteristically nasty in his contact lenses. Tomek called himself my official 'bodywarmer' as I cuddled into his army greatcoat sheltering from the cold.

We rehearsed Ace sending her relatives to safety as the Haemovores did 'Zombie flesh eaters' acting behind us. I worried about running across the slippery ground with a real baby in my arms. Two days earlier we'd filmed the previous bunk room sequence where Ace helps Kathleen and the baby protect themselves from marauding Haemovores. Nick didn't let on what would happen at the end of our dialogue. We knew that monsters would appear at the windows, and I was prepared for something naff. It came as a shock when with a loud crash and a gust of wind, the sugar glass windows smashed and horrible misshapen Haemovore heads and hands waved at us. Cory screamed for real, and grabbed my arm, the baby awoke and started crying, and for a split second I couldn't separate reality from fantasy. The programme which had scared me ▶

command, 'Fetch the heavy rocks!' Immediately, electricians, make up girls, cameramen and costume designers were combing the beach and each Haemovore was soon clutching a heavy rock to help him sink.

Take two. The new system worked well, the Haemovores sank successfully, but the final shot as they passed the camera was not to the director's liking. They had all dropped their heavy rocks and couldn't find them again, so the search moved further along the beach. The tide was coming in and cameras, lights and smoke machines were retreating up a rapidly disappearing beach.

Take three. Success! Now for the real challenge. We had to repeat the shot with the Ancient Haemovore. He was the lion of all Haemovores, with an enormous latex head and mane, and a backpack of hair dryers and various plumbing fittings. There was no way he was going to sink. Eventually his pockets were filled up with stage weights, heavy rocks were fixed wherever possible and he struggled out to sea. The camera recorded and, amazingly he sank. He rose like a spectre and started wading ashore, but to the director's rage, spoiled the effect by scrabbling with his fingers at the mask where it met his neck. The actor was drowning, since his head hadn't emptied!

Costume were called in and instructed to cut drain holes in the head so that he could breath. More weights, more rocks and the crew retreated further up the beach with their backs to the cliff as the tide rose. 'Action!' He sank beneath the waves, then rose into shot. There was hysteria among the crew on the beach. The Ancient Haemovore looked like a giant watering can – water pours from the holes punched round his head!

At this point, the geologists were seen clutching each other for security and inching their way back to their bus to make an escape from, what seemed to us, to be a perfectly ordinary day at the beach.

Ian Dow

Left: The visual effects team were able to wash away the unseasonal snow from the backrounds of shots we filmed.

Top left: Every morning I sat in the spartan make-up hut wrapped in blankets, coats, socks and woolly gloves. Sara scrounged a hot water bottle which I clutched to my shivering body. How did Dee manage to pin those hair pieces with frozen fingers?

Left: My dresser, Sara Wilkinson, introduced me to the joys of thermal underwear which I wore in layers under my costume. For your information, chaps, stockings don't feel sexy and they let in terrible draughts.

Fenric costumes

The dark brown jacket was just a remake of the cream one – same pattern, just different material. The dufflecoat I'd just taken along for warmth, but Sylvester fell in love with it, so that became part of his wardrobe as well. For Sophie I'd found this little 1940s jacket and I had a divided skirt made because she was going under water. We'd picked thin material and we had short sleeves because there was this line, 'It's hot, it's hot'. Of course, we ended up with rain and snow!

The Haemovores were, even if I say so myself, pretty brilliant because they fitted anyone who turned up. We had one set of artistes at Crowborough then a different lot at Lulworth Cove and another lot for the underwater stuff.

I started with the main Haemovore - the Ancient One – and I did some research on Vikings and that sort of stuff, doing designs based on dragon heads – like the prows of longships - but that wasn't working, so I went to Octopus designs. There was a line about suckers rather than Vampire teeth, so I thought about suckers and it evolved from that, really.

The body came from the thought that he was building his own body. On the back of the neck the spine was exposed, then on the chest there was a big respirator built in, with two big tubes that led over the back. It was all rubbish things that you'd find at the bottom of the sea, things people had thrown overboard.

Dee Baron and I decided that a lot of the heads of the Haemovores would be full masks, whereas others would be half-masks. We split our budgets and I did the heads while she did the hands and nails, all of them sculpted by Sue Moore and Stephen Mansfield. Having it all made by one team gave it a very good look, I thought.

For the other costumes, I raided from BBC stock and had everything dyed black and green, not an absolute black or an absolute green, but that sheen of mildew and water. I also found this firm that produced plastic paint, which I dribbled all over some of the costumes. The masks were painted with acrylic paint and to keep them looking wet we used acrylic gloss, but even then we had to keep spraying them with water to keep them shining.

Nick Mallett had said that he wanted two Vikings, an Elizabethan, two Victorian sailors, two Victorian women, a First World War sailor and a flapper. They all got given names. The Vikings were The Grace Brothers, the sailors were Clare Rayner, Mrs Bridges, Errol Flynn, etc. It was actually very useful, because when they were in the water at Lulworth Cove we all knew which one we were talking about.

The baby clothes I got from Maggie Wicks. I rang her up and asked if she had any 30s and 40s baby dresses and she had one that was quite nice. Later, when the show was going out, someone had written in to *Points of View* saying that the baby had a babygrow with a SuperTed on the front, so I ran the tape back to check. The teddy is a knitted one that had been put in by the props buyer and she had checked that it was the right period. I never wrote back to Anne Robinson though.

Ken Trew
Costume designer

Above: Which is the real hair?

Right: Marcus Hutton, Marek Anton and Stevan Rimkus.

Below: Tracey Eddon makes a perilous decent.

Above: Nicholas Parsons at home in a quiet corner of the costume hut.

Above: Janet Henfrey (Miss Hardaker) was at school with my mother and I organised a reunion.

Below: Sylvester and myself in our new costumes.

Above: Tracey Eddon, Tip Tipping and me show a leg on St Lawrence's Church roof.

Left: The chess board on fire (unused).

Below: Mike creates the slimy remains of two Haemovores who had been staked through the heart in another dropped sequence.

Photo: Ian Briggs

Above: At Bedgebury School where I had deja vu – I once played lacrosse here for my school. It seemed churlish to come back and blow it up, especially as I remember their good post-match teas.

The ancient one (Raymond Trickett) takes a tea break, down by the railway tunnel.

Right: Pete Czaijkowski as Sergeant Prozorov, on the beach at Lulworth.

Above: The Russian soldiers in their inflatable boat.

Above: The marines, who were helping with the inflatable boats, tide tables and general sea dog's knowledge, thought we were mad. They wouldn't go into the water, even in dry suits, but the two Jos wore nothing but their period bathing suits and turned blue with cold.

The scenes that never made it

One unfortunate occurrence on *Fenric* was the loss of a tape with various sequences that had been shot on the final day at Crowborough – the fire sequence at the munitions factory. Graham Brown and Nick Mallet had come up with a choreographed sequence to explain how the burning chessboard ignites the rest of the building. As the scene starts, Sylvester drags a table to the centre of the room, sweeping chemicals and equipment to the floor as he does so. When the lightning strikes the chess board (a post production effect) a charge is set off that ignites the board and a trail of spilled chemicals. This trail of fire slowly spreads to other parts of the room until the entire lab is alight.

Several other scenes were lost, but for the usual reasons of time. Most of these were subsequently reinstated for the 'director's cut' of *Fenric* by BBC Video, but some still didn't make it. Following Captain Sorin's successful rescue of Ace from the Haemovores on the church roof, a scene was shot where the commandos pull several wooden stakes from their rucksacks. Later, we return to the church roof where the Haemovores are now smoking pools of slime with stakes sticking out of them. This tied up with an earlier scene where Captain Sorin says that he doesn't believe in vampires, then opens his bag to reveal stakes and hammers.

Needless to say, the slime fell to the effects department once again!

Mike Tucker

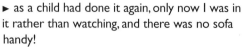

► as a child had done it again, only now I was in it rather than watching, and there was no sofa handy!

After a welcome day off, shooting recommenced on Tuesday at the camp. Due to more rain, the design team's pit head building had sunk at a jaunty angle into the mud. By the end of the day, having played host to Nick Parsons' death, Millington's ruthlessness, and assorted Ancient Haemovore scenes, the soggy mess round the entrance to the 'tunnel' was impossible to walk across. Our final scene here was complicated, involving an explosion and a touching moment between Ace and the Doctor, where he tells her why he had to break her faith in him. A wooden board was sunk under the spot where Nick wanted us to play the scene, as we had to fall forward onto our knees and the mud was like quicksand. On 'action' we ran and felt the explosion. I slipped, falling face downwards and bringing Sylvester with me. We were filthy!

We were glad to see the back of the army camp, and move to our next location – St Lawrence's Church, Hawkhurst. The first person I spotted in the make-up wagon was Tracey Eddon, dressed as me, hair in sprouts, chastising me for doing my own stunts and robbing her of *Doctor Who* work since *Remembrance*. Tip led us up the church tower, and warned us about a loose stone buttress. I assured him I would go nowhere near it! I breathed a thankful sigh that my *Nemesis* experience had diffused my fear of heights as I unfurled the steel ladder, and

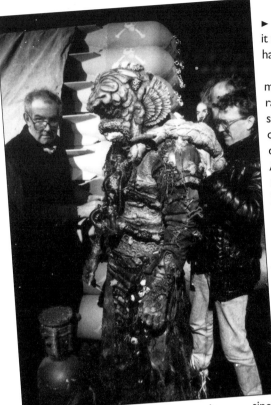

Above: Costume designer Ken Trew and his assistant Andrew Duckett have fun and games with the Ancient Haemovore in 'Sam Fox's bedroom', so called because of the stacked-up shells which looked like 'women's chests' as Sylv put it.

Top right: Tomek Bork and Dinsdale Landen inside St Lawrence's Church.

Right: Getting a hug from my official bodywarmer Tomek Bork who told me I didn't eat enough. 'Now if you were in Poland, you would eat… You English women are crazy!' My suit was already beginning to groan because of eating to keep warm!

Below: Director in action, Nick Mallett, gives Tomek a helping hand.

stuck my leg over the edge. Camera 2 down below had a lovely shot of my thermal knickers! I retired gracefully to remove the offending undergarments and we tried again.

Tracey took over for the descent, a tiny camera strapped to her hard hat. I watched jealously from the church roof, and John Nathan Turner asked me whether I thought I could have done it. Tip had explained that the

difficulty was the narrow swinging ladder which twisted in the wind. When we did the continuation of the scene, I climbed as high as Tip would let me, and Nick used quite a lot of me in the edit as well as the superb shots he'd got from Tracey's headgear.

Tip himself donned Haemovore gear, and we worked out a fight sequence. Tip said I could hit him as hard as I liked as he was padded up, and I took him at his word. As he grabbed me off the ladder, my skirt flew up to reveal rather more than planned!

The following day at the church started in the nave with Nicholas where between takes he regaled us with *Just A Minute* stories. He asked me for reassurance after his scenes, telling me that it was a long time since he took a straight part. I was flattered that he should be asking me.

The afternoon's scenes were time consuming, and we shot a few crypt scenes before the wrap, which meant returning the following morning, and working out the complicated concealed doorway. Sometimes, Sylvester's dedication to detail and logic infuriated me; this was such a moment. Everything we rehearsed was met with, 'No, no that won't work because…' and the annoying thing was that he was right! I was a technical

actress who learnt my lines (usually) and did what I was told (usually) and a useful thing I learned from Sylv was to question. It's the actor who ends up looking silly on screen if something doesn't make sense. I'm glad now that he bothered, but with the minutes ticking away and still no answers, I just wanted to hit him!

There must be better ways of spending an afternoon than down the waterlogged, disused British Rail tunnel which was our next destination. Sylv's wife Agnes had brought their sons Joe and Sam to see their dad in action. After a couple of hours standing around, the boys got bored, and John Nathan-Turner asked them whether they'd like to take part. Those little Haemovores walking purposefully down the mineshaft are none other than Joe and Sam. Next stop, Lulworth Cove in Dorset.

On the last day, his shooting schedule in tatters due to time and tide problems, Nick was a model of calm directorship. He quietly worked out which scenes needed to be done in the next few hours, and we would shoot accordingly. I had to wait until the last moment for my dive into the icy waters, which I assured Tip I was willing and able to do. As Thursday dawned, and I put a tentative hand into the water before boarding the boat out to the cliffs, I wasn't sure whether I was being brave or just plain stupid.

On the rocks, our dialogue complete, I glanced down to make sure of my timing, took off my snood, shook out my hair, and went for it. My main concern when I surfaced was how to get back onto the rocks without damaging myself. I couldn't feel my body, it was so cold. It wasn't until John Nathan-Turner asked me if I was okay that I realised my teeth were chattering so hard I couldn't speak. Quickly, Tip helped me on board the launching craft for the next bit. He bundled me in a pile of coats and hugged me tight in order to bring up my body temperature – or so he said!

Meanwhile, Alan Jessop, who was an experienced underwater cameraman was ready below in his dry suit. We found his floating marker and all too soon, I went up on deck. Tip tapped the surface of the water with a long pole to show me where to dive, and I was off into the water again. I tried to find the camera, but the water was so murky, I couldn't see anything before I had to surface for air. I was hauled back onto the craft, bundled up again and then to my horror, Alan relayed a message that he hadn't got a clear shot. Tip asked me if I could dive again. Beyond speech, I nodded, and Tip tapped the water once more. In I dived, my head screaming with pain. I stayed under as long as I could bear, and the next thing I knew, I was wrapped in blankets once more and heading for the shore.

Then came the worst bit. I'd forgotten the last scene where I waded from the sea towards the Doctor, with some jolly dialogue as we walked off into the sunset… I wasn't sure if I'd ever be able to speak again! The camera lined up the shot, and Nick told me where to wade. Going voluntarily into that water was one of the bravest things I've ever done. I approached the shore and…

'Cut! We'll have to go again. Sophie, a bit further over… Sorry!'

'You will be!' I muttered mentally, trying not to shake.

I mustered up the courage to skip gaily through the water, managed to say my line without gritting my teeth, and with my back to the camera, permitted myself some teeth chatters before a hearty grin, and a walk off up the beach. Best acting I've ever done! **S**

Big bangs and getting dirty... Ace!

After the stunt and bang, Sylvester turned to me and said a rhetorical 'Good one, eh, Soph?'

Myself and Sylvester being re-made up after the big bang.

One of my favourite moments was courtesy of visual effects. Graham Brown and friends found an empty hut to blow up, and Tip Tipping took Sylv and me through our paces for a stunt to go with the big bang. I didn't want to hold Sylv's hand as we ran, as although I've never actually run from a building that's just about to blow sky high, I imagined that holding hands would only slow both people down. Sylv told me not to be so bossy, and to do what Nick Mallet wanted, so I did! We rehearsed a couple of times, then the cry for quiet came and, on 'Action!', we ran hell for leather for a pile of sandbags and mattresses in the foreground, jumping as high as we could as we felt the blast hard on our heels.

'Good one, eh, Soph?' said Sylv as we appeared covered in sawdust and muck from behind the sandbags. I grinned.

The costume people groaned as they watched my costume hit the ground with a splat and thought of their evening scrubbing and soaking. The make-up and costume teams moved in on us for a clean up, and we continued with close-ups. Looking carefully, you can see that Sylv's left hand is black with mud in the wide shot, and mysteriously clean when he puts it on my shoulder a couple of seconds later. The magic of telly!
Sophie Aldred

Above right: Sara Wilkinson ran around with spare stockings, which I laddered with remarkable ease. She also had the dubious pleasure of making sure the line up the back of my legs was straight at all times. She had to wash my two costumes every night, which meant they shrank progressively.

Left: My wellies had to be disguised in post production with computer-generated rocks. Sara found me the black cardy which I wore between takes.

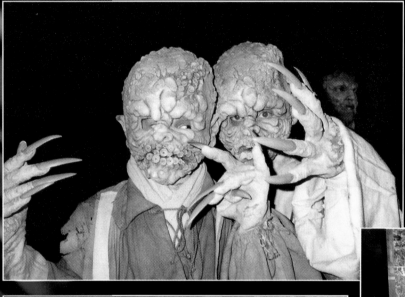

Above: Sylvester and me aboard the boat on the way to do my dive into the sea. Tip gave me my instructions onboard. The tide was lower than he would have liked, and there were jagged rocks under the surface. I had to time my dive according to the wave movement.

Left: I changed into a half wet suit which went underneath my costume.

Top left: Two little Haemovores: Sam and Joe Kent Smith, Sylvester's sons.

Far left: Sylvester with Sam and Joe unmasked.

The Haemovores

Originally, we were just going to do the Ancient Haemovore and the more human ones were going to have bits pulled from that mould stuck onto their faces. We went to a meeting and said that it really wasn't going to work; we were worried about the pieces coming unstuck in the water. In the end we decided that it would be easier just to sculpt other masks. Then it all got a bit out of hand because there were several different versions. We ended up doing five different ones – the old one, a full head with a jaw piece then a simple slush moulded full head, a full face and a half-mask, plus fourteen pairs of hands.

We put seeds in the sculpture to get a quick texture but they germinated with the moisture from the clay which is where we got the idea that this disease that the Haemovores had was going through the blood stream and, if you notice, on the backs of the heads and hands the tentacles follow the pattern of the veins.

**Sue Moore and Stephen Mansfield
Sculptors**

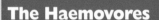

Above left: We made our way gingerly to a rocky outcrop. At the last moment Sara Wilkinson changed my wellies for shoes and gaffer-taped them onto my feet so we wouldn't lose them.

Left: On the beach where I would be filmed coming ashore after my dive.

Above: Recovering in the beach cafe.

Battlefield

By Ben Aaronovitch   Story 7N

4 Episodes – broadcast 6 September to 27 September 1989

The Cast

The Doctor	Sylvester McCoy
Ace	Sophie Aldred
Morgaine	Jean Marsh
Brigadier Lethbridge-Stewart	Nicholas Courtney
Peter Warmsly	James Elliss
Mordred	Christopher Bowen
Brigadier Winifred Bambera	Angela Bruce
Ancelyn	Marcus Gilbert
Pat Rowlinson	Noel Collins
Elizabeth Rowlinson	June Bland
Shou Yuing	Ling Tai
Flight Lieutenant Lavel	Dorota Rae
Knight commander	Stefan Schwartz
Major Husak	Paul Tomany
Doris	Angela Douglas
Sergeant Zbrigniev	Robert Jezek
The Destroyer	Marek Anton

The Production Team

Producer	John Nathan-Turner
Director	Michael Kerrigan
Script editor	Andrew Cartmel
Production manager	Riita Lynn
Production associate	June Collins
Production assistant	Rosemary Parsons
Assistant floor manager	Matthew Purves
Producer's secretary	Clare Kinmont
Finance assistant	Paul Goodliffe
Designer	Martin Collins
Assistant designer	Sophie Boulez
Properties buyer	Sara Richardson
Costume designer	Anushia Nieradzik
Costume assistant	Sarah Buckland
Dressers	Sara Wilkinson
	Debbie Clark
	Ray Greenhill
	Richard Blanchard
Make-up designer	Juliet Mayer
Make-up assistants	Kate Benton
	Renata Strickland-Loeb
Visual effects designer	Dave Bezkorowajny
Visual effects assistants	Chris Reynolds
	John Savage
	Claire Hainstock
	Norman McGeock
Armourer	Ken Bond
Video effects designer	Dave Chapman
Lighting engineering manager	Ian Dow
EM2	Brian Jones
Sound supervisor	Martin Broadfoot
Sound assistants	Peter Hales
	Ken Osborne
Camera supervisor	Paul Harding
Cameraman	Alan Jessop
Vision supervisor	Dave Jennings
Vision assistants	Dick Barlow
	Anthony Kemp
Lighting chargehand	Jim Russell
Video tape editor	Ian Haynes
Production operatives supervisor	Vic Young
Production operatives	Tony Lansdell
	Alan Bennett
	Gary Sigrist
Incidental music	Keff McCulloch
Special sound	Dick Mills

WHEN THE NEW SEASON CAME INTO THE VISUAL EFFECTS ALLOCATIONS office *Battlefield* was to be the first to go into production, with Mat Irvine as the effects designer – his first *Doctor Who* since *Warriors of the Deep*. *Fenric* was to be second in recording order with Dave Bezkorawajny in charge of the effects.

Quite early on, Mat booked me as his assistant and I began gleaning information as to what would be required. Although I didn't see a copy of the script, it was established that we would be involved with the biomechanical spacecraft, the knights' guns and the Destroyer, and so I began on some preliminary drawings. Then everything changed.

The shooting order for the first two stories was reversed in order to accommodate the availability of Nicholas Courtney and Mat was swapped with effects designer Graham Brown. As a result, I ended up as Graham's assistant on *Fenric* instead of Mat's on *Battlefield*.

As always in visual effects, however, no ideas were wasted and although Dave decided not to use any of my designs, some were adapted for use in season 5 of *Red Dwarf*, most noticeably the design for the Destroyer which ended up as Rimmer's self-loathing demon in the story *Terrorform*.

Construction of the biomechanical spacecraft fell to assistant Chris Reynolds who, following ideas of Dave's, came up with a crab-like design in a combination of vacuum-formed plastic and fibreglass resin. The texture of the ship was achieved using a new type of stone finish spray that the department had on trial at the time.

Rather than shooting the model in water – which would have caused untold problems – the spacecraft was shot through a narrow tank, with another shallow tank hung over the miniature set to give suitably 'underwatery' lighting effects.

A wax copy of the spacecraft was made for its final destruction, the sequence was shot on video tape and the slowed down, rather than the more usual method of shooting on film. For Ace's escape to the surface a small hatchway was raised on a thin line with the stream of bubbles added as a post production effect.

The only other miniature sequence for the story involved the knights seen hurtling towards the earth. Two commercially available soldiers were remodelled to resemble Anushia Nieradzik's costumes and the shot put together in the video effects workshop. The subsequent shot of the landed knight elevating from the crater was achieved on location by positioning the actor on the end of a counterbalanced cantilever rig and raising him up manually.

The bulk of Dave's work on location was involved with the, now obligatory, explosive sequences, including a Nitro 9 bang. Rather than just reusing the Nitro cans that I had made for *Dragonfire* I had subtly updated them by adding a clockwork timer, reasoning that Ace would have made improvements to them during her time with the Doctor.

The new prop was due to have made its debut in *The Curse of Fenric* but, as is the nature of effects props, it broke within minutes of getting on location. A repaired and suitably strengthened version of the can thus made its first screen appearance in *Battlefield* and was the only thing that I made for the story.

Below right: Nothing goes to waste at the visual effects dept. Mike's unused design for the Destroyer became Rimmer's self-loathing demon in Red Dwarf.

Bottom: Mike's original destroyer sketch.

Creating the Destroyer

Photo: Sue Moore

Above: Stephen Mansfield at work on the Destroyer's head.

At the beginning of that final year, before we built anything, we had a meeting with John Nathan-Turner to talk about the whole season. He sat there and listened to a lot of ideas and then asked how we would do a race of cat people. I actually modelled up a cat head, with sculpted fur, but it never went any further.

We'd also heard rumours about a story with a devil-type creature, so I'd done a maquette of a devil thing. We discussed whether it had to be a man in a suit or whether it could be a puppet against blue and John took it all on board and had a good think about it. We were then phoned and asked if the maquette that they'd seen was a wearable mask and they were a bit dismayed to find that it was only made out of plasticene. We then went to a meeting about the Destroyer with the designers from visual effects, make up and costume, John and Michael Kerrigan. At the time, the concept was that the Destroyer started off as a little man in a pin stripe suit and it was only when the chains were removed that he transforms into the demon. They were talking about talons bursting through the skin of his hands, but it would have been so expensive and in the end they dropped the entire transformation idea and had the Destroyer in his demon form all the way through.

We had to change it a little bit from the maquette because it had to have dialogue and the original design didn't have any lips. The raised set that they had helped a lot, because it meant that you were always looking up at it.

Sue Moore and Stephen Mansfield Sculptors

Possibly the most daunting of the tasks facing Dave and his crew was the helicopter explosion. Being faced with a very expensive piece of hardware that couldn't be damaged, it was obvious that a dummy helicopter would have to be found and the real one rigged in such a way that it would sustain no damage. Dave's crew fitted a small, electrically initiated smoke charge to the underside of the helicopter, running a firing button to the cabin. The helicopter pilot fired the charge himself so that no member of the effects crew needed to go up.

The final explosion was achieved with a crude fibreglass copy of what was, in fact, a completely different type of helicopter. Fast cutting and a suitably large explosion ensured that no one was aware of the fact.

Most of the other explosions planned by the effects crew had to be scaled down, because of that ever limiting factor – time. Whereas the normal way of setting a battlefield sequence is to plot it first and then dig in all the mortars, this one was done 'on the run'. To cope with this, a set of mortars were permanently rigged with firing lines. Once rehearsals on location were underway there was a frenzy of activity to get the mortars safely bedded down and primed before shooting began.

Because of the safety factors involved, and the minimum time needed to set each pyrotechnic device, the eventual number of explosions in the battle scenes was greatly reduced. This lack of time also meant that non essential close-ups – such as guns being fired – were the first things to be cut, though director Michael Kerrigan was still keen to get them shot somehow. As in *Silver Nemesis*, one of the effects crew ended up in the knight's costume and we got all the shots with a second unit.

The guns themselves were manufactured by Jon Savage, the perspex handles custom made to fit an existing telescopic barrel that Dave had in his personal stock of bits and pieces. The guns were each capable of firing once and were self contained, with a safety switch on the rear end. A larger machine gun version was also used for some scenes.

A number of smaller props were also needed. Bessie's overdrive was a small device with a joystick connected to several LEDs, a similar self contained flashing device forming the basis of the biomechanical control device that the Brigadier steps on. For the Doctor's self propelled piece of coinage Dave merely adapted one of the smaller 'Zoid' toys.

The bulk of the work was involved with the physical effects. For the scenes around the ruined building used as the gateway between dimensions, Dave had his work complicated by the fact that he was unable to do any actual explosions. The building was listed and not in particularly good repair and it was decided that loud noise was not a good idea. All the explosive effects were shot separately and added in post production, tinted green to add to the unearthly feel.

The Brigadier's tussle with the Destroyer was shot partly on location and partly in the studio, the interior of the tower being a set to accommodate the various smoke and lighting effects that were needed. On location an air mortar was used as a stunt man hurled himself through a boarded-up window. In studio the reverse was shot, with the stunt man launching himself off a trampette as an air mortar was set off behind him, at least this was the plan. I was in the studio that day to see various people before we started on the last two stories of the season, and watched as this particular sequence was set up. Unfortunately, the mortar didn't fire – a simple wiring error, it was eventually discovered – but the tight schedule meant that Dave wasn't given the opportunity to have another go – an irritating state of affairs at the best of times, especially when the cause of the failure has been something so simple. **M**

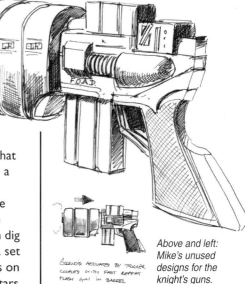

Above and left: Mike's unused designs for the knight's guns.

SOLENOID ACTIVATED BY TRIGGER COUPLED WITH FAST REPEAT FLASH GUN IN BARREL

Dirty deeds and the police

We were setting off some explosions on the lake and the local police came to be on hand while we did this. They decided that they would get wet, so retreated about one hundred yards and stood next to their police car. Visual effects set off this bang and there was the most almighty explosion in the lake, which brought fish to the surface, and a huge dollop of mud took off, flew through the air, completely missed the crew and landed on the policemen who thought they were safe.

We had a helicopter in that one but, being a typical *Doctor Who*, it had to do two scenes in two different places, we only had it for four hours' flying time, and it had to come from Shoreham. Initially, it had to land at the Brigadier's house, which was near Pinewood studios in Buckinghamshire. We set up the outside broadcast van at the house and, right on cue, the helicopter came in and landed. It then flew to Black Park and we had to pack up and race them there with the van.

Three scenes in the cockpit had to take place at night, so we built a tent that we could push the helicopter into, though it nearly blew it over when it landed. I then lit it with lots of little orange lights to simulate instruments.

In the final sequence it had to simulate a crash, so it flew in circles trailing smoke and ducking behind trees. Again, that's typical *Doctor Who*; in two hours shooting time we had to do five scenes in two different locations that were three miles apart! Quite manic.

Ian Dow
Outside broadcast manager

Top left: Mike's early design sketch for the sword, Excalibur.

Left: Mike's original, unused design for the biomechanoid ship.

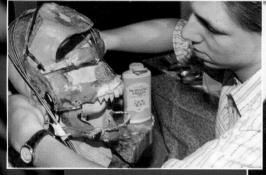

Photo: Andy DeEmmoney

Above top: Stephen Mansfield constructs the animatronic underskull for the Destroyer.

Above: The maquette of the Destroyer's head. The mouth was altered on the final head to allow the actor to speak.

Above right: The clay sculpture of the head.

Right: The finished mask.

Far right: Marek Anton as the Destroyer on set.

Photos: Sue Moore

Right: Sophie shows her Curse of Fenric photos to an unrecognisable Marek Anton, who played the Russian Vershinin in that story.

Right: The Brigadier confronts the Destroyer with a gun filled with silver bullets.

From left to right: Sophie takes a dip in Rutland water for the scene where Ace becomes the 'Lady of the Lake'.

Right: Sophie receives a dressing gown from Sara Wilkinson and a steaming cuppa from Matthew Purves.

Far right: Sophie reveals the sound crew's method for keeping an underwater mike dry... a condom!

Above top: Visual effects assistant Chris Reynolds stands in for one of the knights.

Above: The battle for the convoy rages by the side of the lake.

Left: An impressive explosion is set off as James Ellis and Sophie head for the crash mats.

Another soaking for Sophie

I waded back to shore, where Sara had blankets at the ready, and after the next bit of cheeky dialogue where I handed over the sword, I ran off to shower at the local pub, but not before the sound crew showed me their method for keeping an underwater microphone dry – a condom!

In the next scenes I looked as though I was still soaking wet but I was as dry as toast under those blankets. Renata damped me down for each take with a house plant sprayer filled with water.

An exciting moment for me was the visual part of the explosion in the lake. Visual effect's Dave had problems keeping the explosives-laden raft in one place and Nick and I weren't sure where to look out for it. It seemed an impressive bang, although Dave wasn't sure. As usual with explosions, we ran over to the monitor to check it back. Michael and JNT gave their thumbs up and we cheered!

Talking of explosions, there was of course the blowing up of the archeological dig. First we covered all the scenes leading up to the Nitro bang, including close-ups of the special edition can of Nitro which Mike Tucker had made for my blowing a hole in the cellar wall in *Fenric*, but which I'd broken. This new improved model appealed to my sense of gadgetry; I removed a pin and the clockwork top rotated like a wind-up toy. Shame I didn't get to take that one home.

Then came the explosion, and Michael set up the cameras so that the bang could be seen clearly behind the running figures of Sylv, Jimmy and me. We asked for crash mats to be laid out of vision so that Sylv and I could do one of our spectacular leaps. Jimmy was only too happy to join in the stunt competition! We rehearsed a couple of times so that visual effects knew when to press the button, and then went for a take. My heart pounding as usual with stunt adrenalin, I got ready to run. On 'Action' I went for it, jumping as high as I could when I felt the explosion behind me. We ran over to the monitor and watched the replay. I was pleased that the bang looked a lot closer than it actually was, so I looked even more daring – clever things, camera angles.

The close-ups for the next bit of the scene meant lying on the crash mat while the production team covered us in fake muck and dirt!

Sophie Aldred

I VISITED THE **BBC** DOCTOR (THE TRAINED MEDICAL TYPE, NOT THE MAD bespectacled Scottish one), as for BBC health and safety reasons I had to take a course of antibiotics before my second plunge of the season, this time into Rutland Water. I found the idea alarming. Rutland Water is a reservoir and to my mind should be free from nasty things like Weil's disease. But what do I know? I was just thankful that I didn't have to have any injections.

When we arrived on location, a private house just off the M40, I saw Bessie drive into position, and realised that I was actually going to be driving her. Another childhood dream fulfilled! The next day I drove to Leicestershire to the location where we were filming the Brig's near-death scene. My favourite part of the day was the explosion and Nick Courtney's stunt double hurling himself through a ruined window. The bang was apparently smaller than intended because of the delicate ruins, but it was still big enough to warrant ear plugs and a big smile from me. Is there a psychological dysfunction to do with watching explosions? If so, I'm a definite contender for the title!

Next morning we were driven to Rutland Water and arrived to find a beautiful morning mist over the lake. We'd hardly settled down before word reached us that a BBC pay strike had hit all productions, and that we couldn't carry on filming. Consequently, we were sent home, and with the shooting schedule up the spout, we waited. Finally the phonecall came, and we returned to Rutland.

Above: Ling Tai, Marcus Gilbert (before the Gold Blend ads) and me.

Below right: Sylvester and me sharing our 'tea and a tart' as JNT always put it.

Two words are written in my diary for Tuesday, May 16th… 'The Plunge'. This refers to my Lady of the Lake impression, something I had been looking forward to, particularly since Rutland Water was considerably warmer than Lulworth Cove – I'd tested it with my hand! I tried not to think of rats, and of what creepy wildlife might be lurking on the lake's muddy bottom. It was incredibly shallow, and I had to crouch underwater to give the illusion of coming up from a great depth. Communication with the director was tricky, but semaphore indicated that the camera was rolling. I took a deep trumpet player's breath and plunged. Here was my first problem. It was impossible in the murky water to orientate myself and I forgot which way was up. So Excalibur broke through the surface of the water at a jaunty angle, followed by a waterlogged Ace, who quickly lost her balance, slipped and fell un-Lady of the Lake-like backwards into the water. Take two. This time I took note of where the sky was. Carefully, I raised my arm, and this time Excalibur rose at a pretty good angle. That Lady must have been practising before Arthur bumped into her – it's trickier than it looks.

We returned to North Acton for the studio rehearsal block. It had seemed odd for me to go back to a more gung-ho Ace in this story compared to the deeper nuances of *Fenric*. However, *Battlefield* showed facets of Ace's character, particularly her jealous guardianship of the Doctor, that were important themes. There was an enormous amount to get through in the three studio days, and we gradually fell behind schedule. One problem was our leap through the interstitial vortex. Originally, this was to have been part of the set, but it proved easier to jump into a video effect than through a chunk of scenery. I remember feeling self conscious as I spun towards the camera, having

Ace on the Battlefield

I learnt a lot from working with Jean Marsh who was encouragingly complimentary about my acting. In our Excalibur confrontation I could feel a real frisson of tension between us. Looking back, the only thing I'd like to change is the 'paper knife' line, which doesn't sound like something Ace would say. I liked the argument between Ace and Shou Yuing – Ben's favourite anti-racism theme which he explored more fully in *Remembrance*. It was horrible to be calling Ling Tai, who had by now become a great pal, 'yellow' and 'slant eyed', and it was a powerful scene for us both.

The Destroyer turned out to be a magnificent creation, and all signs of Marek disappeared, save his careful work on the speeches, which I found both touching and chilling. I have admiration for someone who is willing to climb into a monster costume and, despite all the discomforts – being hot and sweaty, not being able to go to the loo, not being able to eat – manages to pull off a performance into the bargain.

At the time I enjoyed the heavy emotional scenes, because I felt I was really working as an actress, whilst the running around with Nitro and being cheeky came naturally.

Sophie Aldred

been assured by Michael that it would look fine in post production. Kind of hard to act with, these interstitial vortices.

The following day I was blessed with the exclusive company of Mr McCoy, which was wonderful fun. Sylv maintains that we're such good friends because I'm the only person who laughs at his jokes, and there were gags aplenty. I watched as Sylv threw himself around the set with no regard

for his personal safety – a man after my own heart – as he pretended to be beaten about by an invisible green snake.

I'd been eyeing up a large glass-fronted container in a corner of the studio which I knew was going to be filled with water and me at the end of the day. I'd also noticed some towels on the floor under the tank, which seemed to be mopping up some leaks, but decided to keep my nose out of other people's business for a change. Eventually, a voice called me over to the tank so that I could get ready while other bits were being filmed. I was lowered into the tank by the visual effects crew who were stationed at the top. I would shout to the Doctor a few times, dive down and grab Excalibur, then they would haul me out by my arms, creating the illusion that I'd burst through an airlock into the lake above. The water started pumping in over my head. I had thought that after my ordeals in Lulworth Cove and Rutland Water that this would be easy, but hadn't realised what the weight of the water would be as it poured out of the pipe onto my head, and the incredible noise it woul make, which cut out everything else. There was a bellow from a McCoy pair of

Photo: Claire Hainstock

lungs, asking me if I was okay and I gave a smile and a thumbs up. The camera seemed to be running, so I shouted my lines a few times, and dived down to pick up Excalibur. There was now a lot of water in the tank, and I was bobbing slightly, my jacket filling with air and acting as a buoyancy aid. I spread my hands on the glass in front of me to steady myself, and a few seconds later heard a loud cracking sound, and felt the glass give way beneath my fingers. Instinctively, I shot my arms into the air, and the crew, alerted by a shout of alarm from Sylv, 'Get her out of there!' hauled me to safety. For a second or two, no one moved, and then suddenly there was a mad dash for the studio doors, as the front of the tank buckled and bowed, and gallons of water gushed forth, spilling onto the studio floor and sending cameramen, actors and crew running for safety – water and electric power cables are not a good mix.

I watched water gushing towards the studio walls, and picked splinters of glass out of my hands. There was little damage done to me, and I didn't even feel very frightened, being of the stoical viewpoint that plenty of nasty things could have happened to me, and they didn't, so there's no point in worrying. So I was surprised when I received a frantic phonecall from my agent the next morning. The tabloids were about to print an article about how my face had been ripped to shreds by broken glass and that I was suing the BBC for six million pounds!

Having been shown the clip, I realised that it was the heroic Mr McCoy who probably saved my life, or at the very least my six million pound face! His reactions were amazingly quick, and his shouts which alerted the studio to prompt action undoubtedly averted major disaster. I owe you one, Mr McCoy. Ⓢ

Above top: A UNIT stunt soldier practises a flying leap for the convoy battle.

Above: The paparazzi arrive to snap away at Sylvester and Jean Marsh's sword versus brolly duel.

Left: Rehearsing with Ling Tai at North Acton for the bar scenes.

Below left: The Doctor and Morgaine come face to face.

Below right: Still trying to get a motorbike scene in somewhere.

At the pub

The many hotel bar scenes were complicated by the effects that were needed – a shaking scabbard, rattling glasses, flashing lights and so on.

The design team nipped in and out of shot, checking continuity, and adding props and effects. Then came the moment that we'd all been waiting for. The shooting schedule said 'Trash the bar' after the Destroyer had been at it. 'Thrash the bar! Thrash the bar!' shouted Riita, waving her schedule like some invading Viking. Everyone burst out laughing at her Norwegian interpretation.

While the design team were busy thrashing, we hurried over to the command trailer set and knocked off a couple of scenes, having to remember continuity jacket carrying from Rutland. Bar succesfully thrashed, Ling Tai and I returned for another dose of debris, courtesy of the production team. I streaked my face with dirt, never being one to do things by halves, but Juliet asked me to wipe it off pretty pronto to avoid continuity hassles. In the finished episode, it disappears suddenly, as if by magic.

Sophie Aldred

Photo: Sue Moore

80

Above: Sophie pretends to be in the water tank, with Riita Lynn checking.

Below: John Nathan-Turner, Nicholas Courtney and Sylvester waiting to shoot the Brig's stunt scene.

Above: The two Brigs.

Left: Things got mad. The technical staff were picking up shots wherever they could with little or no rehearsal. A voice called me over to the water tank – I realised: 'But I'm in this scene, too'. Close-ups completed, I left the set. Who says everyone has to be in the same scene at the same time?

Left: Which way did you say? Sylvester holding another favourite gadget.

Below: Don't shoot! Robert Jezek (Sergeant Zbrigniev) takes aim at Angela Bruce (Brigadier Bambera).

Bottom: Sylvester and Jean Marsh rehearse in the studio.

The Brig versus Ace

Dee Baron had bequeathed my *Fenric* hair extensions to Renata, my make up girl, who fixed them into my pony tail – thankfully a less time-consuming task than the sprouts. Costume designer Anushia Nieradzik and I decided on a sleeker look, and we bought Harry Hall riding jodhpurs from Lillywhites, a green lycra all-in-one and a wrap-around top from Pineapple's dance shop. I wore my Season 26 boots and copper earrings made by my mother in her evening class. Now I'd learnt my lesson in earring continuity, she ran up a spare pair just in case!

In the original script, Ace was to have a run in with the Brig on their very first meeting, and although it was filmed, time pressure meant that it never made it to the final cut. It was the beginning of a minor sub-plot – a mini battle for the right to the Doctor between Ace and the Brig, resolved after the latter's conflict with the Destroyer when he tells Ace:

'I'm getting too old for this. From now on, he's all yours.' It was a funny moment, as the old-style chauvinist Brig got it in the neck from Ace, then Bambera, and finally the Doctor. Luckily the scene was resurrected for the video documentary *More Than Thirty Years in the TARDIS*.

Sophie Aldred

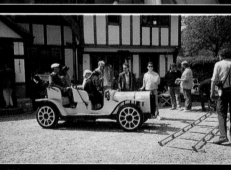

Above top: James Ellis (Peter Warmsly), Ling Tai and Sylvester in the Range Rover.

Above: Sophie gets to drive Bessie for the first time, directed by Michael Kerrigan (in the pink top).

Survival

By Rona Munro   Story 7P

3 Episodes – broadcast 22 November to 6 December 1989

The Cast

The Doctor	Sylvester McCoy
Ace	Sophie Aldred
The Master	Anthony Ainley
Paterson	Julian Holloway
Karra	Lisa Bowerman
Midge	William Barton
Shreela	Sakuntala Ramanee
Derek	David John
Stuart	Sean Oliver
Harvey	Gareth Hale
Len	Norman Pace
Ange	Kate Eaton
Squeak	Adele Silva
Neighbour	Michelle Martin
Woman	Kathleen Bidmead

The Production Team

Producer	John Nathan-Turner
Director	Alan Wareing
Script editor	Andrew Cartmel
Production manager	Gary Downie
Production associate	June Collins
Production assistant	Valerie Whiston
Assistant floor manager	Stephen Garwood
Producer's secretary	Clare Kinmont
Finance assistant	Paul Goodliffe
Designer	Nick Somerville
Assistant designer	Paddy Lea
Properties buyer	Nick Barnett
Costume designer	Ken Trew
Costume assistant	Sally Booth-Jones
Senior dresser	Riley Clark

Dressers	Ray Greenhill
	Sara Wilkinson
Make up designer	Joan Stribling
Make up assistants	Christine Wheeler
	Helen Johnson
	Caroline O'Neill
	Rebecca Walker
Visual effects designer	Malcolm James
Visual effects assistants	Mike Tucker
	Paul McGuinness
	James Davis
	Guy Lunn
Video effects designer	Dave Chapman
Lighting engineering manager	Ian Dow
Planning engineering manager	Brian Jones
Sound supervisor	Les Mowbray
Deputy sound supervisor	Peter Hale
Camera supervisor	Paul Harding
Cameraman	Alan Jessop
Senior vision engineer	Dave Jennings
Vision engineers	Anthony Kemp
	Dick Barlow
Rigger supervisor	Alan Redman
Chief electrician	Jim Russell
Vision mixer	Susan Brincat
Video tape engineer	Steve Grayston
Production operatives supervisor	Vic Young
Production operatives	Brian Roberts
	Alan Bennett
	John Greenham
Incidental music	Dominic Glynn
Special sound	Dick Mills

ALTHOUGH *SURVIVAL* WAS THE LAST *DOCTOR WHO* STORY TO BE TRANSMITTED IT was not the last to be recorded. As was usual with the three-parters the location story happened first, recorded in the same sand pit that had been used for *The Greatest Show in the Galaxy*. Before any of the Dorset scenes, however, we had the delights of filming in Perivale.

From the effects point of view the list of requirements for the story was quite a small one. Basically we just had the atmospheric and physical effects, the animal carcasses – and the cat.

Below: One of the fake skeletons built for Survival *and reused several times – being less maggoty than the real ones.*

Bottom right: Mike models a set of horns, which later adorned the visual effects van.

When the script arrived it was obvious that the black cat – the kitling – could only be achieved with a combination of real animal and puppet. Alan Wareing came over to the effects department to talk over the problems of the cat with effects designer Malcolm James. Malcolm had worked on a comedy programme (*I Lovett*) that had featured an animatronic dog capable of a tremendous range of expression. He arranged to have the dog set up in the model stage on the day of Alan's visit and from this session it was decided to let Malcolm proceed with the construction of an animatronic cat, although this, being smaller, meant that all the movements, major and minor, had to be operated via cable. Most of the shots of the cat were achieved with it in a sitting position and the major movement was in the head – turning, ear movement, eyes up, down, left and right, eyelids, jaw and lips.

The main problem was that it was obvious that we were never going to be able to match the real cat exactly. There were three cats playing the part of the kitling and they were all smaller than our model. Also, the real cats rarely did what they were required to do and we ended up using the puppet far more extensively than had originally been intended.

Among the more difficult shots that we had to achieve were the ones where there was no wall to hide behind to operate the cat. When Sophie holds the cat on the swing there were four of us behind her, out of shot. One scene required the cat to be sitting on the grass watching children play. I ended up lying on the floor covered in a pile of grass just to get minimal movement to the puppet.

The kitling was not the only cat that we had to make for the story. Several cat corpses were needed at the Perivale location, the dead kitten at Midge's flat and Tiger, the dead cat in the back of the shop. The dead kitten was a problem because it lacked definition, ending up more like a toy. With the other corpse I had gone for more realism, using the moulds made for the animatronic cat, but dressing it with ginger fur instead. I bought some offal from a local butcher and dressed this into the slashed corpse. The final effect was too gruesome, however, and although Alan did shoot the scene with this version we also did a suitably toned down version and it was this one that eventually got transmitted.

Our big day in Perivale was on Horsenden Hill, with the explosion of the bikes and the subsequent fire. To achieve the apparent collision of two speeding bikes Dave Chapman came to the location to ensure that we filmed enough material for him to be able to fake the shot in post production. The bikes were recorded separately, one going one way and then one going the other. A predetermined place was set for the explosion and that was set up and shot as a third element.

With all the London filming completed, the crew set off for Dorset. All of our fake animal carcasses were in evidence, scattered around the location to give the impression of a charnel house. A local abattoir had

Sylvester's spaghetti western

I enjoyed *Survival*. We were in a sand pit in Dorset and it was like being in the North African desert – acres of sand and it was well over one hundred degrees. It was a bit like making a spaghetti western and I've always wanted to make a spaghetti western – I even got to ride a horse.

It was incredibly hot though, and the poor people who had to be the Cheetah people were dressed up in all this rubber and fur. One of them freaked out, she just couldn't take it any more so she stripped off her costume and left!

Julian Holloway was a marvellously funny bloke and we had a great time. We had to do this horseriding scene. It was a complicated tracking shot and Julian was terrified of horses, and had a bad back. Now, I'm not a great horseman. I've been on them on the odd occasion, but Roy Kinnear had just been killed in a horseriding accident, so that was on all our minds. It was the end of the day, I had a very long speech, the heat was pounding our brains, Julian was hanging on, terrified, crushing my ribs, and I was trying to control this horse. They'd put us on the edge of a cliff, which made things even worse, but as soon as they said, 'Action' this horse looked into the camera and smiled! It was the horse that they used to advertise Lloyds, so it was a pro. It was all a bit of a performance. We had to keep doing it and the light was going – I don't know how we ever got it all in.

Sylvester McCoy

also delivered crate loads of bones. Although the bones were meant to have been steam cleaned, some of them were still hanging with rotting meat and, after a day in the sweltering temperatures (white sand being an excellent reflector) maggots began to hatch.

I spent a day in the bone strewn valley, rigging the horned skeleton that Anthony Ainley tears strips of skin from, and it was, without doubt, the most disgusting environment that I have ever had to work in. Quite apart from the maggots and the flies, the smell became quite overpowering. The fake skeleton was an aluminium skeleton with a sculpted head and horns. The skin was a latex soaked fabric that tore along its weave very easily, even providing a suitable noise.

The script called for Karra to collapse into a pool of 'moonwater', subsequently being pulled clear by Ace, who saves her by bringing her a handful of glowing liquid. The actors playing the Cheetahs were already suffering in the incredible heat, and make up were having great difficulty keeping the prosthetics attached. Having their principal Cheetah dunk her head in the water was out of the question and so one of the background artistes did it. Karra's close-ups were all done with just a light sprinkling of water on her fur.

The moon reflecting in the water was done by erecting a large lamp on the far side of the pond, painted out in post production. Ace scooping up the glowing water had to be shot separately since Alan Wareing wanted to see her reflection in the surface of the pond and we couldn't get that at the actual location. We dug a small pit, and lined it with black polythene. Filled with water and being dark, it acted as a perfect reflector.

The glowing water was effected by insulating a small quartz bulb so that it could sit in the palm of Sophie's hand, with the wires running down her arm. The water stopped the bulb from becoming too hot to hold.

All the scenes of fissures opening in the ground and burning water were achieved by Malcolm, working with a second unit. He had found several deep cracks in the quarry floor and, while the main unit shot the fight between the Doctor's party and the Cheetah people, he rigged several flares and smoke canisters into these cracks, giving the impression of volcanic activity. Several of the large, shallow pools were rigged with gas lines, weighted down so that the gas bubbled to the surface before igniting. Similar gas lines were rigged around Sylvester McCoy and Anthony Ainley for the climactic battle in the Cheetah camp.

The bulk of the planetary disintegration scenes were achieved in post production. Most of the distant vistas of volcanoes were achieved with Paintbox, though the plumes of smoke and swirling clouds were all shot on the visual effects model stage at Acton. The stage has a black floor and a black cyclorama, so Malcolm came up with the idea of using dry ice vapour, which is white, and then reversing the colour in the video effects workshop to get black smoke against a white sky. Dry ice is heavier than air, so to achieve vertical columns of smoke we suspended the feed tubes several feet off the ground and let the vapour tumble to the floor. As it hit the floor it spread out, and this swirling carpet of mist was inverted and used to create the turbulent skies of the Cheetah planet. Ⓜ

Above: Paul McGuinness operates the animatronic kitling nicknamed 'Sooty' by John Nathan-Turner.

I had to summon up tears for the final scenes. I find it hard to manufacture tears at will at the best of times, and now, with time pressure and an atmosphere of panic, I couldn't come up with the real thing. In any case, I find real tears get in the way of acting; you're so busy wallowing in your own feelings, that you can't act. Chrissy handed me a tear stick that she swore was Tiger Balm – it smelt suspiciously like a Vicks Sinex nasal stick to me – and I smeared it on the tender skin below my eyes. Hey presto! Real tears!
Sophie Aldred

Below: 'Eyes and teeth'. Anthony Ainley as the Master baring his fangs.

Above: Anthony Ainley in his new Master's costume and yellow contact lenses.

Above: Mike Tucker, Paul McGuinness and James Davis operate 'Sooty' on location in Perivale.

Frightening contact lenses

My next appointment with fear came when Joan Stribling, the make-up designer, met me at David Culows opticians in Earls Court. I'm blessed with 20:20 vision; this was my first eye test since squinting at an eye test card in a cold school shower room before being tapped on the knee with a small hammer, along with other mysterious tests carried out by starched white nurses who didn't appreciate our school-girl humour. This time I wasn't nervous so much as curious. I'd always wondered how my contact lensed friends could bear to poke those floppy bits of plastic into their eyes. Now I was about to find out.

The first lens covered my eye completely and felt as though I was rubbing a handful of grit into my face with an electric sander, so the optician whipped that one out and popped in a bright yellow disc. He handed me a mirror and I stared in horrified fascination at my yellow-eyed reflection. We took the lenses.

I went to my boyfriend's house to practise. Perfect for scaring the children next door, I hoped, and inserted the instruments of torture. Minutes later, red-eyed, squinting and tearful, I poked my head over the garden fence and awaited my prey, chuckling as six-year-old Sam strolled down the path towards me.

'Look, Nina, look, look! Sophie's got funny contact lenses in! Her eyes are all sore!'

Despairing at the cynicism of today's youth, I returned to the kitchen. My boyfriend turned to greet me.

'AAGH!' He screamed, leaping across the room.

'What's happened? It's horrible! Go away – you're not my Sophie!'

At least I got a reaction from someone.
Sophie Aldred

Above: Sophie holds the animatronic cat, while the visual effects team operate 'Sooty' out of shot. Working with the fake cat caused Sophie fewer problems than the real felines.

Right: Moving the TARDIS around would be a lot easier if it really did dematerialise.

Above: The visual effects assistants for Survival: (left to right) Mike Tucker, Paul McGuinness, Guy Lunn and James Davis.

Above: The costume team: (left to right) Ray Greenhill, Sally Booth-Jones, Riley Clark, Sara Wilkinson and Ken Trew.

Above: Three members of the make up team: (left to right) Helen Johnson, Joan Stribling and Chrissie Wheeler.

Right: Make-up assistant Helen Johnson surveys her handiwork on Lisa Bowerman.

Above: A Cheetah person's make up nears completion.

Left: Lisa Bowerman in her completed make up plus a natty pair of sunglasses, braves the soaring temperatures in the quarry.

Top left: Mike adds some hoof prints to Sophie's rear using a special visual effects gadget.

Above: Director Alan Wareing and John Nathan-Turner check the recorded scenes on a monitor.

Left: Alan Wareing works with Anthony Ainley and Sylvester on their fight scene.

Riding lessons

Ken kept the jodhpurs theme started in *Battlefield* – after all, I had to get on a horse in this story. He adapted some black cotton drill trousers from Warehouse to fit me properly around the nether regions. I loved the *Battlefield* wrap-over ballet top, and Ken bought a pink version, adding a school tie as a belt.

Rehearsals were great fun. Anthony Ainley's enthusiasm for cricket was shared by Dave John and me, and during breaks we set up a make-shift pitch: three metal poles were stumps, a lump of wood was our bat, and we bowled with a tennis ball.

The producer's 'run' was precisely that for me; I charged up and down the rehearsal room pretending to be chased by Lisa, who was pretending to be on horseback – very surreal, but good for the leg muscles!

On a day off I was booked into a riding stables in Rickmansworth. Although as a kid I had played horses in the school playground, and spent hours dreaming about living in the country and riding *Black Beauty*, I had never sat on a real horse. At first I found the whole thing quite scary. A horse doesn't have a clutch and throttle like a motorbike! Once I'd got used to using reins instead of handlebars, and to the motion of the animal, I felt happier.

Sophie Aldred

Above: The Cheetah people find a shady spot at Warmwell quarry.

STRIKES, AND THE RESULTING RE-JIGGED STUDIO DAYS WITH A READ-THROUGH at North Acton the following morning meant that I didn't have long to brood over my lucky escape from the water tank in *Battlefield*, even if I'd wanted to. I realised from the outset that *Survival* would be particularly fun to shoot – having Ace's 'gang' around meant a young cast, plus the very funny Julian Holloway, and my first encounter with Anthony Ainley. One of my great regrets is that Ace never got to have a head to head scene with the Master – I'm sure she would have had a thing or two to say to him if she had.

Right: With my yellow contact lenses in place. Even though I'd been rehearsing with them, the first time I put my lenses in was agony; and down at the quarry, the bright sunlight made my eyes sting and water.

Above: Savaged by a fake fur cat.

I was delighted to tackle a script written by a woman, Rona Munro, who gave Ace a realistic depth which I found challenging. Ace had strayed somewhat from the cockney rebel created by Ian Briggs all that time ago and now contained a lot more of the real me.

My first glimpse of Perivale, the genuine article, was much as I'd expected – a grim graffiti-adorned council estate. I struck up a friendship with Adele, who played Squeak, and got lots of cuddles. My first day in Perivale ended early, after a scene inside the flat, where Ace is rude about a pop band, and discovers Squeak hiding in the kitchen. I was amused to find Mike Tucker pouring tomato ketchupy goo onto what looked like the sad remains of a cuddly toy. After some rude remarks I beat a hasty retreat.

The next day, to my horror, was a 7.00am start at Television Centre where I was poured half asleep into costume and make up and Sylv, Gareth Hale and I were driven to a pub near Ealing. I was always star struck by our guest performers on *Doctor Who*, and Hale and Pace were no exception. Because of previous commitments, they'd not been at the read-through or general rehearsals, though if memory serves, they did have a session with Sylv. This was our first meeting, and both Gareth and Norman, when I met him

Above: 'Squeak' and me at the council flats on the first day of filming.

later, were great! They both lived in my part of London, Blackheath, and had met at Avery Hill teacher training college. Unfortunately for the youth of south east London, they became comedians instead.

My last scene of the day was with 'Ange' outside a charity shop. Originally, the Doctor took out a strange coin which wouldn't fit the hunt saboteurs' collecting tin, gave it a magical Time Lord's tap, and it would mysteriously drop through the hole. As usual we'd run out of time, and the shot was abandoned.

The next day was another early start. My first shot involved picking up a kitling as I sat on one of the playground swings. This was more complicated than it seems – the animatronic black cat turned out to be a bit ropey and had already been nicknamed Sooty by a frustrated John Nathan-Turner, who had hoped for something more convincing. What made matters worse was that our live animal handlers were not handling the cats as effectively as we'd hoped; as soon as one of the live kitlings was groomed for the camera (gel on the neck fur to give a dishevelled Mohican kind of look) it would promptly lick itself back into shape. Cats are unpredictable at the best of times, and as they kept running off, Sooty was brought into action more often than had originally been expected.

However, we managed to catch one of the real moggies long enough for my scene on a playground swing. Some bright spark piped up,

'Hey, Sophie, wouldn't it be funny if you were allergic to cats!'

'I am,' I replied, 'and it's not that funny!' I'd been keeping this quiet and now steeled myself for a day of itching and sneezing. The frustrating thing is that I like cats, but I can't touch them. This poor specimen sensed my awkwardness, as I grabbed hold of it for dear life to get the shot finished as quickly as possible. Finally, it bolted off my lap back to the love of the cat handler and a reward of Whiskas, and left me with scratches up my arm which quickly turned into large itching welts. There was nothing we could do, so we continued with Sooty and a crowd of visual effects boys at my feet to operate him out of shot.

Above: All the running around in the rehearsal room was good preparation for the location filming, and good excercise too.

Next was one of the horses with Cheetah person stunt rider. I was disappointed when I first saw the cat costume. I thought they'd be menacing and feline like the description in the script, not furry and cuddly. Make up and costume for the actors who played them was a trial – how on earth Lisa Bowerman managed to ride a horse wearing contact lenses and all that fun fur, I don't know. The horse behaved well, rearing on cue, under the expert guidance of one of the riding extras team. I wonder what the horse thought, being ridden by a giant cat!

I spent the next couple of hours being chased round the adventure playground, worried at times at the proximity of dangerous looking hooves, and then came my running shots. I ran the length of the playing field, glancing over my shoulder as if pursued, and alongside me drove an open-sided van with a camera

Above: To Anthony Ainley's delight I love cricket, and I found these nets for practice shots while not being used on set. I also found some local kids for a game of football and kept myself fit for more running.

pointed at me. We made a competition of it, and I ran as fast as I could. The driver kept an eye on the speedometer, and I reached a decent top speed with the van's occupants cheering me on!

We moved onto a housing estate where the TARDIS materialises in episode one. The locals watched our antics with amazement, especially when the TARDIS was wheeled into position by the props boys, and when the large crane arm for the camera appeared, plus a giant wind machine. That's how Alan managed to get those fabulous swooping overhead shots from the horse's point of view, as though it was rearing above the victim.

The last scene of the day was one of those complicated continuity moments when we had to jump to the end of the storyline and film a scene from episode three. Paterson had to look the worse for wear after his brawl with a Cheetah person on the 'planet' without knowing what that would entail. Make up and costume scruffed us all up,

Above: Cheetahs chilling out with plastic fans and umbrellas.

Left: Cat food! Lisa Bowerman on the catering bus trying to eat lunch without getting it in her whiskers.

Right: Gareth Hale, Norman Pace (Harvey and Len) and me outside the shop. Gareth and Norman were pleased with the storyline as they'd had some bad press due to a sketch in their TV show about cats and microwave ovens.

Above: The horse rears up on command in the playground.

Right: Lisa as Karra getting friendly.

Far right top: Julian Holloway (Paterson) trying to keep cool.

Far right bottom: I felt tanned and fit beneath my make up, keeping my swim suit under my costume ready for a spot of sunbathing when not needed.

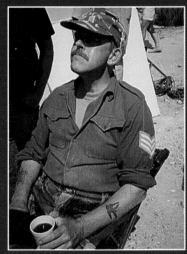

Sophie's good seat

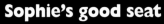

The horses behaved themselves perfectly; mine obligingly walked exactly where I wanted him to, turning his head to camera and trotting out of shot to his handler's offer of a sugar lump without so much as a whinny. My moment of triumph came some years later when a riding instructor friend who had seen me in *Survival* thought that I'd been born in the saddle – at least she told me that I had a good seat, which I took as a compliment.

Sophie Aldred

Left: *Sylvester has a spot of trouble with his new glasses in the youth club.*

Below: *The hand of the Master. Sylvester looks a little worried.*

Above: Sylvester takes to horseback.

Below: Lisa Bowerman had had a nasty riding accident several years previously and wasn't looking forward to riding again, though she'd been an accomplished horsewoman. Now she had the additional problems of restricted, contact-lensed vision and being covered from head to toe in fun fur!

Above: An unusual side effect of one of the visual effects team's explosions.

Tip Tipping

With time running short, John Nathan-Turner and Tip had a dispute which led to Tip walking off the show and Paul Heasman replacing him. This, then, was Tip's last day on *Doctor Who* before his fatal parachute jump in 1993 for the BBC series *999* when his chute failed to open and he fell to his death. I saw Tip many a time before then in many guises, including as a gorilla in the BBC canteen, and we swapped stories about happy times on the series. When I jumped out of an aeroplane in aid of the Children's Society last autumn I thought about Tip. He taught me about courage, fear and accepting my limitations, and I hoped that somewhere, somehow, he was watching me and feeling proud of me too.

Sophie Aldred

Above right: Cameraman Alan Jessop had brought his scuba diving equipment with him and gave me a lesson in the hotel pool where I swam around looking at dead flies and wishing I was in the Caribbean.

Below: The sensationalised News of the World *story reporting the water tank accident on* Battlefield.

▶ including a whole different costume for Julian, and then took continuity Polaroids so they could match them up when filming the preceding scenes the following week! We all felt daft standing in the middle of the road, holding hands, and jumping in the air on 'Action!' Alan reassured us that it would look fine with the addition of the video effects and some spooky music.

The following morning saw us back in the streets of Perivale for a long day with cats and a dog, John's beloved Pepsi, who could also be seen snuffling round Miss Hardaker's cottage in *Fenric*. The old saying, 'never work with animals,' crossed a few minds as we coaxed unwilling gelled furred cats in and out of shot with tasty morsels until they were sick of the sight of cat food and sat in the sun, licking off their hair gel. Pepsi behaved herself impeccably, and I wondered silently if it was too late to rewrite the script for 'doglings' and 'dog people!'

The next day's location was at a martial arts centre, which was our youth club location. We arrived to find the design team putting some finishing touches to the boarded up canteen, and Sylvester and I added some of our own graffiti to the walls. I felt penned 'I luv' and the name of my boyfriend, and Sylv made sure that the poster for *Cats* would be included in shot. As usual, the shooting order was back to front, so we started with the exterior scene where Paterson suggests that the Doctor takes up self defence classes. It was hard to be angry with Paterson, as Julian was so completely unlike the character he was portraying. Some of his pompous lines made us howl with laughter in rehearsals, and Julian knew how to get the most out of them. We moved to the interior scenes, first in the lobby, and then to watch Stuart 'beating up' one of the other poor lads, all out of order as usual!

Our final day in Perivale began with a surprise. Driving up out of the housing estate, the road became leafy and rural, until I arrived at Horsenden Hill, which for all the world could have doubled for the grassy knolls of Hampstead Heath, that exclusive suburb a few miles away. I hoped that Rona Munro wouldn't be upset at her scripted 'urban landscape' and 'wasteground' being translated into grass and trees. There we did one of the most complicated scenes known to man or Time Lord! Episode three, scene 18 was a massive twelve pages long, and included a motor bike stunt, the sudden appearance of a Cheetah person on horseback, a huge explosion, and worst of all, Sylvester trying to ride a motorbike minus glasses! The scene was divided into sections, and Alan went through the order with us to check we all knew what was involved. Tip Tipping, again the stunt coordinator, had booked Eddie Kidd to double for Will Barton, as although Will could ride a motor bike, he couldn't be expected to do the final confrontation, which required both bikers (Tip as the Doctor and Eddie as Midge) to ride hell for leather across the shot, stopping in time to avoid a rather inconvenient cliff edge. It was ironic that although I had passed my bike test years beforehand, owned my own bike, had got the job in the first place on the strength of my esoteric skill, and had nagged Andrew Cartmel relentlessly to let Ace ride a bike in the series, the nearest I got was to sit on one for a few mingy seconds until Sylvester pulled me off and rode off into the sunset. Unfortunately, no one had thought to ask whether he could actually ride, and he didn't realise he couldn't either until it was too late and he suddenly found himself heading for the cliff without knowing how to stop. At the last minute, he decided it was safest to jump off, and luckily nothing

DR WHO GIRL CHEATS DEATH

Sophie is sucked into tank

DR Who's assistant was almost killed and dozens of others had to jump for their lives when a studio stunt went wrong.

The accident happened when actress Sophie Aldred, who plays Ace, was thrown into a glass-lined cylinder full of water.

The glass shattered, sucking Sophie to the bottom of the tank, and sending hundreds of gallons of water flooding on

By CHARLES CATCHPOLE

to electrical cables at the BBC Television Centre in West London.

A member of the production team said: "We could all have been killed, as the floor was covered with live cables.

"We jumped on to chairs or hung on to

camera gantries—anything to keep our feet off the ground."

A BBC spokesman said: "Quick thinking prevented a serious disaster.

"Sophie swallowed some water and was shaken, but not hurt."

An inquiry has been launched, but the new series will be ready for the autumn.

SOPHIE: Dice with death

was damaged. After that, close-ups of both Sylv and Will were taken with the bikes stationary!

A few days later we left Television Centre on a Dorset bound coach at 7.00am on Sunday morning – Warmwell quarry revisited – this time shot from different angles to represent the nameless Cheetah planet rather than clown filled Segonax. As we were driven to our first location, I saw a new side to Warmwell quarry; as Segonax had been a mainly sandy planet, I'd not noticed the trees and bushes which we now used for the gang's hideout. Temperatures were soaring into the 80s, so we were glad to be making a start under the shady trees. I was intrigued by the huge piles of bones which designer, Nick Somerville, had procured from a local abattoir and hoped they had been sterilised properly – we were warned not to touch them just in case. At coffee break someone handed me the *News of the World*. With a wry smile on my face, I read the over-sensationalised 'Doctor Who girl cheats death' in the *Battlefied* water tank. I'd forgotten all about it – although it was only two weeks since the accident, to me filming a new story in a Dorset quarry, it seemed months ago.

Soon I had to do one of my marathon runs. After several rehearsals my legs gave way under me and felt tingly and strange. I had cramp through lack of salt, after sweating in the heat and not drinking enough water. Someone gave me salt tablets, which I then took every day. One frustration was that the catering team didn't seem to understand the meaning of drinking water. It was the one thing we all desperately needed, yet we'd be handed gallon containers of sweet sticky squash, which just made us even more thirsty. Sylvester renamed the location 'The deserts of Dorset' as temperatures continued to rise, and I worked out how I could wear my Ace jacket as little as possible. Luckily, I'd remembered my swimming costume and wore it under my wrap-around top so that I could remove it between scenes for some serious sun bathing!

The following day was nightmarish for the Cheetah people, who were entombed in fun fur from the early hours. I couldn't imagine what it must have been like to be covered from head to foot in that heat – even down to the contact lenses. I sat quietly with Lisa under a shady umbrella, set up by costume. Having lived in India as a child she'd learnt to sit very still – then the heat wasn't so bad. The puny battery powered fans with which the costume and make up teams fanned Cheetah people's necks (their only accessible part) were no match for the airless sandy wastes. As temperatures soared into the one hundreds, tempers flared. We lost a Cheetah person, as she ripped off her mask and disappeared over the horizon, running for the nearest train station.

We had to remount the final scene once a location had been found to match the leafy

glades of Horsenden Hill. There was another mad scramble to complete it, so out came the continuity Polaroids. Rona had written about six million stage directions for Ace, but now there just wasn't time. Alan said he'd insert a shot of the planet disintegrating and to react; I dutifully did one of my famous *Doctor Who* assistant's 'reacting to nothing' faces, and he never put the shot in! I can see the moment when I'm watching volcanoes erupting – I must be the only one!

An extra day's shoot to make up for the strike was mainly the Doctor and the Master battling it out with each other in the heat, exacerbated by the fire torches round them. For Sylvester it turned out to be a nightmare, he decided to put his contact lenses in for the first time, then Anthony hit Sylv's arm with a prop bone by mistake, so all in all the day was a painful one. **S**

Glow worms and picket lines

One night I led an impromptu visual effects night hike up the steep path to Durdle Door, a geological phenomenon that we couldn't miss this time, even if it was the middle of the night. The moon lit our way and the fascinating wildlife we saw included glow worms, which apparently light up during sexual activity – this particular night was obviously party time! Bewildered rabbits crossed our path as we made the descent to the pebbly beach, sploshed stones into the sea and lay on our backs and gazed into the heavens to look for shooting stars. They're a romantic bunch, these visual effects guys, especially after a few pints.

Sylv and I were the sole occupants of the coach home to London, and we were both so exhausted that we fell fast asleep, though in my case it was too much sun and playing frisbee rather than overwork.

I woke to loud shouting, and peering bleary-eyed out of the window, I ascertained that we were back in London outside the closed gates of Television Centre facing a picket line of BBC technical staff. Sylv and I were given a huge cheer as we walked off our separate ways. I felt a bit of a fraud – the striking crowd obviously thought that we were making a political statement by not crossing the picket line. All I wanted was a hot bath and an early night!

Sophie Aldred

Top left: Where are we? We set off to walk to the final location and got hopelessly lost. Eventually we heard Gary Downie's dulcet tones floating across a field and were guided to the right place.

Left: Sylvester doing Buster Keaton.

Below: What on earth is this, Doctor? My non-alchohol days.

Right: Sophie advises Sylvester on how to ride a motorbike.

Barbecue time at Lulworth

There was a very good atmosphere amongst the *Survival* crew; it was a young cast and there were a lot of people who had worked together regularly for three years. The fact that we were at a seaside resort during the summer also helped and, taking advantage of the good weather, John Nathan-Turner organised a crew barbecue. The barbeque itself fell, of course, to the effects crew and John was quite concerned to find us still at the bar, and the barbeque unlit, only half an hour before people were due to start eating. In fact, James Davis had adapted the gas rigs that had been used earlier in the week and we managed to get the barbeque lit, and up to full heat, in about ten minutes! The OB crew provided music and lights and John acted as chef for the evening, cooking a vast amount of food for his assembled crew.

The fact that by this time rumours were beginning to circulate that this might be the last *Doctor Who* we would ever do gave the evening a somewhat different atmosphere – it might be the last time that we would work with this particular OB crew. The design and production teams, however, had to return to London and start work on what would actually be the last *Doctor Who* story to be recorded – *Ghost Light*.

Mike Tucker

On the Tuesday we found ourselves so far ahead of schedule (yes, you read that correctly) that when a BBC pay strike hit us at 3 pm, we knocked off early. With many of the cast travelling home the following day, JNT decided a celebration was in order, and organised one of his legendary parties: a beach barbeque at Lulworth. Cooking implements and the barbeque itself were knocked up from bits of old metal in spare moments by visual effects. Damon Jeffry, our intrepid Cheetah horseman, turned entertainer for the evening and dragged his electric keyboard down to the beach. More traditional bopping music was provided by the sound crew's gear. Visual effects threw some dry ice into the sea, producing an eerie *Fenric* like mist, and the whole party was superbly lit by the sparks team. Sylvester and I waltzed along the beach, and into the sea, then I dried his trouser ends, his legs still inside them, over the flaming barbeque. His linen suit was never the same again!

Sophie Aldred

Above: Sylvester heads off towards the cliff edge!

Left: Two Doctors (Tip and Sylvester) and stunt rider Eddie Kidd on Horsenden Hill.

Above: Wil Barton (Midge) practises riding a stationary bike.

Left: Wil with his stunt double Eddie Kidd.

Far left: A far safer way for Sylvester to ride a motorbike.

Below: Sylvester relaxes after a hard day fighting the Master.

Ghost Light

By Marc Platt

Story 7Q

3 Episodes – broadcast 4 October to 18 October 1989

The Cast

The Doctor	Sylvester McCoy
Ace	Sophie Aldred
Josiah	Ian Hogg
Mrs Pritchard	Sylvia Syms
Inspector Mackenzie	Frank Windsor
Control	Sharon Duce
Light	John Hallam
Gwendoline	Katherine Schlesinger
Redvers Fenn-Cooper	Michael Cochrane
Nimrod	Carl Forgione
Reverend Ernest Matthews	John Nettleton
Mrs Grose	Brenda Kempner

The Production Team

Producer	John Nathan-Turner
Director	Alan Wareing
Script editor	Andrew Cartmel
Production manager	Gary Downie
Production associate	June Collins
Production assistant	Valerie Whiston
Assistant floor manager	Stephen Garwood
Producer's secretary	Clare Kinmont
Finance assistant	Paul Goodliffe
Designer	Nick Somerville
Assistant designer	Paddy Lea
Properties buyer	Nick Barnett
Costume designer	Ken Trew
Costume assistant	Sally Booth-Jones
Senior dresser	Riley Clark
Dressers	Sara Wilkinson
	Lisa Billingham
	Karen Beale
Make-up designer	Joan Stribling
Make-up assistants	Helen Johnson
	Caroline O'Neill
	Christina Webster
	Val Sparkes
Visual effects designer	Malcolm James
Visual effects assistants	Mike Tucker
	Paul McGuinness
	James Davis
	Guy Lunn
Video effects designer	Dave Chapman
Lighting director	Henry Barber
Technical co-ordinator	Richard Wilson
Sound supervisor	Scott Talbot
Deputy sound supervisor	Andrew Down
Camera supervisor	Spencer Payne
Vision mixer	Susan Brincat
Floor assistant	Eirwen Davies
Production operatives supervisor	Martin Carley
Production operatives	Pat McGuire
	Dougie Hancock
	Phil Clark
Incidental music	Mark Ayres
Special sound	Dick Mills

G HOST *LIGHT* ALLOWED ME TO REALISE A CHILDHOOD AMBITION – TO create a monster for *Doctor Who*. Up until now the creatures had always been handled by specialist sculptors, and rightly so. For *Ghost Light*, however, a last minute change of plan for the monsters allowed me to design and build a creature myself – the insectoid husk.

Marc Platt, presented with the studio bound story, took full advantage of the fact that it would be shot entirely indoors by setting it – entirely indoors! The only exterior shots, the establishing shots of the house, had been done by Alan Wareing during the recording of *Survival* at a house near the sand pit in Dorset.

Ghost Light required a full Victorian house, with all the dressing that that entails, and a fully practical lift linking the hallway with the lower observatory. Most of the visual effects involvement was with the spacecraft set.

Following the description in the script, Malcolm designed an asymmetrical console with crystal rods that could rise and fall, apparently of their own volition. The console itself was a timber construction that was handed over to the scenic department so that they could texture it in the same way as the rest of the set. A system was devised involving pulleys and control wires that ran through the back of the set, each wire operating a single perspex rod. The wires feeding the lamps set into the rods were run out the same way.

The membrane was a vacuum-formed sheet manufactured by James Davis. At various points through the story the membrane had to crack and eventually shatter, and James devised a spring loaded rig that was capable of being reset in case of retakes. Smoke jets, air mortars and powerful lights were also set up behind the membrane to augment the effect. The embryonic form of Light was a simple marionette constructed by Paul McGuinness, puppeteered from behind the set amid clouds of smoke, with the intention being to keep the shape as vague as possible.

Early script ideas for *Ghost Light* had an army of husks in the cellar and originally Joan Stribling intended using the fish and frog footman masks from *Alice in Wonderland*. Intead, the husk army was eventually reduced to two and effects landed the job of designing and sculpting the heads and hands for the two monsters. Paul McGuinness handled the reptile while I did the insect. Following the idea that the husks were earlier versions of Josiah as he struggled to become more human, Paul decided that the reptile would be the more advanced of the two, beginning to show human characteristics. He took life casts of Ian Hogg's eyes, nose and mouth. These features were then incorporated into the sculpt, though they are barely visible in the final show. My husk was far more straightforward, a mixture of various different types of

Designing Light

I tried to give Light and Control a period feel because, even though the Doctor and Ace were from the future, it was nice to try and keep everything within that Victorian frame. Control started as a bundle of rags, there were no shiny fabrics, and every time you saw her she was slightly different – she always had the basis of the next change underneath.

Light had this shell on his back which was meant to be where his wings were. Henry, who was lighting the programme, had trouble because there were so many different layers. There was a bright gold, a dark gold and an almost-black with gold in it. When he spread Light's cloak – if it was backlit – all this gold showed up, but they said that they would have needed about twenty minutes to light each shot, so all that went out of the window and they did everything in video effects afterwards.

For their final scenes I had Katherine and Sylvia's dresses copied in a canvas material and then sprayed with grey paint and coated with cement powder so that they could still move in them, but they looked like stone on camera.

Ken Trew
Costume designer

Above right: Mike's design sketches for the insectoid husk with the final design sketch below.

Below right: The husk mask under construction.

Below far right: The clay sculpture for Paul McGuinness' reptilian husk.

THE HUSKS
"Doctor Who - Ghostlight"

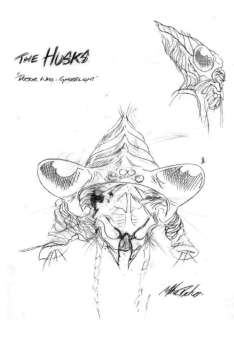
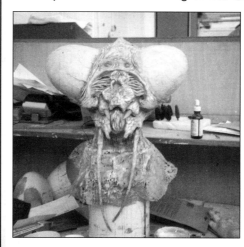
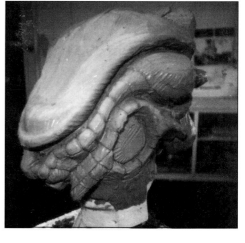

insect.

For the demise of the two monsters – their heads exploding – Malcolm had originally planned to make replicas in wax and blow them apart using pyrotechnics. When the fish and frog masks were still being considered, we had even got as far as making wax copies and conducting some tests. The new designs, however, were far too complex to get a wax version, certainly in the time that we had, and so we had to come up with an alternative. We resorted to making pre-broken versions of the heads, pulled from the original moulds, stuffed with shredded latex and foam. The heads were loosely stuck together with vaseline and fitted to dummy bodies with air mortar tubes fed through the middle of them, and the eventual explosion would be achieved using compressed air.

On the actual day of shooting, we were unlucky and one of the air mortars didn't fire, but we had no time to reshoot and so the eventual explosion was achieved in post production using one of the explosions shot for *Battlefield*.

We also needed the Doctor's Geiger counter, with the specification that it could be mistaken for a gun. Malcolm came up with a shape that was gun-like but that could still pass as a piece of scientific equipment. Having carved the shape in wood, I took a mould and produced a hollow fibreglass version that could take the electronics and batteries needed to make it flash and click, though the noise of a real Geiger counter was eventually overlaid.

One of the more gruesome scenes in the story is Light's clinical dissection of one of the maids. The actress due to be diced came into the effects department and had a cast taken of her arm. A rubber version was then produced with a suitably dressed stump. On the day of recording she lay on a table with her real arm tucked underneath her though, as usual, we were asked to hold back on the amount of blood and gore!

The snuff box was simply a real one provided by the props department. Several powerful bulbs were tucked inside and a mirror fitted into the lid. The attic set where the box glows to life was raised about a foot off the floor allowing assistant Guy Lunn to squeeze underneath and operate the lid by pushing a thin rod up through the floor. In the dim lighting conditions of the set the light from the box was quite dazzling.

Another lighting effect called for Mrs Pritchard's candle to flare up suddenly, affected by the stray energies from the snuff box. James Davis built the prop, basing the mechanism around a gas lighter with a variable flame, usually used for camping. The entire mechanism, including a fuel reservoir, was self contained within a fake candle and candlestick, and operated by Sylvia Syms. The candle was capable of suddenly flaring up to an eight inch flame, but it is only on screen for a few seconds, lost in the confusion of the scene.

The bulk of the effects involvement was in the second half of the story, when Light's energies are beginning to affect everything in the house. In true ghost story tradition, bolts had to fly across on their own and blinds snap shut, all activated via wires from the other side of the set. The bugs eaten by Control were easily effected by manufacturing several liquorish insects.

Control's escape from the house through a window required us to construct a number of balsa wood frames with resin glass panes. Stunts of this type always require a lot of preparation, particularly if one of the artistes is involved instead of a stuntman or woman, and Sharon Duce insisted on doing this stunt herself.

The balsa frame was carefully sawn through in several places so that when she hit it, it would break easily. The panes of fake glass were then glued into place and crash mats positioned on the floor. Although we had a couple of spare windows standing by in case of retakes, Sharon got it right first time. Ⓜ

Writing *Ghost Light*

I think that *Doctor Who* got a bit shallow in the pre-Sylvester years and I wanted to go back to the things that terrified me when I started watching it. I used to have nightmares, which I liked, and I wanted to get back to that. I wanted to have more interaction between the Doctor and his companions, as there was originally. I think that Ace is quite interesting, because one thing that I've always found with companions is that they arrive with lots of nice ideas and quickly get reduced to screaming wrecks that can't do anything. Ace continued to develop though.

Once I knew that I was going to get the all studio story I knew I had to set it indoors. I have this fear of trying to do streets and things in studio – it doesn't work. Another thing I grew up with were the BBC classic serials on Sunday afternoons, and I knew that the BBC could do that sort of thing well. I liked the idea of people being trapped in a small environment.

Light was originally going to have huge wings and be very ferocious. Then he went through a phase where we went in reverse and thought that we should have him dressed in black, like a tall, spindly accountant. Then Ken Trew picked up on the line where Ace says that he's like an angel and designed him in this Pre-Raphaelite style. Alan Wareing took it a lot further with the aura and made him a lot more alien.

Marc Platt
Writer

Top left: Sophie poses with the two husks in the spaceship set.

Above: The insect husk played by Jack Talbot camps it up.

Below: The two photographs of Sylvia Syms and Katherine Schlesinger taken for use in Gwendoline's locket.

Right: Slvia told me she hadn't enjoyed a job so much in years. So much for the prim and proper Mrs Pritchard!

Far right: John Hallam had a tricky job inventing a voice and character for the alien Light.

Below: Light dissects a maid to discover how she works.

Far right: Katherine Schlesinger (Gwendoline) tinkles the ivories.

Right: Sylvester takes a quick nap between takes.

Below right: Filming a scene where Light is confronted by…

Below far right: …The Doctor and Ace.

An embarrassing moment for Sophie

A question I'm often asked at *Doctor Who* conventions is my most embarrassing moment. I can now reveal that it was at the producer's run of *Ghost Light*!

It was a hot day and the rehearsal rooms were particularly stuffy, so I was wearing a pair of black cycling shorts and matching cropped top. We came to the fight scene where I held onto two upright marker posts, used in the rehearsal rooms to designate doorways, and Katherine gripped me firmly round my top, and tried to pull me backwards, as planned. As I resisted her grasp, I looked down and realised that she'd innocently exposed the whole of my upper body, my top coming away in her hands. I shrieked with embarrassment, and covered myself back up as quickly as I could, before realising that the cast were engrossed in Frank's crossword puzzle and hadn't noticed!

Sophie Aldred

Above: Sharon Duce as Control in her costume of multi-layered rags. During rehearsals, Sharon's questions about Control sent Alan Wareing beetling off to ring Marc Platt, cursing and muttering as he went. He'd return fifteen minutes later with a baffling explanation!

Right: Josiah (Ian Hogg) and Gwendoline discuss another 'trip to Java'.

Above: Inspector Mackenzie (Frank Windsor) on the look out for sandwiches.

Below left: The layout of the set was realistic, with a central hallway and grand staircase with the other rooms radiating from it.

Bottom far left: Sophie and 'the boys': (left to right) Andrew Cartmel, writer Marc Platt and Mike Tucker.

Bottom left: I loved all the stuffed animals and bizarre Victorian bric-a-brac.

Below: The Doctor confronts Light.

The steam-powered spaceship

The climax of the story saw the steam powered spaceship in the basement finally take off. Steam in the studio was obviously going to be a problem, while smoke didn't have the ferocity that would be needed. Malcolm eventually used a smoke that dissipated easily, blasted into the set with compressed air. The final scenes were thus very noisy and smoky and the studio doors had to be opened when the smoke built up too much.

At the script stage, it had been suggested that the ship take off through the house, demolishing it as it went, but the simpler and far less destructive version that we saw was chosen instead.
Mike Tucker

ARRIVED AT THE NORTH ACTON CANTEEN FOR A CUP OF BBC TEA. Surreptitiously, I surveyed the members of other productions. In one corner there sat a serious huddle – probably comedians and their scriptwriters concocting some hilarious joke. A gaggle of make up and costume people discussed wigs and frocks, and round one of the larger tables sat a group of distinguished actors, about to embark on some lavish period drama. At 10.00 am I drained my tea, then shuffled into the lift behind them.

I recognised them from posh dramas, and felt insignificant as I listened:

'Darling, I haven't seen you since…' 'How's dear Johnny?' and so on. One gentleman fixed me with a cold stare through horn rimmed bifocals hanging from a gold neck chain, reminding me of a geography mistress I'd had at school. The lift door opened at the second floor and I squeezed past, trying not to tread on any hallowed toes. I realised that they were getting out too, and I glanced at the blackboards outside each rehearsal room to see which lavish period drama series they were to create. I pushed open the door to room 201 and to my astonishment the actors trooped in behind me – they were the distinguished cast of *Ghost Light*!

Sylvester laughed and joked, and made sure we got off to a great start. What a cast! Sylvia Syms, Frank Windsor – not too sure initially about playing yet another copper, even though this was a Victorian sergeant with not a Z car in sight – Sharon Duce, ardent Fulham football club supporter, Katherine Schlesinger whose career I would have killed for… the list was endless. I was intrigued at putting a face to John Nettleton (of the piercing look in the lift) when I remembered *Blue Peter*'s Valerie Singleton introducing a historical picture item with 'John Nettleton tells the story'.

Sylvia Syms was daunting. Sylv leaned over and whispered 'Let's see who can make her crack a smile first!' Needless to say, he won.

The read-through led to expressions of polite bewilderment, and during the afternoon's blocking session, once all the clever script people had left, the questions flew thick and fast. Michael Cochrane had a wicked sense of humour, and like Sylvester, relished inventing business like waving away the 'damned tsetse flies' in the trophy room, and practising with the Masai warrior's spear, played in rehearsals by a broom handle.

Sylvia passed on a handy tip about stunts: in one scene, I was to run past her, and she had to stop me. Sylvia suggested pulling my hair wouldn't be as painful as it sounded. As I ran past, Sylvia put her hand lightly on my head, I felt her touch, and yanked my head back as though in pain. Simple, but effective!

What first struck me on entering the studio was the effectiveness of setting an entire story in a house interior, rather than create an alien planet setting. Nick Somerville and his team had done an amazing job with limited resources, hiring in fantastic props including stuffed animals, sumptuous furniture, and elaborate Victorian bric-a-brac. Marc Platt wandered round with a huge grin on his face, his dream come true at last.

I loved the humour of the first few of our scenes; the initiative test and teasing the 'professor' about his parking skills, and the trophy room scene with Michael. In retrospect, I'd have worked out something better for the moment where I try and grab the gun from Redvers. The props boys heaped a pile of mattresses over one side of the desk and I launched myself over a few times, once or twice to check for safety, and a

Recording in the spaceship

My final scenes the first day were in the Lower Observatory – the cliffhanger for part one and opening of part two. We saw the husks for the first time, and I was amazed at the detail which had gone into the head modelling by Mike Tucker and Paul McGuinness. Beneath the insect head was Jack Talbot, who should have an award for the most used non-speaking artist in *Doctor Who*; a soldier in *Remembrance*, panicking milkman in *Survival*, a Nazi in *Nemesis*, and now making his debut as an official monster complete with *Doctor Who* monster walk. The studio had really hotted up by now; Carl Forgione, who had spent many patient hours in the make up chair being neanderthalised by Helen Johnson, now had her constant attention as his putty nose melted in the heat like Inspector Clouseau's in a Pink Panther movie!

As usual, time was short. These scenes had been difficult to block in the rehearsal room with no idea of the set, so any plans went out of the window. Carl and I, plus the husks who hadn't been in rehearsals, improvised quickly. We tried to speed things up by filming without breaking the action into scenes. I was backing round the console when I tripped, fell over backwards and ended up a giggling heap on the floor.

'Carry on…Carry on!!' Gary Downie signalled, in capital letters, but I'd got the giggles and couldn't stop. No one else was finding it funny. Goodness knows which expletives Alan Wareing and John Nathan-Turner used to describe me up in the gallery as time ticked by and the money ran out.

Sophie Aldred

Above left: Katherine and I showing off our suits. Chrissy plaited my hair as we wanted a boylike look while Katherine's was loose and wild and girlie.

Below right: There's something odd about changing into a nightdress and, in front of loads of people, climbing into bed and pretending to be asleep.

Below far right: Katherine and I working out our fight scenes on the raised set. I can't stand fight scenes where actresses squeak and flail their arms around with no body contact and I found in Katherine a strong advocate of the aggressive approach – though as I rubbed my bruised shins I did wish she wasn't a method actress!

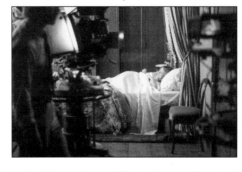

couple more for fun! We were concentrating so hard on whether I could dive over the desk without hurting myself and without ruining the radio mike, that my focus was the stunt rather than grabbing the gun, and so it looks silly. Another mistake is when I run for the door and I'm stopped by Mrs Pritchard and Josiah – something tucked into the back of my leggings, glinting in the light, looks suspiciously like a bit of radio mike transmitter.

My favourite scenes followed – Ace telling the Doctor about what scared her about Gabriel Chase in the future. There's a certain something I can feel when I know I'm doing a good job in the acting department, and I get totally concentrated. The camera was right up close, just a few inches from my face, and I had to think hard so I wouldn't be distracted – difficult with my nose pressed up against the camera lens!

The next morning, the scene where Josiah metamorphoses into a younger version of himself was shot in two halves for the sake of the make up change, and while Ian was having his old dead 'skin' peeled away and a fresh coat applied, I learned the art of sitting down in a corset which, if you've ever had the misfortune to wear one, you'll know is pretty tricky – there were so many awkward bones sticking into me, and none of them my own, that the most comfortable position was propped against a tall stool, half standing, half sitting.

We'd fallen behind schedule again, and scenes originally destined for the study were reset in Gwendoline's bedroom in the next studio. A wildlife expert handled the assortment of awakening bugs and beetles, which were carefully placed in a top drawer of a large cabinet in the study. Sylvester chatted with a beetle, finding them fascinating – I was inclined to keep well away!

After a day off, we ploughed on with rehearsing the rest of the story. Frank and Sylv had struck up a great rapport and became a comedy double act with Sylvester as the straight man for a change. Frank decided that Inspector Mackenzie would be eating

constantly, the minute he was woken, and he and Sylvester worked out moments for spraying assorted sandwich fillings over Sylv's clothes to best comic effect.

My last scene on *Ghost Light* was my last on *Doctor Who*, and was very fitting. The space ship has departed, Light has dispersed, and the Doctor follows Ace to the bottom step of the grand staircase.

'Any regrets?' asks the Doctor.

'Yes,' replies Ace, with a troubled look.

'Yes?'

'I wish I'd blown it up instead.' To which, instead of the scripted, 'That's my girl', at the last minute Sylvester decides to murmur, with more than a hint of mischief in his twinkling eyes, 'Wicked!' **S**

Left: Getting to grips with the part. Ian Hogg and Katherine by the dock door in the studio.

Ace in Victorian garb

The first costume Ken Trew and I tackled was the Victorian man's gear, complete with starched butterfly wing collar – I realised why men have stubble – my poor neck came in for a real chafing.

Then Ken produced a monstrous looking contraption – my corset! This alarming garment would go on first, followed by a multitude of petticoats. We decided that Ace would have worn her own boots and socks rather than tiny button boots which would have been agonising for my wide feet. There was a starched cotton night dress for my bedroom scene, then came the moment to try on the Victorian dress. Ken had originally designed it for *The Onedin Line*, where it had made only a split second appearance. The actress in *The Onedin Line* can't have had my tennis player's biceps nor my broad un-Victorian shoulders.

I braced myself for corset day. Sara, my dresser, who knew me pretty well by now, showed no mercy as she laced me up. Apparently, Victorian ladies used to grab hold of the bedpost while their maids pulled the cords tighter. I held onto my dressing room wardrobe and Sara put her knee into the small of my back to get a good grip. Now I know why young ladies are always fainting at the slightest excitement in Victorian novels – their blood can't circulate! The corset was marginally more comfortable than my arms. Although the sleeves had been let out, the shoulders were still too small, and I couldn't lift my arms without some pain. A decorative flower had been added half way down my biceps, which cut off the circulation to my lower arms. But I have to admit it did look great, even though my tan wasn't Victorian.

Sophie Aldred

Left top: The Doctor finds himself held at gunpoint.

Left bottom: Sylvester fell in love with a visual effects Geiger counter, which made real clicking noises when he pressed the trigger. Sylv spent the rest of the day pointing and shooting at everything that moved like a kid with a new toy.

Season 27

The end... for now

Sylvester was on the phone. 'Are you sitting down?' were his first words. I promptly did so, as Sylvester explained how his agent had heard on the grapevine that there was to be no more *Doctor Who* and our contracts (his for another season and mine for another eight episodes) were not going to be renewed.

I was gutted and bewildered. I knew our ratings hadn't been fantastic, but wasn't that partly because we were scheduled opposite *Coronation Street*, one of Britain's top rated soaps? In my opinion and, it seemed, that of fans and general public alike, the programme was getting back to the darker, more mysterious atmosphere of old and was more popular as a result. Surely the powers that be would wait to see how the next season fared before they pulled the plug.

I waited for the BBC to contact me with the news. It was a long sit – about six or seven weeks. Finally a letter arrived. John Nathan-Turner thanked me for my work on the series and regretted that there would be no more *Doctor Who*. At the time it seemed a brief dismissal – now I see that, as usual, the producer-come-scapegoat had to deal with the crap. Having spent the majority of his career with the programme, John had more to be upset about than a newcomer like me.

In this business nothing is set in stone. You should be prepared for bad as well as good; failed auditions, cancelled productions and... no more *Doctor Who*. Take a deep breath, shrug your shoulders, and set off for the next audition.

With *Doctor Who* it has been a bit different. Not in my wildest dreams did I imagine that six years later I would still have fan mail, be attending *Doctor Who* conventions and working on spin off projects...

Sophie Aldred

The nature of drama production, particularly of a series that takes up a fair portion of the year, means that while one season is being recorded another is in early planning stages. So it was with *Doctor Who*. While the upper echelons of the BBC had, no doubt, already decided that the series was to finish after *Survival* this fact didn't filter down until we were nearly at the end of recording and so Andrew Cartmel and several of the writers had begun work on ideas for a new series.

Of the writers that Andrew had worked with before, it was Marc Platt and Ben Aaronovitch who were asked back, submitting storylines for their second and third adventures, respectively. They were both to be involved in a series of stories that would write Ace out and introduce the new companion.

It was indicated that Marc would be the one who would actually write Ace out, and he was asked which monster he would like to write for. With both the Daleks and the Cybermen having already confronted the seventh Doctor, Marc chose the Ice Warriors, planning to use the characters for the first time since the Pertwee era of the show. Drawing on Ben's experiences with the Dalek story, Marc wanted to set the story in the 1960s.

The idea that had evolved for Ace's departure was that she was to be left on Gallifrey, the Doctor enrolling her in the Academy, determined to rock the Time Lords' cosy existence to its very foundations. The Time Lords agree and send a delegation of business suited agents with a mission for Ace to test her suitability – in the process having a problem solved that they don't want to involve themselves in. The Doctor is furious but can't interfere without spoiling her chances of being accepted.

The concept is radically different from how things evolved in the New Adventures series of books and, it seems, that this particular version of Ace's future will never be realised.

Ben's story was to have been the studio bound three-parter and would have preceded Marc's. The story was to have been set on a large space cruiser and would open with the camera panning around all the duty stations – navigation, engineering, communications and so on. The camera would have come to rest on the captain's chair, containing a uniformed Ace. She announces that she is going to her ready room and leaves the bridge. Her ready room contains the TARDIS and the Doctor, and as he looks up at her she says 'Professor, this isn't going to work!'

The villains for the story were to have been the Metatraxi, a warlike insectoid race that Ben had talked about doing for a long time. He had written them into the version of the *Doctor Who* stage play he and Andrew Cartmel had written (this never got taken up and *The Ultimate Adventure* was eventually written by Terrance Dicks). The only mention that is ever given to the Metatraxi is in Ben's introduction to Marvel Comics' graphic novel *Abslom Daak – Dalek Killer*.

The replacement character was to have been the daughter of a gangland boss who has gone straight. She finds the excitement of her father's former profession far more interesting than her life at the moment, and has learnt how to be a safe-cracker from one of his one-time accomplices. Her introduction was to have been set at a formal dinner in a country house. During the proceedings she was to slip away and find the house's safe. Pulling on a pair of white cotton gloves, she breaks the combination and opens the safe to find the Doctor inside, his first line to his new companion being 'What kept you?'

With the cancellation of the series, no more details were ever worked out, although Marc has indicated that he would have liked to introduce the father in his sixties story, his daughter merely a baby who the Doctor knows will eventually travel with him.

All these plans were eventually superseded with Ian Briggs' epilogue to the novel of *The Curse of Fenric*, leaving Ace in France with the ancestor of Captain Sorin. **M**

Above: Looking to the future?

Surviving Survival

THE CLOSING MOMENTS OF *SURVIVAL* SEE THE **D**OCTOR AND **A**CE WALKING off into the distance, the Doctor's final speech written by Andrew Cartmel to reflect the fact that this might be the last time the public would see the characters. The very last words of the series – 'Come on Ace, we've got work to do!'.

Indeed, the work of the seventh Doctor and Ace has yet to be completed. Refusing to roll over and die, the series has gone from strength to strength, probably with a higher public profile now than when it ended in 1989.

These new adventures of the Doctor have been handled both by Marvel UK's *Doctor Who Magazine* and by the ever increasing range of Virgin books – both keeping the successful partnership of the seventh Doctor and Ace as their lead characters. Even at the BBC it became obvious that even if the drama department wasn't prepared to revive the series, there were other departments all too willing to make use of the characters.

The year following *Survival* I ended up working with both Sophie and Sylvester again, on a children's programme called *Search Out Space*, a special programme in the popular *Search Out Science* series.

The idea was to present basic scientific facts about space to a young audience, in the form of an intergalactic quiz show, and the production had been granted permission to use the Doctor and Ace as their key presenters. Visual effects designer Mat Irvine was allocated to the show and he, in turn, asked for me as his assistant.

At early planning meetings it was mentioned that a non-human contestant would be needed, and the production were quite keen on using a Dalek. Having seen the dialogue that this non-human contestant would have to speak, I voiced concern that they wouldn't get permission to use a Dalek. Terry Nation has always maintained that his creations should always be shown as menacing, and competing in a quiz show is not the most menacing of pastimes!

Mat suggested that K-9 would be a better choice, which delighted the production, who were not aware that he still existed. Now, the last time that K-9 had been used was in *K-9 and Company*, almost ten years earlier. Since then the prop had been sent to America, as part of a mobile *Doctor Who* exhibition, and the original radio control mechanism stripped out of him in order to fit a more robust exhibition mechanism, running off mains. At the end of this American tour all the props had been returned to BBC Enterprises and put into storage.

Mat and I not only managed to track down the original body shell, but also most of the original mechanics, as the

Below right top: K-9 in a bad way. The robotic dog undergoes an extensive refurbishment.

Below right bottom: Mike works on the rebuilt K-9.

An East End reunion

John Nathan-Turner called me out of the blue one day to ask whether I'd be interested and available to take part in a 'little bit of *Doctor Who* nonsense' for the annual BBC *Children in Need* fundraising event. I said yes at once and eagerly awaited the script. When it came through, I found to my delight that I was written into both of the short episodes and I would be working with Colin Baker and Sylvester. The schedule meant that I would film at Elstree on the *EastEnders* lot before a Wednesday matinee of *Lust* at the Theatre Royal Haymarket, and then for a whole day in Greenwich.

I'd never visited the hallowed ground of Albert Square; the Elstree car park was the nearest I'd ever got to the inner sanctum of soap folklore. I arrived early on the Wednesday morning to find the make-up room a hive of activity – or should that read complete pandemonium! 'Pauline' and 'Kathy' were enjoying a healthy application of character make-up for a change, and I mumbled a shy 'hello' in their direction. Having been made-up and dressed I tried to find my way to Albert Square. All roads led to the ladies loo, and it was there I bumped into Carole Ann Ford, who was also searching for the exit!

We rounded a corner and there was Albert Square – smaller and tattier in real life – but then people have said the same about me! John Nathan-Turner introduced me to the director, Stuart McDonald. Both wore ridiculous plastic spectacles which looked like they'd come straight from Toys R Us, though Stuart explained that by wearing them, he could immediately check out the effectiveness of the 3D image on the monitor. Cameras and actors had to be moving in the correct direction, and I could see the crew laying a camera track for my first section with Colin Baker.

Round the square in various states of undress stood assorted *Doctor Who* monsters, some played by fans of the ▶

American refit had been done by an ex-BBC effects designer, Tony Oxley. Tony also had the original moulds for the dog so that Mat and I were able to make a better copy of the shell. With most of the original parts back in the workshop, Mat and I began to rebuild.

The main thing that we had to do was install slightly more sophisticated radio control gear, as a lot of the original parts were no longer available. The chassis we kept from the original prop, the same with the ear mechanism and gun. We had originally planned to give him a new body colour, to distinguish him from the other versions of K–9 that had been seen in the series. Since Dapol had released their K-9 in a green finish, we thought that we might follow their lead, and even sprayed the dog up, to see what it would look like. In the end it was decided to stick with the colour scheme established in *K-9 and Company* – a metallic blue.

The K-9 scenes were recorded at North Acton, and at the Lloyds building in the City, where he prompted several passers-by to ask whether we were recording a new series of *Doctor Who*, with K-9 as the companion. In time honoured K-9 tradition, he also broke down during shooting. I had often heard that he was a pig to work with and here, and on subsequent dealings with the infamous beast, he was no exception!

For Sylvester's scenes, the director had asked that he present the show standing on a small anti-gravity disk, and the construction of the disk fell to me. To give the impression of it floating, several sponge pads were fitted to the underside of the disk so that it would wobble. Sylvester, of course, used the wobble to its full advantage. He was originally asked to wear a space helmet to present the show, but it not only looked ridiculous, but also hampered his performance, and was quickly dropped.

Dave Chapman was, once again, called upon to provide several video effects sequences, and Mat and I spent several days in the video effects workshop, working on the TARDIS scenes. The workshop itself doubled for the interior of the TARDIS at one point, since the production couldn't afford to have the console room rebuilt! Instead, a couple of flats with roundels on were brought in and positioned behind the control and edit desk and K-9's scenes were recorded there.

Most of the TARDIS scenes were achieved using the six inch miniature that I had built for *The Mysterious Planet*, although one sequence where K-9 enters the ship required the doors to open, so the three foot miniature built for *Logopolis* was pulled out of storage and suitably modified.

I continued to bump into Sophie and Sylvester over the years, particularly Sophie with

her regular appearances on various children's television programmes, but it was during the programme's thirtieth anniversary year that I was to work with them as the Doctor and Ace again.

I received a call from John Nathan-Turner asking if I would meet him for lunch to discuss a show that I might be

interested in working on. The show was, of course, *Dimensions in Time*, the infamous 3D extravaganza that formed part of the BBC's annual *Children in Need* telethon, and was the only new *Doctor Who* to be produced in the anniversary year.

The idea was to mix the fictional worlds of *Doctor Who* and *EastEnders* in two short, fast-paced episodes to be shown on consecutive nights. Not

Above top: An unpainted K-9 awaits completion.

Above: The metallic pooch ready for action.

show. They alternated between excitement at being involved and nervousness in case they made a wrong move. Andrew Beech, head of the DWAS, stood resplendent in his very own Time Lord costume, having been responsible for lending many original props and costumes from his collection. Finally, there were the stars of the show – Colin Baker, Peter Davison and the granddoctor of them all, Jon Pertwee.

It was fun to be playing assistant to Colin's Doctor, although as usual we were recording back to front and had no idea what the previous action was going to be. I racked my brains remembering how I'd played Ace, and hoped that it wouldn't be too different after a four year break.

The other day's filming was much nearer home, in Greenwich, south east London. It was a beautifully misty morning down by the river though a bit nippy too, and I took an extra jumper to hide under my Ace jacket. Sylvester took my arm and we wandered through the mist towards the catering wagon under the looming prow of the ancient dry docked tea clipper, the *Cutty Sark*. As the mist cleared and the masts of the *Cutty Sark* became visible, I investigated the camera track which the crew were laying down by the TARDIS. Stuart showed us our position and where the camera would be, and Sylv and I went through our lines a few times.

Squashed together in the TARDIS, Sylv and I were giggling and missed our first cue. We then pulled ourselves together, and picked our way over the strategically placed coils of rope and debris. Timing was crucial. We had to arrive at a carefully placed newspaper at the same time as the camera. On the first rehearsal we ran out of lines before we got to the mark, and the second time we walked too fast and the camera couldn't keep up. On the next take I stumbled over the rope, but carried on anyway, even though I thought it must look terrible. Stuart was happy, and my 'big mistake' turned out to be something which looked fine on screen.

Hours later the cameraman reset for our final scene, and I met K-9. Mat Irvine and Mike Tucker were despairing; true to form, their robotic pal had been functioning without a hitch until he was needed in shot – now he was playing up. My first and last scene with this mechanical marvel, and he's pulled through shot on a piece of string!

Sylvester muttered his fiendish lines over and over while we worked out the action for the scene. It was his bright idea to pile my arms high with heavy metal objects. We did several takes; first I dropped the whole pile, then something rubbed against my radio mike, and finally I walked into the TARDIS, then couldn't shut the door!

Weeks later, I sat in a room, surrounded by hundreds of American Whovians. As the applause rang round the room I felt a twinge of disappointment that, due to time, Sylvester's last piece of improvisation as the Doctor had failed to make it to the screen.

As Ace and the Doctor turn to survey the explosion, Ace murmurs a faint 'Excellent!' The Doctor looks at her approvingly; 'Wicked!' he concludes.

Sophie Aldred

Above: Sylvester stands on the floating pad in front of a CSO blue screen.

Right: Sophie, back in Ace's jacket after four years, for Dimensions in Time.

A matter of dimensions

I got no pleasure from the cancellation of *The Dark Dimension*, however I felt that the whole idea had been stolen from me – not the script, but the idea of a special to be made by BBC Enterprises – and I told them so. A special had been budgeted twice and I was then asked to be script consultant on *The Dark Dimension*, which I declined because I felt that it was an insult, but I hate to see any project go down.

Then I was asked to do *Dimensions in Time*. Nick Handle is an old friend of mine and he said that he was doing *Children in Need* and was aware that *Doctor Who* was thirty years old and what started as a one-off five minute insert developed into a two-parter with part two in *Noel's House Party*.

What made it for me was getting all five living Doctors in costume, including Tom, and all those companions. I didn't think that we'd get Tom into the costume. When he arrived in the studio there were a few things that he wanted to adjust in the script, so we took him off to the executive office and I asked Michael Purcell, who was Ken Trew's dresser, to bring up the costume. Tom and I chatted and went through the script. Then Michael turned up. Tom didn't know that the costume still existed, but I told him that it had been pulled out of mothballs especially and asked if he wanted to try it on. He said no, he would wait until it was time to go down to the set, and I still didn't think that he would wear it. When he eventually came down he was in the whole attire.

John Nathan-Turner
Producer

content with merely having Sophie and Sylvester reprise their roles, John managed to persuade all the surviving Doctors, as well as a huge list of companions, to appear; in the process he finally arranged that elusive meeting between the sixth Doctor and the Brigadier.

John also managed to re-form a large number of the crew on the other side of the camera. As well as myself on effects, Gary Downie would be production manager, Ken Trew would handle costumes, Keff McCullough for the incidental music, Dave Chapman on video effects and, coming back out of retirement, Dick Mills on special sound. The director for the story was Stuart McDonald, who I knew from his work on *Bodymatters*, several years earlier.

Having discussed various ideas for portraying the first and second Doctors with John and Stuart, we eventually opted to have two portrait heads sculpted by Sue Moore and Stephen Mansfield. They very kindly gave their work for free, simply asking that the wigs be provided by the BBC make up department.

The show also required the first overhaul of the TARDIS console for several years. I got a BBC engineer to give the wiring a good look over. Even though the six control panels were in good condition, this wasn't much help since the script called for the console to be the Rani's, with a black and red colour scheme, tying in with the colour scheme designed for her costume.

I had all the upper parts of the console reproduced in black fibreglass from the original moulds, adding buttons and switches stripped from a number of junk computer keyboards that were lying around the department. The rest of the console was redressed with black fablon (I would say sticky-backed plastic, but that smacks too much of *Blue Peter*!).

The console room scenes were all recorded at Fountain Television Studios in New Malden. Since this was the only studio day that we had, it was also used to record Tom Baker's SOS message that comes at the beginning of the show. Although originally conceived as a large close up of Tom's face, John had the burgundy costume from Tom's final season brought to the studio. On the day he managed to persuade the actor to wear not only the coat, but the hat and scarf as well.

Tom came up with the idea of speaking into a microphone instead of looking directly at camera, and the futuristic prop was quickly cobbled together out of whatever we had lying around the studio! As it turned out, it looked awful on screen and we eventually replaced it in the post production session.

The rest of the story was recorded at the Albert Square backlot at Elstree and around Greenwich. Although I had a number of props to look after (such as a futuristic parking meter for the futuristic scenes!), the bulk of my work was taken up with the flashes that accompanied the change of Doctor and companion. The constantly moving

Above: Louise Jameson (Leela) finds herself partnering Sylvester in Greenwich for a segment of Dimensions in Time.

camera shots that were required for the 3D to work properly meant that some nimble footwork was needed to get to the right place at the right time.

Once the monsters arrived on the scene, I was responsible for ensuring that they all had a weapon of some sort. Having been given a list of what monsters would be present, I was able to do some rooting about at the effects department and most of the creatures ended up with the correct prop – not an easy task given the age of the stories that some of them originated in.

One extra effect that evolved on the day was the explosion at the feet of Peter Davison and his companions. Having seen a run-through of the action, I suggested that we add a bang, since I wasn't needed to do anything else in that scene. John and Stuart agreed and the charge was swiftly set in place. On action I set off the effect and the bolt from the Cyberman's gun was added later by Dave.

The only potential disaster on the show was when the Rani's gun is shot from her hand by Mike Yates. The prop was made of perspex, and quite brittle so I volunteered to catch it as Kate O'Mara dropped it. On the first take I missed, and there was a disturbing smashing sound. Fortunately, developments in super glues meant that the prop was back on set for a retake in seconds, but the looks on several faces around the lot were worth seeing.

The final day of shooting was at Greenwich, starting with the scenes in and around the *Cutty Sark*. The crew assembled around the breakfast truck and watched as the TARDIS, Bessie and a truck load of props were unloaded. Given that most of the *Cutty Sark* sequence is meant to be set in the 1970s, Stuart and John were very relieved to find that an early morning mist had completely obscured Canary Wharf and they had no problems with shots looking over the Thames.

The opening shot of the day was Sophie and Sylvester emerging from the TARDIS and, once again, I was crammed inside with them to operate the light – it was as if no time had passed at all. With the TARDIS scene out of the way, I had nothing to do until the flashes for the scene with Jon Pertwee and Deborah Watling. By this point, Mat Irvine had arrived, (this time acting as my assistant!) with K-9.

Mat kept passers-by and photographers entertained by running the dog around for a while, and Jon Pertwee even posed with him for several publicity shots. Throughout all this, the prop behaved perfectly – I should have known at this point that he wasn't going to play ball later!

With the material around the *Cutty Sark* recorded, the crew set off for the Royal Naval College to record the scenes with the helicopter while Mat and I began to set up at the Queens House for the final scenes of the story. I made up a number of charges to be dressed onto the Rani's TARDIS prop for its climactic destruction while Mat did some fine tuning on K-9. I also began to set up the various pieces of scientific junk that the Doctor has supposedly stripped from the TARDIS.

By the time the rest of the crew arrived it was lunchtime, and we spent the next hour lounging in the park at Greenwich in front of the Royal Observatory, old cast members like Richard Franklin and Louise Jameson mingling with the newest members of the TARDIS crew, the *Doctor Who* family having expanded somewhat since their day.

With lunch over, we began recording the show's final

Costumes for Dimensions

Dimensions in Time was done very quickly – more quickly than normal! At one point there was a line about keeping heads covered because of radiation and it just happened that there were dozens of Russian hats in stock, so I grabbed them. That's why everyone in Albert Square is in hats and ponchos.

I'd never worked with Tom Baker before, and because of all the big auctions there was nothing of his left in stock. It was only because Lorne Martin of the *Doctor Who* Exhibitions had the stuff in a lock-up that we were able to do it. I spent two days there, getting the stuff for the Doctors.

Kate O'Mara's costume was the only thing made especially for the show. She just said, 'Oh, you know my size, darling, just make it'.

Ken Trew
Costume designer

Below far left: Sophie and Sylvester record their scenes for Dimensions in Time *with K-9, who, true to form, had to be pulled along on a piece of fishing line after stripping its gears.*

Below: Gary Downie checks his running order in the Rani's TARDIS set.

Below bottom: the models used in Dimensions in Time*: the Rani's TARDIS, the space station and the futuristic tube train seen in Albert Square.*

Above: Jon Pertwee poses for pictures with K-9.

Below: Stephen Mansfield adjusts the first Doctor head on the turntable.

Bottom: The two heads of the first and second Doctors, created by Stephen Mansfield and Sue Moore.

Photo: Sue Moore

moments and, as if to emphasise that shooting on *Doctor Who* never changes, we began to run out of time. Sylvester was appearing on stage in *The Invisible Man* and had to leave the location by 5.30pm at the latest. Similarly, Sophie had to be in her West End dressing room for that evening's performance of *Lust*. The fact that the scene between him and Louise Jameson as Leela was so complex, both in terms of lines and camera moves, meant that it took the bulk of the afternoon to set up and shoot, and against this frantic scenario K-9 decided to strip his gears.

Mat and I turned him over but realised that, although he could be repaired, it was going to take time. Fortunately, no effects toolbox is without several reels of fishing line and, choosing a heavy duty one, I hauled the dog unceremoniously through shot while Mat dealt with the steering by remote control.

With the finale over, Sylvester was whisked away by taxi and I began setting the pyros. Unfortunately, we had exceeded our time limit at the location and they pulled the plugs on our power! A few minutes' frantic activity by the outside broadcast crew provided us with a battery powered camera and we completed the shot using that, with all the charges kept quite small so we didn't disturb the tranquillity of Greenwich.

With the show complete, several of the crew retired to a nearby pub for a well earned pint. Although short, the shoot had brought back a lot of memories of the 'good old days' and it seemed a great shame that we weren't allowed to do something a bit more spectacular.

A few days later John, Stuart and I descended on the video effects workshop to deal with the post production effects that the story required. All the model work was to be shot on video so that a constantly moving background could be inlaid, again for the 3D effect. Although the police box miniature was one of the existing ones, all the other models were specially made for the story, albeit using several old models that were still in existence. The Rani's TARDIS was needed in two forms – the monolith and the space station – and there was also the tube train, the asteroids and the two portrait heads of Hartnell and Troughton being brought straight to the workshop by Sue and Stephen.

Dave and I began with the space shots, shooting the asteroids in several variations that could be overlaid to give the impression that there were many more. The TARDISes were then both set up on a turntable and those shots dealt with, including one where the Doctor's TARDIS dematerialised seconds before it would have been smashed by a huge meteor, a shot that never made it to the final cut of the show. With the space shots completed, we were eager to start work on the head shots. On cue, Sue and Stephen arrived.

The two heads, suitably dressed with wigs from the make up department, were also shot on the turntable. Once Dave had enough tape of the spinning heads he could then begin putting them into their appropriate scenes. While the effect is only on the screen for a few seconds, it took most of the rest of the day to achieve the half dozen scenes that required the heads, since they had to pass both in front of and behind the Rani and Cyrian.

The last shot involving miniatures was the tube train sequence. Because of the length of shot that Stuart wanted, we ended up having to extend the length of the train electronically, as the model only had three sections. Since all the other shots were purely electronic, my involvement with the show was over.

As I was packing up, an old friend of mine, Kevin Davies, popped into the effects workshop and asked if I would phone him about a show he was doing. I duly did so, only to discover that he was the director on the *Doctor Who* documentary, *30 Years in the TARDIS*, and had some work for me. It seemed as though my involvement with the series was not yet over!

I met up with Kevin in an office at Television Centre and he explained that the format of the programme was to be a mixture of interviews and drama sequences, the drama recreating classic moments from the series' history. Kevin had some spectacular ideas but, with only a documentary budget, even less money than we normally had. We went through a lot of his ideas and came up with the ones that we thought would be feasible. In the end, I was involved in several of the locations and the studio days, mainly with the Auton and Cybermat sequences, though I helped out with a few other shots as well.

Kevin wanted me to recreate the Auton hands for a number of linking sequences, including one where they burst from a shop window. The hands had to be able to fire in a manner similar to the originals, and we had wanted to show the explosive effects on the unfortunate victims, but this fell foul of the usual cost limitations. The actual pyrotechnic devices used for the Auton guns are no longer made however, and I had to come up with a suitable alternative. At the time I had no decent reference of what the hands looked liked but careful study of the two television stories meant that I was able to have a good stab at them. I was also lucky in that we had a mannequin hand at the effects department that was in exactly the right pose. Typically, as soon as I had finished making the guns loads of really good colour reference photos turned up! The final props (there were two) had a firing stud on the back end and the batteries were hidden in the pockets of the Auton's coats.

The other main constructions that I had to deal with were the Cybermats. Unlike the Auton hands, that had to be exact copies of the originals, Kevin was keen that the Cybermats were updated so that they still had similarities with the ones seen in the Troughton era, but that echoed the features of the John Nathan-Turner era Cybermen. I showed Kevin the design that I had done for *Silver Nemesis* and, using that as a starting point, we came up with a design that we were both happy with.

Two Cybermats were eventually built. One had to be radio controlled, but rather than custom building a chassis, I found a good radio control racing car toy and adapted that to fit inside the prop. The shells of the Cybermats were fibreglass but with aluminium powder in the resin to give them a solid, metallic feel. I had originally wanted them to be entirely metallic, but Kevin specified gloss black eyes and a bright red 'sting' on the tail.

The second Cybermat was rigged onto a stand and could curl its tail underneath itself. Kevin had always thought that, as weapons, they were not very menacing, so he planned to show one hovering into the air so that the sting was at eye level.

Both Autons and Cybermats were shot in and around the steps opposite St Pauls cathedral that had been used for the classic scenes in *The Invasion*. The Cybermat was seen emerging from a drain cover and scuttling towards Colin Baker and Nicola Bryant, the hovering one being added in post production. For the Autons, Kevin had permission to use an empty shop that was dressed up as a seventies clothes boutique called 'Magister and Splink', and tight camera angles and fast editing made it look as though the 'male' Auton (in reality the then *Doctor Who Magazine* editor, Gary Russell) had actually smashed the window.

The main problem for these shots was that I would be using pyrotechnics in the middle of London. At the time, we were in the midst of a fairly intensive IRA bombing campaign and the police were understandably nervous about anything involving explosives, no matter how small. In the end, they gave us a one hour window in which to shoot the sequence, and a police woman came along to keep an eye on the proceedings. We ended up doing several different shots of our two Autons firing that were edited in throughout

Above: The Dimensions in Time *production team.*

Below: Constructing the new cybermats for More than Thirty Years in the TARDIS. *The Auton hand can be seen under construction to the right of the picture.*

Bottom: The finished cybermat.

Above: On location with the TARDIS on the wharf by Tower Bridge, originally used for filming during Resurrection of the Daleks.

Photo: Marcus Hearne

Above: The Auton shop dummies outside the ficticious store Magister and Splink.

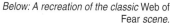

Below: A recreation of the classic Web of Fear *scene.*

the documentary.

The two other London landmarks that we filmed at were Tower Bridge and Westminster Bridge. The Tower Bridge shoot – on the wharf where *Resurrection of the Daleks* was shot – was relatively easy, since it was bitterly cold and there were very few people about. My only involvement was covering author Adrian Rigelsford with cobwebs for his rôle as the news vendor in the recreation of the scene from *The Web of Fear*, though trying to use spray-on cobwebs in a high wind is not the easiest of tasks. The rest of the day was taken up with interviews – notably with Mat Irvine – and with the complex motion control shot of the TARDIS, starting outside and ending up in the control room, all in a single, moving shot.

To achieve the shot, Kevin had called on the services of cameraman Peter Tyler, who set up his portable motion control rig on the pavement for the first part of the shot, with the latter half being shot at Television Centre some weeks later. I've known Pete for years as he and his crew have handled the model photography for every season of *Red Dwarf*, though usually in the relative warmth of the effects model stage at North Acton and not the windswept south bank!

Whereas the Tower Bridge shoot had been relatively undisturbed, the Westminster Bridge shoot couldn't have been more different. I was there at the request of the BBC safety office to ensure that the Daleks – none of which were BBC props – were safe for the actors to use. As is usual with fan-built props, they were all in much better condition than their BBC counterparts, though the fact that they were all built by different people meant that we had a vast variety of colours and heights. We started early one Sunday morning hoping to miss the tourists, but several Daleks being wheeled across a pelican crossing is bound to attract some attention and our solitude didn't last for long. Matters were made worse by the press insisting on a shot of the Daleks ranged over the entire width of the bridge, which didn't go down too well with the motorists.

Kevin had originally wanted to have a shot of one of the Daleks hovering up the stairs in pursuit of Carole Ann Ford, but rather than just have a glow from the Dalek's base he wanted a blast of vapour. To achieve this we locked off the camera and I ran up the steps firing a CO_2 fire extinguisher. We planned to remove me electronically and add the Dalek in post production but Terry Nation decided that he wasn't going to give permission for hovering Daleks and so Kevin had to change his shot to the one of the hoverbout that made it to the final version of the show.

Several other planned effects sequences never made it either. During Verity Lambert's speech she makes a comment about the Doctor being an anti-establishment figure and at that point, in the background, a Dalek saucer was to have fired on the Houses of Parliament. I even got as far as building the model of the saucer, basing it on the *TV Century 21* comic strip of the sixties, but the money for post production ran out before that shot was completed.

Of the various cliff-hangers that could have ended the show my favourite was one in which Elisabeth Sladen was to have morphed into a Zygon, but the cost of recreating the costume meant that this never got any further than a discussion with Kevin in a pub. Similarly Sophie was to have reverted to a Cheetah person at the end of her sequence with Sylvester, but here we simply ran out of time. The interviews were shot at Quasar in Slough with various monsters from the McCoy era plaguing Sophie and Sylvester as they wandered about in the gloom. Although most of the creatures were played by Gary Russell, I did manage to play the Husk and, although it didn't make it into the documentary itself, it did get seen in one of the five minute 'shorts' that preceded each repeated episode of *Planet of the Daleks*, being shown to commemorate the anniversary.

The anniversary year also played host to the saga of the aborted special *The Dark Dimension*. Rumours had been floating around for a long time that some form of special story was being planned. Things got a little more definite when Tony Harding was allocated as effects designer and the first draft of the script – at this point referred to as *The Environment Roadshow* – turned up.

Even with this early version of the story it was obvious that there was going to be a lot of effects involvement, though it seemed as though the creatures would be handled by an outside company. Things then got more definite when a second draft of the script,

Working with my fellow Doctors

I was very disappointed that we hadn't been able to do a thirtieth anniversary *Doctor Who*. I was very sad about that because I'd always wanted to do a complete Doctors one, because the others had done it – *The Five Doctors, The Three Doctors, The Two Doctors*, etc. So I was really looking forward to the thirtieth anniversary but for various reasons it never happened. So when *The AirZone Solution* came up I thought 'great!' because I'd be able to work with Jon Pertwee and Colin Baker, and Peter – who I didn't know, so I was very keen to work with him. I also thought it was a good story. I quite liked the atmosphere, it was quite like a *Twilight Zone*, and it was nice that we could play non-Doctor roles.

I thought *Dimensions in Time* was rather pleasing just to see everyone appear, but I got totally confused all through it. I'm sure that anyone who didn't follow *Doctor Who* very much would have been utterly confused by the end of it, but the actual making of it was great fun. I'd just opened in a play and so was completely exhausted, but it was great filming it. There was a lovely buzz on the streets, everyone was excited that *Doctor Who* was being made again. They saw the TARDIS, and all the bits and bobs and Bessie, and when we went to film at the Greenwich Naval College there were Admirals coming out asking for autographs. They were very excited, and we had helicopters flying about the place – a great buzz. It felt great to be doing it again, but I don't think that it translated too well to the screen. I've only watched it once, very late at night, having been with John Nathan-Turner in the pub for a long time.

I enjoyed the 3D work as well. The funny thing about it was that everything had to be kept moving – technically that's what had to happen. There had to be movement all the time whether it was from the performers or the camera. When I was working with Louise Jameson – that was a real delight. I mean, of all the companions, apart from Sophie and Bonnie, the one that I really wanted to work with was Louise. We did a scene with the two of us talking the camera going round and round us. The camera was, of course, attached to loads of wires and we were trying to remember our lines and keep our eyes on the camera! It was a really mind-bending experience, but pleasantly mind-bending because as the camera went round, it completely tied us up! It was a really good day for me.

Sylvester McCoy
Actor, the seventh Doctor

now entitled *Doctor Who – The Dark Dimension* arrived at the department and Tony was asked to attend a pre-production meeting. Following this meeting, which had included director Graeme Harper and video effects designer Dave Chapman, Tony allocated several assistants to the show including Alan Marshall and myself, and we began doing preliminary design work, Alan doing some sketches of a new special weapons Dalek while I did some research into the old wood panelled version of the TARDIS console, as this was the required design for the script. Before we had got any further, however, the show was pulled.

To this day the exact facts surrounding the rise and fall of the production seem to be shrouded in mystery. It was a great shame that nothing ever got filmed since some of the design work indicated that it would have been a very slick looking production indeed, and rumours still abound that it will resurface in some form or other; time will tell. Until then, *Dimensions in Time* and *30 Years in the TARDIS* remain as the last two *Doctor Who* related programmes made by the BBC, and with the programme's future seemingly based firmly in the United States, they are the last two *Doctor Who* projects that I shall work on as an effects designer. Ⓜ

Above left: Alan Marshall's design for a new special weapons Dalek for the aborted special The Dark Dimension.

Books and Comics

AS WELL AS BEING THE LONGEST RUNNING SCIENCE FICTION SERIES IN THE world, *Doctor Who* also has the honour of being the longest running comic strip based on a television series. From its beginnings in the pages of *TV Comic*, through magazines like *Countdown* and *TV Action*, the strip has run alongside the television series, finally finding a permanent home in the pages of *Doctor Who Weekly*, *Doctor Who Monthly*, and now *Doctor Who Magazine*.

Since the early days, the strip has switched between having the Doctor accompanied by companions of its own making and characters from the television series. Among the more infamous of the 'invented' companions have been the first Doctor's grandchildren, John and Gillian, and Frobisher, the shape changing penguin that accompanied the sixth Doctor during his comic strip stories. Television companions have been included sporadically with Jamie, Liz Shaw, the Brigadier, Sarah Jane Smith, Leela, and Peri all having brief lives in the comic book medium. But just as it was considered inconceivable to have the fourth Doctor's comic strip without K-9 accompanying him at some point, so the seventh Doctor would be equally naked without Ace.

In an effort to forge closer ties with the television series, then editor of *Doctor Who Magazine,* John Freeman decided to introduce Ace as the regular companion in the comic strip. Not only that, but he also decided to have the story written by the script editor who had overseen her creation, Andrew Cartmel.

Smoothing over the continuity between the television series and the comic strip, John commissioned two text stories, one by Andy Lane and the other by Paul Cornell, to act as prologues to Ace's debut in the strip. *Fellow Travellers* started in issue 164 with art by Arthur Ranson. The strip also introduced the concept of the Doctor having a house in the country, a feature subsequently used by several of the New Adventures writers.

Links between the television series, comic strip and books became very strong over the next few years with writers Ben Aaronovitch and Marc Platt both submitting ideas for books and strip stories. Virgin Books editor Peter Darvill-Evans even made use of the comic strip character Abslom Daak Dalek Killer in his novel *Deceit*.

Deceit also introduced the new look Ace. Right from their inception, the New Adventures had given Ace a major rôle, taking the character much further than had ever been done within the confines of the television series. The conflict between Doctor and companion had been taken to new heights culminating in Ace's departure from the series with Paul Cornell's *Love and War*. Peter Darvill-Evans reintroduced her to the Doctor four books later, with three years having passed for her. This new Ace was a much harder character, a battle-scarred mercenary who had spent years fighting the Daleks.

Here again Virgin and Marvel forged close ties, with artist Rodney Ramos providing a set of visuals that were used as the definitive look for the character. This new version of Ace also made it into the comic strip and great efforts were made to keep good continuity links between both sets of stories.

As with any good character, however, there is always a limit to what can be achieved without retreading old ground, and it was eventually decided to have Ace written out of the New Adventures, leaving her in 19th century France, a scenario that had been set up by Ian Briggs in his novelisation of *The Curse of Fenric*. Kate Orman was given the task of writing Ace out in her novel *Set Piece,* though in such a way that there is the option of

Right: The worlds of Doctor Who *and comics collide! A piece of artwork to publicise* The Two Doctors – *a meeting between the Doctor and Doctor Strange due to have been written by Andrew Cartmel.*

Ace joins the comic strip

Introducing Ace into the comic strip was a deliberate move to increase continuity between the strip and the television series. The strip was always an oddity and seen as something that people wouldn't necessarily read. The fans were fans of the television series, so by making the strip more like the series I thought it might get a better reception - and it worked. We introduced Ace via a text story. *The Happiness Patrol* had introduced the idea that she wanted to go off and see some dinosaurs, so we had a story that revolved around that, illustrated by Cam Smith. She rejoined the Doctor in *Fellow Travellers*, written by Andrew Cartmel. Again, it was a conscious decision on my part to involve people who had been involved with the television series and Andrew had offered to write a comic strip.

In many ways, without being derogatory, the seventh Doctor was a very comic strip character. Andrew was very influenced by things that you could do in comics – fast action and good characterisation rather than sitting about in the TARDIS.

The story that Andrew wrote had lots of undercurrents about Ace not being very confident and being messed around by the Doctor, who knows what is going on and manipulates her from one end of the story to the other. He sends her off simply to get her out of the way whilst the real things begin to happen. That was the first time that we saw the Doctor's big old house in the country which also appears in the novels but was created for Marvel. Andrew always liked the idea of the Doctor owning a big house in the country.

John Freeman
Editor, Marvel UK's
***Doctor Who* comic strip**
1990-93

bringing her back as a guest character.

I was even lucky enough to be able to write for the character myself. Marvel Comics commissioned Robert Perry and me to write a short story for one of their specials that we were able to write Ace into. We were subsequently asked to write a story for the *Decalog 2* collection and, of course, we chose to write for the seventh Doctor and Ace.

Even though Ace is no longer an on-going character in any medium it seems unlikely that she will vanish for ever, but for now, with nine television stories, 32 novels and countless comic strips behind her, it seems that she has finally got a well earned rest! Ⓜ

Above: Four of the New Adventures books which featured Ace.

Doctor Who – The New Adventures

The following is a list of New Adventures up to the end of 1995 that feature Ace.

Timewyrm: Genesys – John Peel
Timewyrm: Exodus – Terrance Dicks
Timewyrm: Apocalypse – Nigel Robinson
Timewyrm: Revelation – Paul Cornell
Cat's Cradle: Time's Crucible – Marc Platt
Cat's Cradle: Warhead – Andrew Cartmel
Cat's Cradle: Witch Mark – Andrew Hunt
Nightshade – Mark Gatiss
Love and War – Paul Cornell
Deceit – Peter Darvill-Evans
Lucifer Rising – Andy Lane and Jim Mortimore
White Darkness – David A. McIntee
Shadowmind – Christopher Bulis
Birthright – Nigel Robinson
Blood Heat – Jim Mortimore
The Dimension Riders – Daniel Blythe
The Left Handed Hummingbird – Kate Orman
Conundrum – Steve Lyons
No Future – Paul Cornell
Tragedy Day – Gareth Roberts
Legacy – Gary Russell
Theatre of War – Justin Richards
All Consuming Fire – Andy Lane
Blood Harvest – Terrance Dicks
Strange England – Simon Messingham
First Frontier – David A. McIntee
St Anthony's Fire – Mark Gatiss
Falls the Shadow – Daniel O'Mahony
Parasite – Jim Mortimore
Warlock – Andrew Cartmel
Set Piece – Kate Orman

The seventh Doctor and Ace also appear in the following book, also published by Virgin Publishing:

Decalog 2 – Edited by Mark Stammers and Stephen James Walker

Comic Strips

The following is a list of comic strips published in Doctor Who Magazine *that feature the seventh Doctor and Ace.*

Fellow Travellers (three episodes) – Andrew Cartmel / Arthur Ranson

The Mark of Mandragora (four episodes) – Dan Abnett / Lee Sullivan and Mark Farmer

Party Animals (one episode) – Gary Russell / Mike Collins and Steve Pini

The Chameleon Factor (one episode) – Paul Cornell / Lee Sullivan and Mark Farmer

The Good Soldier (three episodes) – Andrew Cartmel / Mike Collins and Steve Pini

Seaside Rendezvous (one episode) – Paul Cornell / Gary Frank and Stephen Baskerville

A Glitch in Time (one episode) – John Freeman / Richard Whitaker

The Grief (three episodes) – Dan Abnett / Vincent Danks / Adolfo Buylla and Robin Riggs

Memorial (one episode) – Warwick Grey / John Ridgway

Cat Litter (one episode) – Marc Platt / John Ridgway

Final Genesis (four episodes) – Warwick Grey / Colin Andrew

Time and Time Again (one episode) – Paul Cornell / John Ridgway

Cuckoo (three episodes) – Dan Abnett / John Ridgway

Metamorphosis (two episodes) – Paul Cornell / Lee Sullivan

Under Pressure (two episodes) – Dan Abnett / Vincent Danks and Cam Smith

Linking the comic strips and the New Adventures

My understanding when I came to Marvel was that John Freeman was very keen to tie in the Doctor and Ace with the television series and the New Adventures. I did a time line that showed how these comic strips and the New Adventures interlaced that was originally going to be used in the Jean-Marc Lofficier *Programme Guide*, but was used in Marvel's thirtieth anniversary special magazine instead.

Lee Sullivan did the visuals for Bernice from Paul Cornell's description, and as a result of that he then got the cover commission for *Love and War*. We also designed Ace's and the Doctor's new looks. An artist, Rodney Ramos, took the descriptions from series editor Peter Darvill-Evans.

I always think that Sharon – the Doctor's comic strip companion from the Tom Baker era – is Ace. Ace was created in 1987, but we'd already done this kick-ass schoolgirl, rebellious with an attitude of 'Let me at them!' in 1980. Sharon is very much a predecessor of Ace. A very, very similar character.

I confess to writing Ace inconsistently in my New Adventure, *Legacy*. I was unaware of the state of Ace's mind at the time the book is set. The aggressive Ace didn't work, she wasn't getting on with anyone and so I sent her off on a little adventure of her own. However, by that point she was happy and balanced again which would have suited me, because in *Legacy* she is relegated to a tacked on plotline. I'd much rather have written for that nicer, more mature Ace.

Gary Russell
Editor, Marvel UK's
***Doctor Who* comic strip 1993-95**
New Adventure author

Right: Two of Lee Sullivan's thumbnail sketches for Metamorphosis.

Right: The same two pages of the strip at rough pencil stage.

Drawing Ace

Drawing comic strips you are trying to bring to life images that the writer has already conceived. It also has this thing called a plot! I know some artists are very free with the plot, but I feel that the plot is what it's all about. Comic strips for me are illustrations of stories, they're storyboards for a film, if you like, they just happen to be the end result.

For *Metamorphosis* I did costumes that were based loosely on stuff that had appeared during *Frontier in Space* from Jon Pertwee's time. The story featured some space guys and their costumes all had large foam rubber shoulder pads and knee pads. I had to do something similar for the Benny visualisation because of some tie-in with that story and I'm more than happy to take advice and inspiration when it comes to visuals.

I found Sylvester very difficult, at first and I'm not really sure that I ever really captured him. I think that when the shadows are long over Sylvester's face then I'm happiest with those. As for Ace, the programme had just finished and John Freeman and I decided that she should be something a little more comics orientated, and in comics the best kind of guy and the best kind of gal are the ones that are dressed in Spandex, which means that you can see their muscles and body structure, and that is really nice for artists to draw. Naked, shiny heroes are really what it's all about! Generally, the comics audience tends to be early to late teens and they want to see gorgeous people, so I decided to show Ace as she hadn't been seen before and that entailed a shiny jumpsuit made, curiously enough, of Spandex. Only the Doc Martens hung on from the original characterisation. She was a tough action girl and a great comic strip character because she's got a nice face, the attitude and – in this strip – the look.

The Daleks are, for me, a dream come true. I happen to have been associated with a lot of Dalek stories and that couldn't be nicer for me. I remember their very first appearance, and they are still my nightmare. It's that turret that works independently of the direction in which they are travelling.

I've always been a big fan of the Dalek strips from *TV Century 21*. I love the way that they were conceived and executed, and I finally got the chance to show Daleks flying through the air.

The cliff-hanger is great because it's a real pin-up shot. It has a nice stark image of the Dalek looking down at you, but from a technical point of view it's the pick up page that has the most going for it. You have to show Ace shooting at, and being shot at by, a Dalek that is on the tip of an airlock that is losing its air, you have to show her tumbling backwards with the ▶

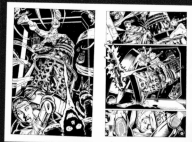

Above: The inked pages awaiting their text bubbles.

Left: The almost-complete pages awaiting colouring.

Bottom: The final coloured pages as printed in the Marvel Doctor Who *Yearbook 1993.*

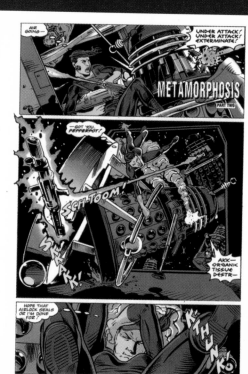

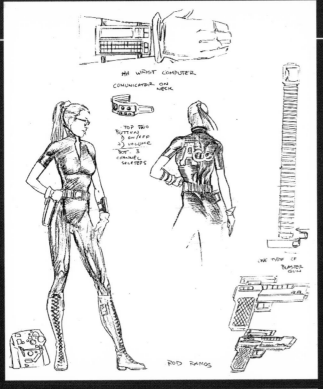

Dalek, that is now dead, and you have to show her staying alive in that kind of environment. For the trivia buffs, this is what the underside of a Doc Marten looks like. I don't do a lot of research, but when I do it's frightening! It's the page that I'm most pleased with because you don't often get the chance to do great images and great story-telling.

Lee Sullivan
Comic strip artist

Far left: Rod Ramos's sketches, showing an older Ace in her combat suit, for use in the comic strip and New Adventures books.

Left: Sophie dons a copy of Ace's combat suit especially created for the photographs used on the jacket and inside this book.

Above, right and far right: Sophie poses for a special set of photographs in Ace's new Adventures outfit. The guns featured in the pictures were built by Mike Tucker to the design of the weapons that appeared in the comic strip.

Conventions

Above: Coming home from a weekend convention appearance in New York, extremely jet-lagged.

Below: I nearly choked to death by cramming a whole doughnut into my mouth at once in an attempt to win a round of a game show. Everyone thought I was joking – it was nightmarish – until Tomek Bork realised I was in trouble and brought me a glass of water. John, the compere, looked on as the doughnut came up and said, 'Never mind, we can auction that off later'!

MY FIRST EXPERIENCE OF FANS EN MASSE WAS AT THE ANNUAL *DOCTOR Who* Appreciation Society clan gathering, PanoptiCon, at Imperial College, London in 1987. I'd completed filming for *Dragonfire*, and had moved into a flat in south east London. I thought, misguidedly, that the convention would be a few anorak-clad students who would chat to the guests, get out their autograph books and watch scratchy old black and white *Doctor Who* episodes. I got a shock when I arrived to discover hundreds of people. I suddenly wished I'd smartened up a bit; the jeans and T-shirt I had donned hastily at home after cleaning out a kitchen cupboard seemed to undermine the occasion. I was escorted into the hospitality room by a couple of smart polite young men, who insisted on calling me 'Miss Aldred' in reverential tones. I was introduced to some of my fellow guests, and was amazed to find myself shaking the hand of none other than the Brigadier, looking a little older than I remembered, and moustacheless now, but nevertheless top dog of UNIT and a man to be reckoned with.

'Lovely to meet you, Sophie,' bellowed Nick Courtney in those cultured tones I remembered so well, 'have you met John Levene?' (Wow! Another UNIT man!) 'and of course, Richard Franklin', (and another one!) 'What a shame, you've just missed Pertwee!'

This was more than I could cope with. Suddenly, I was allowed into this magic circle where I could rub shoulders with my childhood idols including my Doctor, the great Jon Pertwee! I realised I was just as star struck as the polite young men who were now offering me tea and cakes and treating me like a valuable piece of porcelain, as I parked my bottom on a nearby seat and listened with fascination to some choice Courtney anecdotes.

Once I had recovered, I was escorted to the back of a huge lecture theatre, and I was informed of the cunning plan hatched in order to spring me on the unsuspecting audience. I gazed down to the stage area where Colin Baker and Nicola Bryant were answering questions from the floor. Nicola was radiant in a brightly coloured silk jacket, her hair beautifully styled and make up meticulously applied. I wished that I'd at least washed my hair.

The MC was one Gordon Roxburgh, and having led Colin and Nicola from the stage followed by tumultuous applause, he asked the audience to examine their entry tickets for a special prize-winning number. And the prize? A visit to the set of *Doctor Who*. Acting like mad as the lucky number was announced, I waved a scrap of paper above my head as I ran down the steps to the stage. A smattering of jealous applause rippled through the audience. Gordon greeted me and shoved the microphone to my face.

'So, how do you feel about winning a visit to the BBC to see *Doctor Who* being made?'

'Well, actually, I've got a confession to make… I've already been there.'

'Ladies and gentlemen, I'd like to introduce the new *Doctor Who* girl, Sophie Aldred!'

Cue thunderous (if shocked) applause, and blinding camera flashes. I stood in the middle of the stage feeling bewildered as a sea of people rushed forward towards me to get a better look. I was led off stage surrounded by fans who wanted to shake my hand or to grab an autograph. An hour or so later I managed to escape from the crowd – outside in the real world, I was meant to be taking delivery of a new bed for my flat and should have been at home. But such feeble excuses don't deter the average *Doctor Who* fan. Eventually I had to ask for assistance to make my getaway to the tube station.

By the time I was invited to my first American convention, I thought I knew more or less what to expect. I should have known better! Sylvester, his partner Agnes and I were guests of New Jersey Network, the Public Broadcasting Station responsible for *The Making of Doctor Who* documentary. The weekend bash celebrated the documentary's launch and brought Sylv and me together to the States for the first time. I could only stay for the weekend due to my *Corners* schedule. Sylv, Agnes and NJN producer, Eric Luskin, met me at the airport. Having confused the immigration official with the bizarre reason for my weekend visit, and carrying only one small bag, my hosts took me on a tour of downtown New York. We ended up in a Greenwich Village jazz bar, and stayed until my head drooped (with jet-lag, not over consumption of alcohol) and we decided to leave. On returning to the car, we found that someone had tampered with the boot breaking the lock, so I turned up at the hotel and checked in wearing the clothes I was standing in and clutching a toothbrush. More confusion arose as the hotel porters refused to believe that I had nothing to carry to my room except my coat, and consequently would receive no tip!

The convention itself, which started early next morning, was structured round a New Jersey Network pledge drive, one of the main sources of funding for the PBS stations in the States. It's a Telethon-like event; viewers ring in and pledge a certain amount of money so that the station can buy in shows like *Doctor Who*, *Monty Python*, *Absolutely Fabulous* as well as home grown documentaries and children's programmes, watched by a discerning minority of the population fed up with news, violence and the ubiquitous commercials.

After a day of meeting fans and answering questions in the hotel, Sylv and I were driven to the NJN studios. I was given the heaviest ever make up, and Sylvester, who was busy calling me Joan Collins and Sue Ellen, then spent several frantic minutes in the loos trying to wipe off some of the heavy brown tint with which he'd been plastered, while I stifled my laughter. Our job was to persuade as many people as possible to ring in and pledge their cash in the live 'pledge breaks' between the screening of *The Making of Doctor Who* documentary.

I've 'conventioned' in Manhattan, Newark, Long Island, Chicago, Denver, LA, St Louis, Boston, Baltimore, Indianapolis, Florida and a cruise round the Bahamas and the Mexican Gulf. And in Britain I've used up a road map with all the places I've been to.

It was while I was attending the Dreamwatch convention in London in 1994 that something spooky occurred to me. I was standing in the hospitality suite with some of the other cast members of a video science fiction project, *Shakedown*. I turned to one of the organisers and said, 'Isn't it amazing that five years after filming the final *Doctor Who* here I am still surrounded by people who are interested in the programme and who think of me as Ace!' The guy turned and pointed across the room to where Carole Ann Ford was signing a huge pile of video covers.

'And where do you think you'll be in thirty years time?' he asked, eyebrows raised. I wonder. ⑤

Exploding Daleks on stage!

Ever since Tom Baker took over as the Doctor the phenomenon of conventions has been associated with *Doctor Who*. The main organiser of these events was originally the *Doctor Who* Appreciation Society, though with the passage of time, more and more organisers have come onto the scene and the British *Doctor Who* convention circuit is now huge, with barely a month going by without some event or other.

The effects department has always had some involvement with the convention circuit, our main spokesman over the years being Mat Irvine, who regularly used to attend DWAS events with a vast selection of props and slides. My own involvement with this side of *Doctor Who* was at a DWAS event at Imperial College, London, where I was part of a panel covering the making of *Dragonfire*. It was then several years before I got involved again, this time at the huge thirtieth anniversary celebrations held in Hammersmith, organised for the DWAS by Andrew Beech and Dominitemporal Services. In sheer scale and number of guests this has to be one of the biggest events there has ever been in this country, beaten only by the twentieth anniversary convention organised by BBC Enterprises at Longleat.

Alan Marshall and I set up a small exhibition and did two talks a day to audiences ranging in number from seventy to three depending who was on stage in the main hall. (The afternoon that we had three people we were up against Sophie and Sylvester!)

At the end of the event we cornered Andrew Beech and expressed a wish to be more involved if we ever attended again, and he took us at our word. The following year we were invited to the 1994 PanoptiCon convention in Coventry, and given free reign to come up with something for the evening's entertainment. Alan and I reasoned that people wanted to see what we did, not hear us talk about it, and so we decided that we would blow up a Dalek on stage.

Now setting off pyrotechnics that close to an audience is not advisable so we adapted a technique that had often been used to blow up Daleks at Television Centre. The dome of the Dalek was sprung loaded so that it could be triggered on cue, and a number of small charges were rigged into the hollow neck. Judging from the surprised looks on the faces of the people in the front row, it was quite effective.

Conventions tend to be a good time for the cast and crews of various eras of the programme to get together, and I've always found that memories are more easily jogged if several of us are all lumped together at once, certainly a lot of the incidents in this book I've been reminded of by colleagues while at conventions.

Mike Tucker

Left: The exploding Dalek trick done for PanoptiCon '94.

Right: Mike and Mat Irvine *after a visual effects demonstration.*

Far right: Sylvester *meets an American fan with a colourful Time Lord costume.*

Around edges of page: *Just a handful of Sophie's* Doctor Who *postbag.*

DEAR ♡ ACE
I ♡ HAV ♡
RECORDED.
911 ♡ THE ♡
DOCTOR ♡ WHO...S
♡ THAT ♡ YOU
are ♡ in
♡ THANKYOU
AND ♡ I
WHEN ♡ I
♡ AM ♡ A.
♡ LITTEL ♡
♡ OLDER ♡ BIT
WILL ♡ I
MARE ♡ YOU
♡ THANKYOU ♡

Left: *I get to do my Davros impression.*

Below left: *On stage with the Master, Anthony Ainley.*

Below: *Discussing the cover of a New Adventure book at a autograph session with Peter Davison.*

Bottom: *Colin Baker and me.*

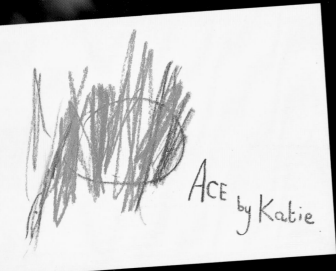

ACE by Katie

Above: Phoning home from the streets of New York.

Above right: Sylvester tries to make sense of the New York subway map.

Right: Posing by my little run-about in America.

Below: At the top of the Empire State Building.

Below right: Jon Pertwee and me.

Above: Modelling the latest fashions, a replica sixth Doctor frock coat in America.

Questions & Answers

Q: What's your favourite story?

Hooray! The old chestnut! Well, I used to say it had to be *Fenric*, because of the demanding acting and the development of Ace as a realistic and emotional character, but with hindsight, I'm not so sure. It has been an interesting exercise to look back at all the stories in fairly quick succession, and now I have to say that my fave is probably *Ghostlight*. I just think the quality of the story as a whole was great – rich and multi-layered writing, great humour, fantastic production values, a wonderful cast, and that dark brooding feeling about it which used to be so much a trade mark of classic *Doctor Who*.

Of course, that's answering the question in terms of which story I thought was best; another way to answer it is which one I enjoyed doing most, and again that's really difficult to answer. They were all so completely different from each other – each new cast brought a different atmosphere, different personalities, a different sense of humour. Having said that, I probably had greatest fun on *Survival* – all that sun bathing and partying – and that's the one where I felt cast and crew gelled completely.

Q: Would you ever reprise your rôle as Ace?

Just you try and stop me! No, seriously, I still think it's a great shame that there has never been a satisfactory ending to this story. Just walking off through a hedge in a Dorset quarry isn't the fireworks you'd expect from Ace really, is it? It seems hugely unlikely that I'll ever be asked back now, sadly. I'd love to go out in a blaze of Nitro 9 as a warning to all those kids who wrote to me asking for the recipe so they could blow up their school teacher. And when I used to write back a sensible grown up reply like 'Ace only ever used explosives or violence on alien beings…' I could imagine the response, 'Yeah, but my teacher *is* an alien being!' I don't fancy Ace's chances of marrying and living happily ever after, like some of her predecessors. I think she's destined to a life of falling in love with strong men who get killed or go to the bad!

Q: What do you think of the New Adventure novels?

Now here's the embarrassing moment when I have to own up to having read precisely three of them; *Timewyrm: Genesys*, because John Peel kindly asked me to write the introduction, *Set Piece* because I was asked to write an afterword, and *Deceit* because Peter Darvill-Evans gave it to me to read when we first talked about doing this book! I must say, it's very strange to read about what is, in effect, myself in a novel. I mean, all the authors have had their own ideas about how Ace would have developed and also about how they perceived my characterisation of her on television, but when I read the books, I did get an odd sense that it really was a part of myself that I was reading about. Maybe that's just megalomania! People have told me different things about the books; that they do or don't like the way Ace grew into a gun toting sexual bundle of aggression, but all I'm really aware of is that the books seem to sell extremely well, so someone must like them. My only regret is that the kids who are now growing up watching the videos don't have any new material written for them – I wouldn't like young kids to read the New Adventures, put it that way!

Above: My first professional steps, modelling clothes for the Mothercare catalogue in 1964 with model Celia Hammond.

Q: Who's your favourite Doctor?

This just makes me think of when I was invited up to Birmingham to do *Pebble Mill* soon after I'd been on air as Ace. There I was sitting between my Doctor, Sylvester McCoy, and my other Doctor, Jon Pertwee! I was nearly speechless, I was so star struck. I have a theory that in your heart of hearts, your favourite Doctor is the one you grew up with. Now, I must have seen Patrick Troughton, because I'm older than I look! But the Doctor I really remember from my childhood is Jon. I just remember that wonderful curly hair and the nose and his frilly shirt. I also remember that the rector of our local church looked a bit like Jon, and I used to get ever so confused about that. There was also a police box in Greenwich Park where I played a lot when I was little, and I always expected the Doctor to walk out of it. And I loved Sarah Jane Smith as well, though I did confuse her for a time with Carol Chell from *Playschool*! When I got to meet Lis Sladen at Marvel Comics some time ago, I rushed up to her and said how much I used to love her in *Doctor Who*, and she said 'but I think you're fantastic, you never scream!' A mutual admiration society. And now Lis' daughter, Sadie, is really into *Doctor Who*, and I'm immensely proud of the fact that she's a member of my fan club!

Q: What's the difference between British and American fans?

Surprisingly little. In the States, there are more female fans than over here, and a lot of them seem to be incredibly brainy people who work for NASA or the CIA, or have high powered management jobs. Luckily, they share a British sense of humour, i.e. they understand irony and laugh at my jokes… or are they just being polite? I find that fans in general do tend to be incredibly polite and once you get through people's initial shyness I find that they're interesting people. I mean we all know the stereotype of the anoraky long scarf type fan, who can quote facts and figures at you over a pint of shandy until you fall asleep and then they still don't stop. But I find people in general fascinating, and if they're prepared to watch me on television and be loyal enough to still be interested in something I did six years ago, then I say thanks!

American fans on the whole tend to be less shy than British, and I'd say they are larger in build, but I guess that's true of the average American anyway. Conventions in the States invariably have a costume parade, and I'm always amazed by the time and money people have put into intricate hand sewing, and not just on a *Doctor Who* theme; one convention I attended was held in a kind of bizarre mock Tudor motel and the fans had stitched amazing Elizabethan costumes and wore them all weekend. Then there was the time when I was judging a costume contest and onto the stage bounded an Ace lookalike. The contestant had gone for the more figure hugging *Battlefield* look, which was all the more startling as he turned out to be a long haired man, who actually had much nicer legs than me! These are no ordinary costume contests, because the participants are allowed to speak to the audience if they want, and most do the most confident acting or dancing or whatever – a British fan would curl up and die rather than do that!

Q: What have you been doing since you finished *Doctor Who*?

It had crossed my mind that there used to be this classic thing of *Doctor Who* girls never working again after their time on the show, though actually that's complete press fiction and depends which section of the 27 or so companions you're analysing. I mean, look at Frazer Hines, Louise Jameson or Bonnie Langford! I was lucky enough to have got this children's presenting thing going at the BBC, and so for three years my work consisted of *Doctor Who*, *Corners*, *Doctor Who*, *Corners*, like that, so that nearly every day I'd be going to the Beeb for something. It was a bit like going to school! In that time I was also asked to do things like *Jackanory*, and a quiz show called *Knock Knock*. One of my strengths is that I'm pretty versatile; I'm first and foremost

Above: This was my publicity photo for Corners *for Children's BBC – a programme that answered children's questions, which I did concurrently with* Doctor Who.

Below: Two of the many attractive characters I played during my time on Corners.

Above: My name is Sophie Socket, I mend the Ratkan rocket. There's something in my pocket, can you guess what it is?. It's Droibee Time *for The Children's Channel.*

Above right: Presenting Tiny and Crew *for TCC, a pre-school children's programme.*

an actress, but I sing as well and did music up to 'A' level, which has really helped for the teaching shows I've done, like *Music Workshop* on the radio. I've also taken to presenting well – I believe presenting's one of those things which you either can or can't do – and as well as having done a year on *Words and Pictures*, and several years of pre-school programming for the cable television company, The Children's Channel, I did a very adult programme called *Love Call Live* for Anglia Television, in which we discussed people's sexual problems and issues, and found dates for our studio guests. The funniest thing was realising that I was presenting in exactly the same way as for the children's programmes I do!

A couple of years ago, I had my West End debut playing the lead in a wonderfully bawdy musical called *Lust* at the beautiful Theatre Royal, Haymarket. *Lust* was based on the restoration comedy, *The Country Wife*, and I played a seemingly innocent young country girl, Margery Pinchwife, who finally succeeds in cuckolding her jealous old husband in a wonderful song which Denis Lawson and I played behind a curtain on a huge four poster bed, and which left everything up to the audience's imagination. That really was a fantastic thing to be in, and we got very good reviews, but sadly, the audiences dwindled and five months later, we had to close.

Apart from that, I've done panto, played Daisy in *Daisy Pulls It Off*, filmed two series of a mad children's television show involving music called *Melvin and Maureen's Music a Grams*, as well as voice-overs (Kotex Panty Pads amongst others!) radio, and I do live links between the children's programmes on the British Forces Television station, SSVC. So you could say I'm keeping myself busy!

Below: Theatre programme for Daisy Pulls It Off at Theatr Clwyd, Wales.

Theatr Clwyd Company

DAISY PULLS IT OFF

by
DENISE DEEGAN

Theatr Clwyd

Q: Which job of all those have you most enjoyed?

That's a very difficult question, because I can honestly say that I have had a great time with everything I've ever done. I've always loved the people I've worked with, and have rarely if ever come across this bitchiness and backstabbing that's meant to be so much a feature of the acting profession. Now I know this sounds a bit corny, but I think the job I miss most is *Doctor Who*.

Q: There have been quite a few spin-off projects since *Doctor Who* ended. Have you enjoyed working on those?

I did a BBC schools programme called *Search Out Science* which used the Doctor and Ace. It was hardly a reunion, because all our bits were filmed separately. I was in the middle of a run of *Daisy Pulls It Off* at Theatr Clwyd, but luckily my day's filming was at the Jodrell Bank radio telescope, so I could travel there and arrive back in Mold in time for the evening performance. It was one of the most amazing places I've ever filmed, and I was allowed right up inside the dish – the cameraman and I climbed up inside and peered over the edge! The trickiest part was roller skating through shot, as I hadn't been on skates since I was a kid. The roller skates were also very ropey – well that's my excuse anyway – and I kept falling over – very embarrassing! I was never quite sure what I was meant to be doing, and the director didn't seem to know either, so I think the resulting programme was quite confusing! Steve Johnson from *Corners* played the part of an alien, so it was all very incestuous!

My next spin off was a Bill Baggs project called *More Than a Messiah*. Colin Baker had told me that he and Nicola Bryant had enjoyed working on the first video, *Summoned by Shadows*, so I thought, why not? We rehearsed at North Acton and I was impressed with the way Bill handled the actors – in fact, I got more notes on character and acting than I had in all my time doing *Doctor Who*!

My first day's shooting was down in the New Forest. I was delighted to be playing an alien for the first time ever. I had a bit of trouble finding the location – I'd driven down at breakneck speed after a lunchtime launch party for Children's BBC – and I arrived late at a log cabin in the woods, where I recognised a few faces as they scrabbled around in the dusk. I was handed a lycra body suit and squashed myself into the toilet cubicle to work my way into it. I loved my make-up, which was mainly green and squidgy, and I also insisted on a rather fetching copydex scar on my cheek. We decided the easiest thing to do with my hair was to gel it back with green colouring for added alien effect. Nicola Bryant and I huddled round a heater – it was December – and tried to keep warm, and eventually, later than advertised, Bill came and found me for my first scene. I had to peer through some undergrowth, and as it was by now quite dark and very cold, I perfected a method of hiding a nice warm blanket and a thick jacket round my legs just out of shot. My scared features were motivated more by the first stages of hypothermia than by good acting!

My next bit of filming was scheduled to be filmed on a beach near Brighton. However, when we arrived at the cliff top pub, the Telscombe Tavern, which we were using as make up and costume base camp, there was a force nine gale blowing. The sea was pretty ugly and fearsome, and blowing up so much spray that it would have been dangerous to venture down to the beach, so we ended up shooting behind a car door in the pub car park. After lunch the wind had died down a bit, so with great difficulty we made our way down to the beach – a tricky manoeuvre which involved letting yourself down a small cliff face on the end of a piece of rope. Colin and I shivered our way through our lines without being able to hear ourselves speak, with a background accompaniment of crashing waves and a howling blast. We just hoped the radio mikes would pick up our voices, as the wind whipped our words away across the Channel. I beat a hasty retreat as soon as I'd shivered my way through the shots, and commiserated with Nicola as she struggled past me on her way down to the beach.

The last bit I had to do was a month or so later somewhere near Cheddar Gorge in Somerset. I gave Nicola a lift down in my car, and we arrived terribly late, having missed the turn off the motorway because we were so busy chatting and putting the world to rights. Most of the filming was done over three days in one of the Wookey Hole caves, which was strange as we had no idea of time down there. I managed to squeeze some thermals under my body suit, but even so it was pretty dank and cold. Colin and I had a risqué little scene where Bill wanted us to look naked. I'm sorry to disappoint everyone, but I'd brought a strapless bikini with me – the shot was cropped so that you couldn't see it. Also out of shot I was clutching a blanket and my jacket round my waist; Colin quickly took his shirt off for the take, and we got it all over with as fast as possible because of the cold and a good measure of embarrassment!

Above: My West End debut in Lust *with Denis Lawson.*

Below: The poster for Cinderella *at the New Theatre, Hull, in 1989.*

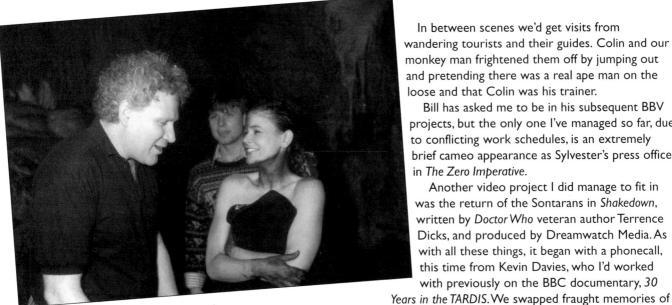

Above: Filming inside the extremely cold Cheddar Gorge for the spin-off project, More Than a Messiah, *with Colin Baker and director Bill Baggs.*

In between scenes we'd get visits from wandering tourists and their guides. Colin and our monkey man frightened them off by jumping out and pretending there was a real ape man on the loose and that Colin was his trainer.

Bill has asked me to be in his subsequent BBV projects, but the only one I've managed so far, due to conflicting work schedules, is an extremely brief cameo appearance as Sylvester's press officer in *The Zero Imperative*.

Another video project I did manage to fit in was the return of the Sontarans in *Shakedown*, written by *Doctor Who* veteran author Terrence Dicks, and produced by Dreamwatch Media. As with all these things, it began with a phonecall, this time from Kevin Davies, who I'd worked with previously on the BBC documentary, *30 Years in the TARDIS*. We swapped fraught memories of my day's involvement with that epic production at the Quasar game centre in Slough; Sylvester's cab driver had dropped him off miles away from the location by mistake, and he turned up irate and demanding coffee, having had to pound the deserted early morning suburban pavements for an hour. As usual, this outburst didn't last long, especially when he discovered the *Doctor Who* pinball machine, and then when called upon to improvise with an assortment of Haemovores and a smoke machine.

Kevin suggested I might be interested in playing a part very much against type, namely Mari, the spoilt daughter of a rich industrialist from another planet, who would scream a lot, run away from monsters and cling helplessly to her adoring boyfriend. 'What fun,' I thought, and Kevin duly sent me the script. I was unavailable to do the readthrough, so the first time I met the rest of the cast was actually on board ship! Filming took place entirely on the wonderful Aliens type set provided by HMS *Belfast*, an ex-battleship, now a tourist attraction, moored by Tower Bridge. This turned out to be problematic for sound, due to the patter of tourists' feet that could be heard clanging down the iron work three decks up, the public announcements that boomed out over the tannoy system from time to time, and the noise of boats going past on the Thames! I can honestly say that it was the most stressful time I've experienced at work, because of a lack of scheduling, and the tiny budget, which meant that most of the work was carried out by willing friends who weren't exactly sure what they were doing, but I must say that the end product is astonishing!

Below: More Than a Messiah. *I loved my green make-up and latex scar.*

Considering that us actors were threatening mutiny at one point, because we just couldn't see how we were going to finish in time, I think everyone did remarkably well. I loved my slinky dress costume, which had been made by someone who usually designs lamp-shades, and I hated my green overalls which were conjured up from an oversized man's pair by a fantastically inventive and industrious Helly, who sat in a corner with her sewing machine and sewed constantly for two weeks as far as I could see.

One of the nice things, as usual, was the cast; as well as actually working with Carole Ann Ford, it was lovely to get to know some science fiction cult figures, and to initiate Rory O'Donnel, an actor new to the camera, into the world of *Doctor Who*.

I found myself actually gasping at the end result, which was previewed a couple of months later at the Dreamwatch convention in Earl's Court. Mark Ayres had done wonders with the music, and I couldn't quite believe that such good quality had been achieved by one lighting cameraman, a superbly enthusiastic director, a talented make up designer, a genius of an editor and loads and loads of good will!

Q: Did you ever have any involvement in *The Dark Dimension* special, rumoured to be in production at one stage?

I was sent a nice chunky script via my agent, who'd been rung by the BBC to see whether I'd be interested. He told them that at the time I was just about to start my run in *Lust* in the West End and that any filming would therefore have to fit in with my theatre schedule. They assured him that my scenes would take place in London locations, and so it surprised me when I received the script to find that not only was my part pretty substantial, but that a lot of it was set in a country house. There followed many phonecalls between someone at the Beeb and my agent, who tried to explain over and over again that I just wouldn't be available for evening shoots or to go far away from London. I was a little surprised at the lack of parts for Doctors other than Tom Baker, and soon found out that Colin and Jon in particular were not at all pleased with the script. Looking back, it seemed to be a story written with one Doctor in mind, and then fiddled with to produce a script for all of them. The story was also suspect with regard to my character; I would start off as a boring school teacher type called, yes you guessed it, Dorothy, and then gradually the revelation would come that using a kind of parallel universe theory, Ace would materialise and take over. I now question just how interesting the general public who wouldn't know about Ace's background would find this idea, and indeed it all looks like a fan's script rather than a commissioned 'special'. There are many theories regarding *The Dark Dimension*; all I know is that my agent received a final call from the BBC which told him that my filming days would start at 8.00pm somewhere miles away from London which showed how much listening had been going on. I don't think we'll ever know what really happened. But I did hear that Tom Baker actually got as far as signing a contract, and was therefore paid his entire fee!

Q: Have you any regrets?

Well, I'm not really one for regrets – life's too short – but one would be that I never got to meet Patrick Troughton before he died. And from the sublime to the ridiculous: the only other one I can think of is that I wish Richard Croft and I had bought a smaller Ace jacket! I wanted to have a sort of 'bum freezer' type, and when I tried it on in that shop in the Kings Road, it fastened neatly round my waist. Trouble was, after a few scenes in the rain, all the stuff I used to cram in the pockets, and a couple of soaks in Lulworth Cove, all three jackets sagged, and I ended up looking like a Michelin man. Many people comment on how much smaller I am in real life than on television, and I'm sure a lot of it has got to do with that darn jacket!

Above: My extraordinary dress created by a lamp-shade maker for Shakedown.

Below: The first and last Doctor Who *companions together. Carole Ann Ford and I both appeared in Dreamwatch media's* Shakedown, *written by Terrance Dicks.*

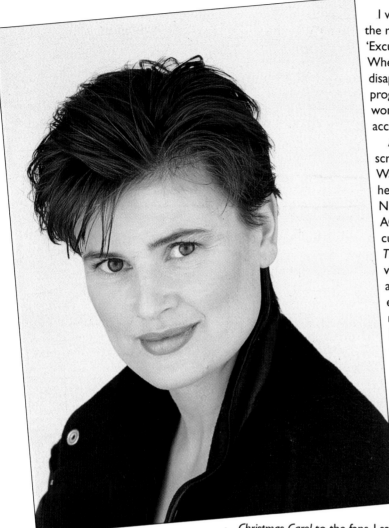

I was in the lift at North Acton one day, and was sharing the ride to the canteen with a well known actor who said, 'Excuse me, aren't you Sophie Aldred from *Doctor Who?*' When I replied in the affirmative his face fell. 'Oh, what a disappointment!' he said. 'My son and I love you on the programme, but we thought you were this huge Amazonian woman, and you're really quite tiny, aren't you!?' There's no accounting for taste.

And one more mini-regret: in my original *Dragonfire* script Ace was to have a beloved stuffed toy dog called Wayne. His mission in life became clear when he came to a heroic end having been stuffed with a good sized chunk of Nitro 9 and used on the baddies. Ace also spray painted ACE 4 WAYNE on a wall somewhere, but this was also cut, along with a reference to spray painting and graffiti in *The Happiness Patrol* because of potential copying by viewers. Hope no one took it into their heads to beat anyone up with a baseball bat! Although Wayne never even made it to the readthrough as far as I can remember, Ian Briggs was good enough to put him back into the novelisation, but I must say I would have liked the irony of the stuffed toy-become-weapon he afforded.

Q: What's the oddest thing that's happened to you because of *Doctor Who?*

My first was meeting Tom Baker for the first time! We were both invited to an 'event' in Baltimore (so called because Tom refused to do 'conventions') which involved a pledge drive for the local PBS station and a one day gathering during which Tom would read Dickens' *A Christmas Carol* to the fans. I saw Tom at Heathrow, in cricket gear and much taller than I'd imagined, but I was too shy to introduce myself. We were picked up at the other end in a huge stretch limo. There I was in my scruffy old jeans, purring along the freeway in a car the size of a house with Tom Baker sitting opposite. He didn't seem to notice me at all, didn't acknowledge my presence either in the car or the following day at the 'event'. But that evening at the television station, we were sitting waiting to go on and Tom was holding forth about journalists. I made some vaguely intelligent comment and suddenly Tom stopped in his tracks and looked at me in an astonished kind of way as if to say, 'My God! This girl's got a brain!' and from that moment on he didn't stop talking to me, asking me questions, giving me advice about my impending role in *Daisy Pulls It Off*, and discussing his 'Marshwiggle' in the next of the *Narnia Chronicles* he was filming. A few months later, back in London, I was asked to do a schools radio programme with Tom and Danny John-Jules from *Red Dwarf*. I arrived to find Tom talking to the producer, who turned to introduce us. I was just about to explain that Tom and I had already met, expecting that Tom would have forgotten who I was, when he strode over, put his arms round me and said to the world at large, 'I'm thinking of adopting Sophie!' in loud booming tones. He is undoubtedly one of the most wonderfully strange people I've ever met!

Another odd moment was also in the States. I was at a convention in St Louis, and had been taken out for a very nice meal by the organisers. It was quite late when we got back from the restaurant, and I flopped down on my bed and turned the television on to see what late night trash I could catch. The first thing I heard was, 'Aldred does all her own stunts…' and there on the screen was a ten-minute documentary all about yours truly! I laughed out loud in amazement – here I was thousands of miles away from home watching a programme about myself. I owe a lot to *Doctor Who!* Ⓢ